LIVING
ON EARTH

ALSO BY PETER GODFREY-SMITH

Metazoa: Animal Minds and the Birth of Consciousness

*Other Minds: The Octopus
and the Evolution of Intelligent Life*

Philosophy of Biology

Darwinian Populations and Natural Selection

*Theory and Reality: An Introduction
to the Philosophy of Science*

Complexity and the Function of Mind in Nature

LIVING
ON EARTH

LIFE, CONSCIOUSNESS AND THE
MAKING OF THE NATURAL WORLD

PETER GODFREY-SMITH

**WILLIAM
COLLINS**

William Collins
An imprint of HarperCollins*Publishers*
1 London Bridge Street
London SE1 9GF

WilliamCollinsBooks.com

HarperCollins*Publishers*
Macken House
39/40 Mayor Street Upper
Dublin 1
D01 C9W8, Ireland

First published in Great Britain in 2024 by William Collins

First published in the United States by Farrar, Straus and Giroux in 2024
as *Living on Earth: Forests, Corals, Consciousness, and the Making of the World*

1

Printed and bound in the UK using 100% renewable electricity
at CPI Group (UK) Ltd

MIX
Paper | Supporting
responsible forestry
FSC™ C007454

This book contains FSC™ certified paper and other controlled sources
to ensure responsible forest management.

For more information visit: www.harpercollins.co.uk/green

For the guides and spotters who helped me see

PENSIVE, on her dead gazing, I heard the Mother of All,
Desperate, on the torn bodies, on the forms covering the battle-
   fields gazing;
As she call'd to her earth with mournful voice while she stalk'd:
Absorb them well, O my earth, she cried—I charge you, lose not
   my sons! lose not an atom;

. . .

In blowing airs from the fields, back again give me my
   darlings—give my immortal heroes;
Exhale me them centuries hence—breathe me their breath—let
   not an atom be lost . . .

   —WALT WHITMAN, *from* Drum-Taps, *1865*

CONTENTS

CONTENTS

LIVING

ON EARTH

SHARK BAY

Driving

We got back into the car for the drive away from Shark Bay. This bay is right on the western tip of Australia, where the continent looks out across the Indian Ocean toward Africa. In the clear, extra-salty water of the shallows are what appear for a moment to be hundreds of outsized aquatic mushrooms, their heads perhaps a foot or so in diameter. They are interconnected, forming an irregular landscape of shapes and channels, sometimes nudging above the water, sometimes submerged.

The mushroom-like clumps are made up, in part, of microorganisms, including countless *cyanobacteria*. These are tiny, nondescript, and pivotal in the history of the Earth. Specifically, they are pivotal in the transformation of the Earth by one of its products: life.

Cyanobacteria (pronounced with a soft "c," as in the color cyan: *sy-an-o-bacteria*) are an old group of organisms. Sometime around 3 billion years ago, they or their ancestors invented a particular kind of photosynthesis. Like other kinds of photosynthesis, this process uses energy from the sun to power the building of living material. But in this case, oxygen gas is released as a byproduct—the oxygen that animals like us breathe.

Standing above the bay, taking in oxygen from the dry Western Australian air, we had organisms like these to thank. Pulling in carbon dioxide, breaking water molecules apart with the power of light, splicing the elements to build living material, and releasing oxygen gas in tiny puffs, they slowly transformed the atmosphere, and the planet along with it, until Earth could power the organic engines of animal life—muscles, nervous systems, brains.

The cyanobacteria colonies at Shark Bay are themselves thousands of years old. The mushroom-like mounds are called *stromatolites*, and this is the largest living stromatolite system in the world. Small fish, tails flicking, threaded through the maze of channels—beneficiaries, like us, of the atmosphere those tiny, ancient cells had generated.

We drove away on a road framed by red-orange earth. The land looks rusted. It *is* rusted—that is exactly what has happened. Redness in earth and rock is usually due to an interaction between oxygen and iron: iron oxide, rust. When the cyanobacteria started breathing out oxygen, initially it did not accumulate in the atmosphere. Much of it reacted with rocks, which contained various elements, including iron, waiting to take it up. Red desert landscapes were painted, and are still being repainted, by life in this way. The particular stretch of red rushing past our car was most likely laid down by later oxygen-producers, but cyanobacteria started the process.

Eventually, with this coat of color laid, oxygen started to hang around as gas. Farther north in Western Australia, you reach earth that does not look rusted or red-orange; instead it is intensely red, close to the color of blood—blood that is red in us because of the same bonding of oxygen and iron.

Cyanobacteria also became the germ of forests, as trees and other green plants contain domesticated descendants of those tiny organisms. The cells in a forest leaf are descended from algae that had engulfed cyanobacteria, and worked with them in building living matter from sunlight, water, and air. Cyanobacterial remnants were still inside those algae when they embarked on the multicelled collaborations that gave rise in time to ferns, pines, oaks, and grasses. The painting of the Earth now saw a spread of green, from plants that exhale oxygen as they grow.

Animals climbed onto land from the sea, their first home, when the greening of the Earth was in its early stages—mosses, not trees. The animals' move began with arthropods, the group that includes insects, millipedes, and spiders. Vertebrates and others followed. Plants had made their way from wetlands and liminal places. Once they gained a footing, their solar-paneled towers turned the land into a place where the flows of energy from sun to living matter intensified. With plants and animals came soil, the Earth's new surface.

Eventually, trees became home to primates, along with birds and other animals. Later still, some of those primates came down and started living on broad savannas. They formed bigger groups and then societies: talking, dancing, building. They forged technologies and social forms, embarked on collaborative projects shaped by reflection and foresight, and eventually re-engineered the world as no animal before them had.

As our car rolled along, fuel from its tank ignited with some of the air's oxygen. The fuel was made from compressed plankton and other marine organisms, settling in still water and then buried many millions of years ago. The car's steel was made from iron and carbon with the aid of vast amounts of heat, produced by burning other fuels in distant furnaces.

Think again about that sequence—let's run through it speeded up. Cyanobacteria begin emitting oxygen into the atmosphere. Oxygen drives animal life, first in the sea and later on land. Descendants of cyanobacteria become part of plants. On land, a more intense energy flux evolves in the blazing light, along with a tangle of coevolution between plants and new animals. And then, in our own evolutionary line, an initially unremarkable mammal starts to change in new ways, forming societies and technologies. This leads eventually to change in the atmosphere itself, as carbon that was buried and formed into oil is deliberately burned with life-derived oxygen to push our car along the highway north.

This Book

The history of life includes a parade of new organisms—new bodies and minds, new ways of living—and also a procession of new actions and their effects, new ways that life remakes the world. The history of life is not just a series of new creatures appearing on the stage; the new arrivals change the stage itself.

This book originated as an attempt to work through those themes: the history of action, and the history of how life has changed the Earth. The aim was to see the history of life through that lens or from that angle, to work through a history of organisms as causes, rather than evolutionary products. This gives us, in one sense, an alternative history of life, a history on the what-is-done side, rather than the what-comes-to-exist side. It's not really another history, though, but an alternative perspective on a single history. The two sides are in there together; the constructive activity of animals and other organisms is part of the history of life on Earth.

Looking through this lens alters our perspective on a lot of things—on animals, on the mind, and on our place here. One result is a dynamic picture of the Earth, a picture of an Earth continually changing because of what living things do. Consider oxygen again. The air we breathe, with its high level of oxygen, is in some ways an "unnatural" atmosphere for a planet like ours. Oxygen is reactive, aggressive, prone to interact with whatever is around it. When scuba diving on "nitrox," air enriched with extra oxygen, there is a maximum safe depth for each level of oxygen in the gas you are breathing from your tank. Below that level, you will be poisoned by oxygen itself. The oxygen is concentrated by pressure as you descend. The ordinary O_2 molecule, although reactive, is not toxic, but oxygen gas, through collisions with itself and everything else, continually gives rise to deviant forms, "oxygen radicals," and those careen about like electrical wrecking balls. So although diving with enriched air is often a good thing, as you go beyond certain depths, there needs to be less oxygen, proportionally, in the tank. Even the amount of oxygen in ordinary air becomes toxic if you go deep enough. When I was taking a course to learn to dive with nitrox, the manual said, with a hint of poetry, "Oxygen is an unforgiving gas."

The oxygen-rich atmosphere that we depend on is something that life put in place. It's not due to "life" in general, though; that concocting of our atmosphere took place through a specific historical path.

Once one starts looking at our planet from a life-as-cause angle, many things look different. The first part of this book, especially, goes down this path. It describes an accumulation of new forms of engineering and transformation, and especially the role of action in this process, along with the minds that guide it.

Whenever minds enter the story, philosophical puzzles follow. One familiar set of puzzles constitutes the classic mind-body problem: How can felt experience or consciousness exist at all in nature? A slightly different question runs beside it: What are minds *doing* here? What is their place within the totality of the world's goings-on?

The start of an answer to that second question is that minds—through perceptions, thoughts, plans, and intentions—guide action. Actions serve the interests of organisms, and whether this is intended or not, actions can also transform the world. Deliberate human action continues and extends a long tradition of organisms transforming nature, and the history of the Earth includes a sequence of different forms of such reconstruction. This history begins with single-celled organisms, spans the early evolution of animals and their actions, sees a transition with the move onto land, and extends through to the development of social life, collaboration, and culture. An animal is a nexus where perception and action meet. It's also a nexus where past meets present, through the traces of the past laid down in memory. Actions, in turn, have consequences beyond the life of the actor, and as minds become more elaborate, they change the reach of animal action. Human action, in its social organization and technical complexity, is one especially powerful form.

This idea of a history that puts minds, especially human minds, into a lineage of transforming agents, and treats those agents as part of the history of the Earth, was the seed of the book and gave rise to its central stem. As that stem extended, other themes branched off from it. Often, a place reached along the main development of ideas offered a vantage point from which some quite distinct topic or question looked different from before.

This includes the traditional mind-body problem itself. *Living on Earth* is the third book in a series. The first two, *Other Minds* and *Metazoa*, were partly about that puzzle. *Other Minds* was organized around a particular feature of the history of animal life: an ancient split in the genealogical tree, leading on one side to us and on the other side to the octopus, along with many other invertebrate animals. That book was organized around comparisons between our lives and theirs, and used this comparison to explore how minds came to be. The second book, *Metazoa*, looked at a wider collection of animals and gave a fuller account of the evolution of felt experience. This third book is mainly concerned, as I said, with another side of the story, the mind as cause rather than product (and this book is not written in a way that assumes you have read either of the others). But when we reach humans, the place of our own species in the story, it becomes possible to return to the mind-body relationship and make further progress on it.

We have, I think, mostly moved past "dualist" views that sharply separate mind from body—or so I will assume. I won't say more in this book about why we should see the mind as a biological phenomenon as opposed to a ghostly addition of some kind. But there is a lot to say about *our* kind of felt experience, the human kind. Human conscious experience is the product of ancient and broad features of animal life, along with what has happened to our species through language and culture, these peculiarities of our evolutionary line. Felt or conscious experience is probably widespread in animals, and one part of the story of consciousness involves the way that nervous systems make felt experience possible at all. Another part involves what happens in humans and no one else, as far as we know; it involves what came to exist when the eccentricities of human evolution, especially our immersion in culture, came into contact with animal experience, an older phenomenon. The combining of these, the ancient and the new, yields the tangled glories of human consciousness.

We humans have come out of this long series of events—in evolution, and the shaping of the Earth itself—with minds that feature self-awareness, foresight, and the ability to step back and reflect. We can look out over the whole, and when we do, we find ourselves in the middle of what often feels like a headlong process. The world feels smaller and tighter, with smoke from wildfires unwantedly connecting distant places. Too much of the world, it seems, has come under human influence during a time when we're not very good at working out how to exercise this power. The portion of Earth occupied by wild nature, its place in the whole, shrinks and recedes.

In the last part of this book I want to think about how we should, or might better, handle some of the choices that confront us. The main topics will be our relationships with non-human animals in farming and experimentation, and policy choices around the environment and wild nature—extinction, climate change, and habitat preservation. We'll turn to the unique challenges of our time, the "Anthropocene."

The aim of these chapters is not a "biologized ethics," or a biological moral code. This can be a temptation—trying to directly read a set of moral principles or policies off our scientific picture. I don't think that if we had a clear and accurate view of us, the Earth, other animals, and so on, it would suddenly be clear *what we have to do*, or what we should do if we are at all sensible. The view I develop in this area acknowledges a kind of inherent freedom of movement in our situation. But the view of life on Earth, including our lives, outlined in this book can help us make choices. We can reflect on the picture, and then choose our response.

One other theme runs through the book. It is broad and philosophical, and in some ways hard to describe. I left it to this last part of my outline for that reason. As I said a moment ago, this book aims to help us to think about the Earth as a whole, and the role of minds and agency in that whole. I want to defend, in this setting, a kind of *ecological* outlook. Saying that probably seems quite innocuous. The term "ecological" has various meanings, and often refers to a recognition of connectedness, of whole systems, within the living world. That is fine, and I do intend to convey that, but the point also goes further. I want to defend an orientation that embraces, and stays with, the idea that we, the world's living agents, are *all here together*, as parts of a single system. We all have different perspectives on that whole, but we do so while remaining within it and contributing, each in our way, to how it is and how it changes.

I realize that this will still sound very abstract. How *else* might we think of things? What does this view contrast with? Sometimes in this book, when working through ideas about animal minds, perception, and action, we'll encounter views that do depart from the ecological mindset I am defending. Especially when writing about perception, both in humans and in other animals, a common tendency has been to move toward a view that installs each animal in a sort of private world. This is a mistake, but it's not a baseless or senseless one. Minds are agents of transformation, and this is transformation of a public, shared world—that is a central theme of the book. But the mind is also the home of privacy, particularity, and the unrepeatable quirks of each person's history and situation. Points of view are private. Thoughts are private. The world encountered and acted upon is not.

Similarly, there's a tradition, in philosophy and elsewhere, of saying that consciousness "makes the world"—or that it makes each person's world, as we each make our own reality. We don't; we live in a shared reality. That reality is continually transformed and to some extent constructed by living activity, including action, and consciousness is part of that story. Rather than making our own reality, we all have a role in shaping our common reality, by means of action.

Those are all questions and themes we'll encounter in the chapters to follow. There is more, as well—communication and culture, beauty and valuation, life and death—with some of these encountered at stages along the book's main stem, and others coming off to the side.

Stems, branches . . . the metaphor is arboreal. This is also much of the setting for the book. It is a forest book, through many of its pages, though one interspersed with returns to oceans and reefs. A lot of the thinking that lies behind this book took place in those settings. The path of this book is often on land and among trees, but with forays back to the sea, where it all started.

TRANSFORMATION

2

EARTH ENLIVENED

Time and Space

Some years ago I went to a university seminar about the evolutionary history of animals, and heard a talk by a dinosaur scientist. He started by setting up the big picture, in a familiar sort of way. Human life is a tiny sliver, a scrap within a larger span. If the history of the Earth were compressed down to a year, our species would arise in the last thirty minutes or so of the final hour.

My mind wandered a little. Versions of this thought experiment can be done on different scales: we can think about the Earth, or about the universe. And the "we" might be humans, *Homo sapiens*, or might be something larger than that—animals, perhaps, or all of life.

If we stick to our species, then we do rush on in a half-dressed flurry at the very end. That is true on the time line of the Earth, and even more so for the universe. But suppose we think of "us" as life as a whole—living beings. Life does not look like an insignificant scrap in the history of Earth, and not even in the history of the universe. The age of the universe, as far as we can tell, is a bit under 14 billion years. Life has existed on Earth for something like 3.7 billion. That is over a quarter of the total span.

We, in this very broad sense of "we," have been around a while. Living organization is one of the longer-running features of the universe. It has existed only in a tiny spatial region, as far as we know, and even if there are other inhabited planets, the whole of life's extent will probably remain tiny in spatial terms. But within that small region, life is not something that scrambles on at the end of a vast dead stretch. Instead, life is a long-term tenant.

Perhaps this broad conception of our place in things, using a sense of "we" and "our" that includes bacteria, won't resonate with everyone. We might think instead about animals. Even animal life is not too fleeting a part of history. Animals might be 650 million years old or so, which gives us about 5 percent of known time. But I do want to think in those broader terms, about life in its entirety.

Given that living beings are long-term tenants within the total span of the universe, we take up a much larger fraction of the history of the Earth. The Earth is about 4.5 billion years old. So life has been around for most of the time the Earth has existed, a good majority of the time.

In this sense, life is a significant part of the Earth's story. And it is even more so in other senses—when we think of what life *does*, what sort of engine it is, what sort of factor in the whole.

Origins

How life arose is still uncertain. There's not much progress or consensus, as far as I can tell, about the likely details, the where and how. But we know roughly what sort of things had to happen, and that gives an overall shape to the story.

A living organism is a pocket of order, a cluster of chemical processes that maintains itself, self-perpetuates, keeps re-creating its otherwise improbable organization. Energy and other resources are required for such a thing to arise. The processes also have to be confined, so they don't diffuse away and become lost into their surrounds.

One setting in which this might get started is around ocean vents, where a natural flow of energy and materials comes up from beneath the Earth, and porous rocks provide compartments in which reactions can be partly confined. From there, some of these cycling tangles of activity could start to produce boundaries—rough and imperfect—that are self-made rather than externally provided. The result is something increasingly cell-like.

The more stable of these cell-like pockets of order will persist, and might bud off new ones, like daughters, containing small samples of these interacting chemicals. The budded-off daughter systems themselves might drift away, or accumulate into clumps. Each one is self-perpetuating, maintaining itself through cycles of chemical reactions, and occasionally creating new systems of the same kind.

Perhaps the story does not involve deep-sea vents. Darwin imagined a warm pond as the site; Graham Cairns-Smith suggested an environment of damp clay. All these scenarios do include a role for water—it can't happen on dry land. A similar general picture can be seen across these hypotheses: pockets of organization, making use of a source of energy and some initial way for reactions to compartmentalize, leading to cell-like self-maintaining beings that proliferate within a more chaotic and disorderly sea around them.

Not everyone thinks the sequence of events has this shape. In those sketches over the last page or so, I took sides on a divide between two camps. I treated the "metabolic" side of life as basic and original—chemical reactions forming cycles, using energy, becoming marked off into cells. Another framework sets out from a different view of what is fundamental. In Richard Dawkins's 1976 book *The Selfish Gene*, life begins with *replication*, with some molecule arising that produces copies of itself. These copying molecules spread, become numerous, and can also have effects on what's around them that influence their chances of being copied. Some are better at this than others, and through this initial Darwinian competition they become able to form cells and control metabolic processes, slowly bringing more of the world under their control. One form of this scenario is the "RNA world" hypothesis. RNA, a molecule found in all cells today, might be the original molecule of replication and control, with DNA and all the rest coming later.

The choice between the origin stories I compared just now can be described as one between "metabolism first" and "replicator first" scenarios. Eventually, we need both—molecules that are copied, and the energy-using processes of metabolism. The details can go in different ways. I have always had a nonexpert attraction to the metabolism-first approach, and a suspicion that replicator-first views will come to seem traceable to the preoccupations of the twentieth century—the "century of the gene," as the historian of science Evelyn Fox Keller has called it. But even if the replicator-based view is a reflection of a gene-centered mindset, that does not preclude it from being right.

Metabolism, those energy-using chemical cycles, might have grown up around replication, rather than metabolizing systems arising first and then making themselves a molecule, RNA or DNA, that works like a cellular "memory," enabling these systems to push their organization onward through time.

Alternatively, perhaps the two activities were bound together from the start. Somehow we get both, metabolism and reproduction, a package of features tied together. What we call "life" usually involves both of these phenomena—the use of energy to maintain order, and the production of new living beings from old. These two activities can still come apart; viruses are packets of genetic material that use the metabolisms of others to reproduce, and have no metabolic activity themselves. Are viruses alive? They have a part of the usual combination, and whether this is enough for them to be *alive* is not something to argue about. The idea of life as a sharp and definite category has been replaced by a view that accepts gradations and gray-area cases.

Another feature that seems to run deep through the history of life is sensing, and responding to what is sensed. This is not known for sure, but sensing is so common across widely divergent forms of life now, including relatively simple ones, that it is probably very old. Recall the start of this chapter, with the dinosaur talk and the idea of life as a long-term feature of the world. If you think of early life as a sort of inert mold or slime, then perhaps its duration is less notable. But when sensing and responding are also very old, that changes the feel of things. Someone has been looking out, just a little, for all that time.

A further feature is also ubiquitous, perhaps more inevitably so. This is having *effects*, changing one's surroundings. Initially this might involve no more than the consumption of nutrients and the emitting of waste, but life, from the start, does not leave things as they were.

If early life involved the formation of pockets of order, pockets of improbable patterning, with this comes the formation of *selves*—the marking-off of self and other. The origin of life is the origin of new divisions in nature. With these divisions comes a kind of complementarity—the creation of complementary roles. Here is an organism, a self-maintaining pocket of order, and here is the environment it depends upon and transforms.*

When I talk about "selves" originating with life, the simplest picture is one where those pockets of order have clear boundaries. There has to be traffic across those borders—hence gates or portals—but we might still picture the divide as pretty sharp. But often—perhaps always—an image with sharply drawn lines is not right and the border is vaguer.

One place to see this is a coral reef. A coral is an animal, a relative of jellyfish and anemones. Huge numbers of these animals live in colonies within a reef. Those coral animals, the polyps, often have symbionts living within them that absorb energy from the sun. The polyps themselves also build a rock-like external body or support, which is responsible for the hardness of the reef. Doing this—building rock, essentially—requires a delicate chemical balance. Some of this takes place within the

---

* I hesitated initially to use the word "complementarity," because of its history in the physics and philosophy of Niels Bohr, one of the pioneers of quantum mechanics. For Bohr, complementary properties of an object cannot be measured or observed simultaneously, and that is different from what I have in mind. This is the best term to use here, though. For Bohr, complementarity is a relation between two properties of one object; here, it's a relation between intertwined beings: organism and environment, self and other.

cells of the coral, while other parts of the process take place just outside, in a kind of controlled space just beyond what would usually be seen as the border of the animal. Living activity often extends some way into a semi-transformed or controlled zone of this kind.

Cycles and Burial

I am sitting out in the garden, being cooked by the sun in a black shirt. Thinking, as best I can, about energy.

Large amounts of energy come in from the sun to the Earth. Much is radiated back, but not all. Some is absorbed and stays around. This energy can do different things according to the form it is in. A simple wash of heat can't do much. How does energy make its way into more useful forms, the forms that can power our lives?

In photosynthesis, the sun's radiation is transformed into chemical energy. This can be done in a few different ways. In all of them, light is absorbed by a molecule of some kind that uses the light's energy to excite its electrons (the charged particles that orbit the nucleus in atoms). If sufficient light comes in, this initiates a cascade by which electrons move from molecule to molecule. By means of these cascades, various kinds of processing and pumping can be achieved.

Crucially, the electrons that are sent off onto an "electron transport chain" by the incoming light need to be replaced. In the main kind of photosynthesis, the kind seen in plants today, this is accomplished by splitting water into its constituents, hydrogen and oxygen, and extracting electrons from the hydrogen atoms as this is done. You start from light, carbon dioxide, and water, and at the end you have chemical energy, in all its useful, portable controllability. You also end up with oxygen gas, which so far in the story is a mere byproduct.

To invent the water-splitting, oxygen-producing form of photosynthesis, two molecular machines from other simple organisms were brought together into a combination. (These are called photosystems 1 and 2. They did originate in a single invention, further back, then diverged and reunited.) This trick seems to have evolved just once.

Not all photosynthesis is like this. Scattered over Earth now, in twilight zones and marginal places, are single-celled organisms that do it differently, organisms with names befitting their exotic lifestyles—the green gliding bacteria, the purple sulfur bacteria. These use other substances as sources of electrons, instead of water. That means that not all photosynthesis is "oxygenic"—not all gives rise to oxygen gas. The special kind was invented by cyanobacteria (or their near ancestors), in the momentous event commemorated in the previous chapter at Shark Bay.

As time passes, over decades of research, this particular reaction has come to seem more and more important. Its place in Earth's history becomes clearer and the language used about it gets stronger. Andrew Knoll, a Harvard biologist who works on early life, says that the bringing together of the devices needed to make oxygen-producing photosynthesis might be regarded, from an ecological perspective, as "the central event in the history of life." Without it, life would have remained more a fringe dweller than an Earth changer, confined to chemically special environments like those deep-sea vents. James Barber, who admittedly worked for much of his career on photosynthesis itself, says that the splitting of water molecules, that difficult step, is simply "the most fundamental reaction on Earth."

Writing this book made it necessary to read and learn in areas I'd never looked at closely before, and this is one of them. By the end, I found myself picking up some of the awe seen in those who spend their lives unraveling the tiny conveyor belts and turbines of photosynthesis, a multitude in every leaf. This is awe at what life came up with, and awe at its consequences. On a lifeless planet, or even one without photosynthesis, energy pours in continually but radiates away as heat because there is no way to convert it into chemical energy. The light-harvesting molecules in bacteria and plants take the whole system into a new place because they absorb and accumulate energy from several incoming photons, and make the transition to chemical energy possible. The sheer amount of energy present on a living planet is greater than on a dead one, as energy has been converted and held. This feeds not only living activity, but geological cycles and processes as well. Life starts storing the sun, and everything is affected.

In photosynthesis itself, oxygen gas has no role; it is left behind when the more "useful" parts of the water molecule have been taken away and put to work. Oxygen is used in other reactions within organisms, including organisms that photosynthesize, but its creation is as a byproduct.

The history of oxygen on Earth, from this point onward, has several stages. Cyanobacteria began to quietly produce the gas. For a while, not much happened. The oxygen was absorbed by rocks, as seen in those red deserts of the first chapter, and taken up in various other ways. But it slowly began to accumulate. Later still, cyanobacteria were incorporated as symbiotic partners inside other organisms, and eventually made their way into plants. This ancient engulfing is similar to an event in which some bacteria were swallowed up by other cells and became mitochondria. These are the powerhouses that lie within us, and within plants, and aid in respiration, which is the biological flip side of photosynthesis; it burns fuels with the aid of oxygen. So animals (and also fungi, and some others) are carrying around one kind of bacterial remnant, mitochondria, and plants and algae are carrying around two.

Back during the early stages, oxygen levels were only a few percent of the atmosphere (at least most of the time—they may have jumped around). That is nowhere near what animals like us, and perhaps just about any animals, need. But this change was still important enough to be called "The Great Oxygenation," beginning roughly 2.4 billion years ago. The levels rose again much later, perhaps near the start of the Cambrian period about 540 million years ago. Fitful increases continued, until we reached the sort of chemical environment in which lives like ours, with muscles and brains, are possible. This enveloping of the Earth in oxygen also had other consequences, on a geological scale, changing the chemistry and geology of the planet. New kinds of minerals—new "mineral species"—came to exist, including semiprecious stones like azurite and malachite, formed through processes featuring the reactivity of oxygen, or through the chemical action of life itself.

With the early history of oxygen in place, it's time to bring carbon to the fore. As the ongoing dance between oxygen and carbon is so important, and as it has taken me a long time to understand it even imperfectly, I will take a pretty slow walk through it.

We have two main players at the level of chemical elements: carbon, with its versatility as a building block, able to form all sorts of complicated molecules; and oxygen, with its reactivity. We also have two pivotal gases they make up: oxygen as a gas, O_2, and CO_2, carbon dioxide.

All through here, we are dealing with a combination of processes working at different scales—fast and slow, biological and geological. What new factors like human behaviors do is nudge, perturb, push, against a background of many others.

The picture we are sometimes given is that plants breathe in carbon dioxide and breathe out oxygen, and we depend on this, day to day. The rainforests are the lungs of the Earth, it is said. Or, the Earth's lungs are the forests plus the oceans. But plants "breathe" in two ways. They take in carbon dioxide when growing, but they also respire, as animals do, to keep the processes of life going. When plants do this, they use oxygen. As long as a plant is growing, it produces more oxygen than it uses. The growth of plants is a process gently out of balance, in a way that adds oxygen to the atmosphere and stores carbon in living matter. But a forest as a whole, when mature and in a steady state, includes not only the growth of plants but also their ongoing existence, their breakdown by microbes and fungi, and also all that animals within a forest do. These are oxygen-consuming processes. A forest is a great producer of oxygen, and also a great consumer. That to-and-fro in a mature forest is pretty much *in* balance—except when the breakdown of plants does not happen. If trees, once built, are buried and squashed before they can break down, then some of their carbon is interred in the Earth, and oxygen that might otherwise combine with this carbon remains above.

These processes act against a background of others. Carbon and oxygen are also tied together in a to-and-fro involving the weathering of rocks, the laying down of sediments in the sea, and the action of volcanoes. In this slower cycle, carbon dioxide in the atmosphere is absorbed into rain to make a weak acid, rainfall over land runs into the sea, weathering rocks as it goes, and this flow contributes to a mix of chemicals that is used by marine organisms to make carbon-rich shells. That carbon is laid down into rock, eventually pulled deeper into the Earth, and released back into the air by volcanoes. This slower "inorganic" carbon cycle involves life, not just because the sediments that store carbon in rock are full of seashells, but because life on land has a big effect on the weathering stage. Plants and fungi can increase the rate of erosion and weathering considerably, by holding water against rocks, making stronger acids, and slowly fragmenting rocks with roots and fungal strands.

We breathe oxygen made by plants and plankton. But if you instantly took all the plants and plankton away, we'd be able to keep breathing for a long time (millennia at least). This is possible because there's now a huge reservoir of oxygen in the atmosphere. That reservoir came from life, from a slight imbalance between oxygen-making and oxygen-using processes over long periods. It is being cycled, used and replaced; the breath you take now could contain oxygen that has not been in the atmosphere for long at all. But the reservoir is huge.

If we suddenly burned all the known accessible stores of fossil fuels on Earth, this would also have little effect on the oxygen reservoir. Humans and other animals don't have the kind of impact on oxygen that we have on other things, especially carbon dioxide. Carbon dioxide is much rarer in the atmosphere than oxygen—only about one-twentieth of 1 percent, whereas oxygen is about 21 percent. But when the level of carbon dioxide goes up or down, even at that smaller scale, this can have dramatic effects. If we burned all those known fossil fuels right now, we would have a big impact, proportionally, on the carbon dioxide in the atmosphere, and that would make a difference to all sorts of things.

This idea that the forests and oceans are our lungs—the real-time source of the oxygen we need—is one that people are sometimes reluctant to correct, as it helps with our sense of the urgency and importance of environmental protection. In this book I want to cover every part of these problems as accurately as I can. The Earth has some features that life (the long-term and continually renovating tenant) affects over long spans, but human choices don't, very much. Oxygen levels are an example. It also contains processes that human choices do affect—the production of carbon dioxide. And all this takes place against a background of processes on an even larger scale, with the sun getting brighter, the Earth slowing in its orbit, and the galaxies moving apart.

This part of the story of the Earth is often told in a way that positions oxygen as the crucial factor—oxygen making animal life possible. I don't disagree, but just as fundamental is the way the invention of photosynthesis led to large amounts of the sun's energy being captured and held in chemical form. The Earth became infused, crammed, with energy in a way that would not happen without life. Bonds were built between atoms in new kinds of molecules, bonds that stored the sun's energy. That energy, with the aid of oxygen, could then be released, sending life swarming over the Earth.

A Circus of Forms

From single-celled life arose collections, colonies, and collaborations of many kinds. The multicellular organisms we are most familiar with are plants and animals, and also fungi (who are closer to animals than plants), but these are just some of the ways cells come to live together, forming blends and fusions, symbiotic and antagonistic.

Earlier I mentioned corals, animals with photosynthetic algae living inside their bodies. Those algae are of a kind called *dinoflagellates*. (This is the same group of algae that cause red tides.) The dinoflagellates themselves contain remnants of cyanobacteria, as you might expect, given that they engage in photosynthesis. But those are not the only layers in the system—it's not just cyanobacteria, dinoflagellates, coral. To acquire their ability to photosynthesize, the dinoflagellates engulfed *another* kind of algae that had previously engulfed a cyanobacterium. Some corals have also been found with cyanobacteria living inside them "naked," as if to remind the corals of the debt they owe to these tiny and more ancient organisms.

This willingness on the part of life to form collections and collaborations engenders a circus of forms, a great diversity of larger units, all making use of those basic ingredients—the living activity of cells, sensing and responding, taking material in and emitting waste, and changing over time. One lineage that pursued a multicellular experiment gave rise to animals. Cells came to live together, as they did often elsewhere, but in this case they did so in a way that invested in controlled motion, in action. To coordinate this, they evolved nervous systems and brains.

Animals arose initially in a low-oxygen environment, much lower than what we experience now. As oxygen levels increased, they were able to become more active. This is part of what happened around the "Cambrian explosion" about 540 million years ago. The explosion was a "coevolutionary" event, one in which evolution in one kind of animal provided an impetus to evolution in others, and vice versa, but all this may also have been set in motion, or at least facilitated, by an infusion of oxygen into marine environments. The amounts of oxygen were still well short of present-day levels, but enough to make a difference. And then, millions of years later, some animals moved onto land.

Much will follow from this—from the animal investment in action, the move onto land and the different lives possible there, and the environmental transformations that result. First, though, I want to return to a theme from the very start of the chapter.

I said back there that although the human species rushes on in the last small part of the total span of time, *life* is not like that, and we can think of ourselves as part of life as a whole. I want to say a bit more about the "part of" idea. Once cellular life exists (bacteria, animals, plants, and so on), cells come always from cells. It is cell giving rise to cell, over the millennia, through all the evolutionary changes and the new species that arise. And when a cell produces a daughter cell, there is a material continuity between them. Membranes, for example, come materially from other membranes; a new cell membrane has part of an old membrane within it. This process is mixed up and more complicated in some cases (as when sperm meets egg), but cells come from cells, with material continuation. It's not that you will have inherited particular material parts from some ancient life-form, but that there is a chain of such relationships—the cells in you containing parts of earlier cells, which contained parts of earlier ones, and so on.

When we look back, then, it's not just that we are living organisms, examples of life, and such things were around back then as well. And it's not just that the link of reproduction has been present since then, with old organisms somehow making new ones. We are also a *material continuation* of what was here before. This relationship stretches back through our ancestors, through lizard-like beings, fish, worm-like animals, to single-celled life. Our ties to ancient life-forms are not just a matter of causal connection. A stronger bond connects old and new organisms, projecting life through time, and this bond has been in place for most of the history of the Earth and much of the history of the universe.

Gaia

The scene coming into view is one of a dynamic Earth. The Earth is not an inert stage, or something that only changes under its own steam; it changes as a result of the actions of life. Once we have come this far, a gestalt switch is possible, a way of taking things further. Back in the 1970s, James Lovelock and Lynn Margulis introduced the "Gaia hypothesis." The Earth, they suggested, is itself an organism, or at least organism-like. It regulates itself, a huge system with a metabolism that spans the plant and animal world along with parts of the Earth that we usually think of as inorganic. Earlier in this chapter, we already found the need to talk about borderline and partial cases when thinking about the origins of life. Maybe there's another phenomenon of this kind, on a much larger scale?

Lovelock, who died at 103 as I was finishing this book, was a chemist and inventor. He devised a detector that picks up tiny traces of pollutants in the air, and spent most of his career as an industry consultant rather than an academic. He was led to reflect on the ways that life, on any planet, will tend to modify its atmosphere. The atmosphere found on Earth, especially with all that oxygen, would be noticeable from far away in space as abnormal, as marked by life. We should be able to work out whether other planets contain life by looking for the same sort of signature.

From there, Lovelock introduced the idea that perhaps a planet like Earth can have the metabolism of a living organism—*is* something like a living organism. The novelist William Golding (*Lord of the Flies*) suggested the name Gaia for this idea, from the ancient Greek goddess of the Earth. The American cell biologist Lynn Margulis, like Lovelock a rebel in science, became an early supporter and co-developer of the theory. In this book, I've treated the idea that remnants of cyanobacteria found themselves inside plants just as something that happened, a historical fact, but it was Margulis who rescued this idea from near-oblivion in the 1960s. She made the same claim about mitochondria, the powerhouses found within the cells of animals, plants, and others—Margulis argued that they, too, are descended from free-living bacteria. Margulis didn't invent these ideas about the origins of our cells, but she brought them back from the fringe. When I was a student in the 1980s, her revival of this view was just starting to triumph over skeptics.

The Gaia hypothesis, in its original form, held that Earth is a huge self-regulating system that acts to maintain life. This is, without question, a radical idea, but points that can be raised in support of it do look intriguing, to say the least. (Ford Doolittle, one of the early critics of Gaia, always acknowledged these; Gaia is not just gratuitous storytelling, or a poetic invocation of natural harmony.) One example is Earth's temperature. Life requires liquid water—water on Earth can't be all ice, or all gaseous vapor. And although we are a suitable distance from our sun for the temperature to be roughly in the right place, the sun's own temperature is not a constant; it has become a good deal hotter over the time that life has existed on Earth. Somehow, the overall temperature on the planet has been kept in a fairly narrow and life-friendly range.

Another example is the saltiness of the sea. Salt is carried to the sea in runoff from rain and rivers. Although salt water is in many ways friendly to life, if the sea was much saltier than it is now, most life could not cope. When a history of liquid water was discovered on Mars, this seemed encouraging to the idea of Martian life. But it looks like that water might have been too salty. And while we can easily see how more salt will keep running into our oceans, it's hard to see how much gets *out*. Might Earth build itself evaporation pans that trap salt in solid form and keep the ocean's salinity at a reasonable level? In his original Gaia book, Lovelock wondered whether the Great Barrier Reef in Australia might be a "partly finished project for an evaporation lagoon." That is a startling idea, but in this case and others, we do need *some* explanation for the ongoing life-friendliness of Earth.

Let's look, then, at what it would be for Earth to be an organism. Not all versions of the Gaia idea are committed to this view, but let's start here. We agree that Earth is a complex system, full of interactions. That is not enough for it to be an organism. A global war is an interconnected system, but not an organism. We need, at least, a high degree of cooperation. The parts of a system must work together to keep it going, to keep the arrangement in place, maintaining order in the face of tendencies to fall apart.

The biologists David Queller and Joan Strassmann take this idea further by classifying systems using two dimensions: cooperation and conflict. Systems are more organism-like— more "organismal"—when their parts show a high degree of cooperation and low conflict. Isn't one of these the flip side of the other? No, they say; a system can contain a lot of cooperation and a lot of conflict at the same time. Human societies are like this.

The form of cooperation that is relevant here is also a special kind. It involves working together in a way that maintains the integrity of a system, maintains its organization in the face of forces of decay. A living animal, such as a giraffe, is a clear case, but if we take this approach, there will be a lot of partial or gray-area cases, rather than a sharp divide between organisms and non-organisms. We saw the same thing in the discussion earlier in this chapter of the origins of life. So, as a next move, the question we should be asking is not a simple "Is the Earth an organism?" Instead, we can ask whether the Earth has organism-like features, whether it organizes itself in something like that way.

A system with organism-like features can arise through a coming together of parts with diverse origins. Much research in recent years has been directed on the close relationships between human bodies and the beneficial bacteria living in our guts. Some people think the human organism itself is a combination of animal cells and bacterial cells. A better example might be a cow, which has a stronger dependence on internal bacteria to digest its food. A cow is a bit like the corals we encountered earlier with photosynthetic algae living inside them. An example with more "looseness" is a collaboration that has been found between ants and acacia trees. These acacias build living quarters and provide food for ant colonies that live inside them. The ants, in turn, protect the tree from other animals who would like to eat it. This is not as intimate a connection as the cow-bacteria case, but although the ant houses are clearly part of the tree, they are there for the ants to live in. If we ask whether the cow-plus-bacteria really *is* an organism in its own right, then whether the ant-acacia combination counts as well, or whether these are all just collaborations between separate organisms, this question looks for a defi-

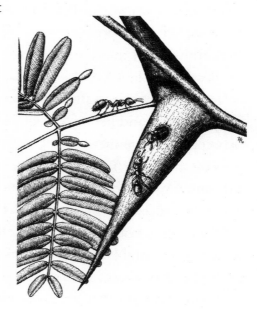

nite dividing line where none exists. What we find is differences of degree, borderline cases as well as clear ones, and a great variety of ways that a system can be organism-*ish*, or organism-like.

When Lovelock and Margulis suggested that the Earth is an organism, they did not say much about how this situation might arise. That led to objections from evolutionary biologists. Organisms have to arise from Darwinian processes, unless deliberate design is going on. God is not supposed to be in the picture, so it would have to be evolution. Evolution by natural selection requires a population, one in which reproduction takes place. New variants arise by chance in the population, and the ones that are better at keeping themselves going and reproducing may proliferate and spread. This also requires that the quirks that give one type an advantage over others are inherited over generations. Those that do well can then become a platform on which further rounds of variation and selection take place. A Darwinian process is a kind of grand trial-and-error, spread over a population.

In the case of the Earth as a whole, the universe does have a collection of planets, but no reproduction, no inheritance, and no competition among them. So there's no Darwinian process, biologists said, and hence no way for something like the Earth to become an organism.

This for a time seemed an important objection to Gaia, but I think now it is not so good. First, the way life initially arose on Earth, especially on a metabolism-first view, has to be somewhat different from the usual kind of Darwinian process, although the "many experiments, a few successes" side still has to be in place. As we saw a moment ago, organism-like things can also arise through the coming together of parts with different origins, and these will have their own distinct, but connected, evolutionary histories. The ant-acacia collaborations are an example. A version of the Gaia hypothesis might work along similar lines. It might say that the Earth as a whole includes organism-like cooperative setups; it is like an ant-acacia system on a huge scale.

Is this possible, at the scale of the entire Earth? It's not impossible, but *very* unlikely. This is partly because there will be continual opportunities for breakout, for a loss of a cooperative balance. In cases like the ant and acacia, we have cooperation between initially surprising partners, but those cooperative relationships are forged in conflict with other organisms. The ant-acacia relationship makes sense because the plants would like a defense against other animals who would like to eat them. It is very hard for *everyone* to be—and especially for them to *stay*—part of the same cooperative project. The ants-and-acacias say: It's us against the world! Against the herbivorous world, anyway. On close inspection, this is not much of a model for Gaia.

Living things do sometimes have mutually compatible needs, but often they have antagonistic ones. The Earth, and anything on a similar scale and inhabited by organisms that are products of Darwinian processes, will always be a different kind of system from an organism. A big, complex system in which life plays an important part does not *itself* have to be organism-like—another organism, with the same features seen again at the new scale. It can be a different kind of thing, one that organisms are a part of, along with other parts. This is an example of what I referred to as complementarity earlier in this chapter. In this view, we can still acknowledge that the

Earth is a special kind of system, one where life matters and there's much feedback between the living and the nonliving.

The Earth-as-organism idea might also be seen as a metaphor rather than a claim to be taken literally. Some people certainly find the image appealing—it takes us back toward a mother-like Earth. But then we have to ask whether the metaphor helps us more than it misleads. People often seem to think that the metaphor has a positive role because it gets us to recognize and care about the whole. I am not sure about that; it might be quite unhelpful. Talk of Gaia invites us to think the Earth will *take care of itself*, if given time to adjust. It invites us to think there's something big and thoughtful in the neighborhood that can compensate for our errors. It will know what to do, and will find a solution. This is not a good way to be thinking, because there's *not* something big and thoughtful around on this scale, and no reason to expect future changes to head in a helpful direction all by themselves. This sort of vague hope is encouraged by talk of Gaia.

In recent years, some defenders of Gaia have moved away from the Earth-as-organism picture. They think Lovelock and Margulis went too far in that respect. Sometimes people just want to use talk of Gaia to emphasize the connections between living and nonliving parts of the Earth system (a view sometimes called "weak Gaia"). Another way of seeing the Gaia hypothesis is not just an acknowledgment of connections, but a claim about a tendency for various processes on Earth to regulate conditions in a way that is helpful to life, without the system being organism-like. The British scientist Tim Lenton defends this view.

The life-friendly features of our planet do have to be acknowledged. In the case of temperature, one puzzle is that the sun gets warmer while the temperature on Earth does not change much. Earlier in this chapter, I said that carbon dioxide levels are affected both by a cycle that runs through living activity in plants and animals, and by a slower "geological" cycle—rain, weathering of rocks, seashells, more rocks, volcanoes. This cycle has "negative feedback" built into it. That means there's a process in place where, as the level of some factor increases, it triggers events that push it down again, and vice versa (when its level drops, it triggers something that pushes it up). In this case, when conditions are warmer, this turns up the activity in the carbon-storing part of the cycle—more rain, more weathering, more carbon locked away. But the parts of the cycle returning carbon dioxide to the atmosphere are not much affected. Since carbon dioxide traps heat in the atmosphere, when its levels go down, the Earth's surface is cooled. Given all this, hotter conditions tend to lock up more carbon, and that exerts (very slowly) a cooling effect. Cool conditions, on the other hand, reduce the weathering that locks carbon away, and this pushes temperatures up.

I also noted back then that plants and fungi on land increase the weathering of rocks. This is relevant to the stabilization of temperatures. Plants cool the Earth, both through this effect and through the laying down of coal. Our early atmosphere seems to have had a lot more carbon dioxide, leading to a strong "greenhouse effect" that warmed the Earth, preventing the seas from freezing when the sun was fainter. Since then, the sun has gotten hotter, but much of that carbon, thanks to life, has been taken out of the atmosphere. All this is a combination of negative feedback and an alignment between processes that are just going on their own path without life affecting them. The sun slowly gets warmer, no matter what we do.

How about the salt in the oceans? This case is interesting because scientists, at the moment, seem a bit uncertain about it. Sometimes people say the salt level is not held stable, but only changes very slowly. Either way, it has stayed in a life-friendly range for a long time. The main way that salt can be removed from the sea is through evaporation, in places where, for some reason, water does not get replenished and salt is left behind. If this happens on a large enough scale, it forms a "salt giant," a deposit of solid salt whose depth is measured in hundreds or thousands of meters. Around 5.5 million years ago, much or all of the Mediterranean Sea dried out in this way, before water came rushing back in. Why should a combination of this sort of process, with the ferrying of salt to the sea in runoff, lead to a roughly stable salt level? Is there some potential for negative feedback here, or are the two processes just separate, and (from our point of view) helpfully aligned?

Some life-relevant features have not been stable at all. Oxygen levels in the atmosphere have gone up and down a lot, in part due to changes in those "cycles and burial" processes I looked at earlier. Sometimes more carbon is buried and oxygen levels increase; sometimes things tend the other way.

Our picture, as far as I can make out, is that the Earth has indeed tended to stay in a fairly life-friendly range for a long time. It won't always do so—the sun, it seems, will eventually cook away the oceans completely. But for a fair while, conditions have been friendly. This is not because a vast organism is regulating things in a goal-directed manner. Instead, a collection of processes, quite disparate ones, operate in tandem and do keep things—or *have* kept things, at least—in a life-friendly state.

Why do they do this? Is it a matter of luck? This is not luck in the usual sense, not like a lottery or game of roulette. In each case, a huge mechanism lies behind things, one involving physical principles and the history of the Earth.

We might have a story for each factor (temperature, salt, etc.), but what about the fact that all of these helpful mechanisms are in place together—is *that* just luck? In a sense, yes; I can see what the word "luck" refers to there. It refers to the fact that there's no overarching explanation of why all these processes (each big, and ancient) head in a direction that is suitable for life. Does this show a failure of understanding on our part? Must there be more to it?

Some of it *does* have to be luck, in this broad sense, including important parts. Tim Lenton, the Gaia-friendly scientist I mentioned earlier, notes that a planet with life has to have water, in good amounts, before life appears. I'm not talking here about whether the water is ice or liquid, but just its abundance. Earth had plenty of water. Why? Much of it was probably brought in on asteroids, Lenton says. If so, this has to be a matter of luck no matter what one thinks about Gaia. Even a living planet can't call in asteroids bearing water. An articulate Gaia would have to say: "Yes, that thing with the water and asteroids is pretty good, but it's not one of mine."

A role here is also played by "observation selection effects," as they are sometimes known. Suppose we do need water-bearing asteroids for the evolution of complex and intelligent life. Then intelligent beings will only be around to ask these questions on planets that have gotten lucky in this way. If there are many planets that can be seen as "experiments" of this kind, with different amounts of water coming in to each, and a small number of planets have a life-friendly quantity of water arriving, then any intelligent beings on those planets will say, "That's remarkable; conditions here had to be just right." But there were many such experiments. In such a scenario, someone will end up noting their good luck, and it happens to be us. This only helps remove a sense of mystery about the life-friendly conditions on Earth if there *are* a lot of experiments, and hence a reasonable chance of someone being alive somewhere and able to reflect on their good luck. Otherwise, we do have to accept that a low-probability event has occurred. (If a million people play a gambling game that has odds of success for each person of a million-to-one against, someone will probably end up happy. If only a hundred people play, then any win is surprising.)

Is it then likely, as in my scenario above, that someone, on some planet, will end up saying, surrounded by ample water and friendly temperatures, "Look how lucky we were!"? That is a good question. If an Earth scientist who knows more than I do about all this says *no*, it was not at all likely, then I must take that seriously. Then either there was, indeed, a stroke of something like luck, or perhaps we don't know the whole story.

Where does this leave us? Some of our planet's stabilizing, life-friendly effects are not just intriguing; they can look a little uncanny. The combination of factors that have kept our water from freezing or boiling away is like that—or seems so to me, anyway.

Lenton would say: To believe that these feedback connections are there, and helping life survive, *is* to accept the Gaia idea, in a more modern form. I would respond that the Gaia idea can certainly change—can evolve. An echo of pervasive cooperation does still come with the term, and that is misleading. So is the suggestion that there's a single center of control at work, something like a single agent. Whatever language we decide to use, the right picture to have in mind is, I think, one that uses that idea of complementarity introduced earlier in this chapter. As you walk along, you are a living part of a larger system, one that has living and nonliving parts. That system is not much like an organism, but it is a system in which the nonliving is closely tied to the living. The Earth has been enlivened by its organisms, even though it is not itself alive.

Goals

One thing that can make the Gaia idea exciting is the suggestion that events in the atmosphere and broader environment happen for a reason, in a particular sense of that term. They don't just have causes—things that make them happen—but purposes.

The idea of purpose in nature is occasionally criticized as unscientific, but *some* of what goes on is purpose-driven. Humans can act with a goal or purpose in mind. And, a bit more controversially, an event like a flow of adrenaline has a purpose within our bodies even when we don't consciously decide to produce it. Adrenaline flows prepare the organism for fight or flight—that is what they are *for*.

If the whole Earth was an organism, this is part of what we'd get. All sorts of subtle activities might go on in order to keep conditions on our planet within a suitable range for life, just as all sorts of processes within us go on to keep our body temperature in the right range. I argued against this view of the Earth, but purposes and goals are important in their own right, and they are going to appear often in the chapters to come.

Goals, purposes, and functions (in one sense of that term) are often referred to as *teleological* concepts. In the ancient scientific/philosophical framework of Aristotle, influential for many centuries, just about all natural processes have something like a goal, a natural end. The model of a growing tree, going through a sequence of events that manifests its nature and purpose, was applied very broadly, even to inanimate objects. This way of thinking was readily taken over into a Christian framework, when it arose centuries later. Purpose was still everywhere, and now reflected God's creation and will.

The scientific revolution in seventeenth-century Europe included attacks on the overuse of teleological ideas, even though the scientific revolutionaries were generally not atheists. This continued in the eighteenth-century "Enlightenment" period. A picture of the world as driven by physical mechanisms, impacts, and push-pull causes seemed to leave little or no place for purpose. Darwinism, when it appeared in the next century, was sometimes seen as reviving a role for purpose in nature, because "natural selection" is a bit like choice, and sometimes seen as continuing teleology's banishment, because natural selection is a physical process with no conscious guidance. I think the right interpretation is that teleological ideas did get a low-key revival within Darwinism, and something similar happened within cybernetics, a field that arose a century or so later.

In outlining how all this works, I'll make use of ideas from the American philosopher Larry Wright, who wrote about the scientific place of teleological ideas in a very insightful way. I augment his ideas with modifications of my own.

Some things, Wright said, happen because of their effects. That sounds odd, backwards, impossible—and in a pure form, it is. The actual effects something has can't reach around through time and cause it to happen, or to come into existence. But there are a couple of approximations to that situation. One is where we *think* about an effect, something we want to happen, and act accordingly. We act in a way that we think will bring the effect about. I think that if I put this wedge of paper under the table leg, it will stop the table from rocking, so I put the paper there. Maybe it won't work, but that was my goal, and that is why a bit of paper is now under the table leg.

Some non-conscious, less intentional processes can have a similar feature. Suppose you are looking at a biological organ like a heart, or an event like an adrenaline flow. What you are looking at is the latest member of a long line of similar objects or events. A long line of beating hearts was there in other animals before this one. A long line of adrenaline flows went before this one. In cases like this, earlier members of the line have done something, have had effects, that help bring newer members of the line into existence. Earlier hearts helped keep animals alive, and that has led to hearts being kept around, and also refined, in evolutionary processes. Hearts don't directly give rise to more hearts, but they do play an indirect role in new hearts being produced. The same is true of adrenaline flows. The useful effects that earlier members of the line had can play a role in explaining why things are the way they are now—why hearts, and adrenaline flows, have continued on. Adrenaline flows, hearts, and mating displays exist, roughly speaking, because of their effects.

Hearts are there because they pump blood—that is their function within the body. The bit of paper is under my table's leg because it will stop the table's rocking. That is its function, and that was the goal of my action in putting it there. This is a low-key rehabilitation of concepts that used to be used in more adventurous, all-encompassing ways. This rehabilitation does not carry over the idea that for something to perform its function is *good*, in a moral sense. That is left behind.

So far I've talked about two kinds of processes that can give rise to functions, purposes, and so on. One is evolution by natural selection and the other is deliberate, conscious choice. There are a few others—processes that are similar to evolution, or similar to deliberate choice. One is learning by trial and error, doing something today because it worked yesterday. You might have done it entirely accidentally the first time (it was a "random mutation" in your behavior), but it worked, so you continue to do it. This case includes a role for choice, but it also has similarities to evolution, and the choice need not always be conscious.

Larry Wright suggested that many of our ways of talking about purposes and goals originate in what is sometimes called a "dead metaphor"—a metaphor that has lost its metaphoricalness and given rise to a new way of using language literally. He thought that the conscious cases, where we do something with a goal in mind, are the starting point, and the nonconscious processes of evolution by natural selection, and some others, are treated as analogous to the conscious case. When hearts have been kept around by evolution because of their useful effects, this is like a person choosing to install a fan because of its useful effects.

In none of these cases is it literally true that X happens because it leads to Y, or X comes to exist because it does Y. Something can't exist because of what it *will do*, an effect it *will have*. That would be backward causation, or a kind of perfect teleology. Instead, the idea is that "X happens because it will lead to Y" gestures toward some phenomena that are real and that are close to the impossible case in different ways.

The history of our ways of talking about these things, according to Wright (and I think I agree), starts from the case of conscious planning. In nature, it goes the opposite way; it goes from unconscious evolutionary design, to learning, then to conscious planning and decision making. There's been a transition in nature between different ways in which the world can be shaped by goals and purposes.

In this setting, once again, we can find borderline cases, faint glimmers of what is seen more clearly elsewhere. Think back to those negative feedback cycles, discussed earlier when we looked at the temperature on Earth. As the system moves away from some state it's usually in, such as a temperature, it gets pulled back again. It gets pulled back because of an effect that the move away has had. The world gets warmer, that leads to more carbon being locked up in rock by the geological carbon cycle, and this (eventually) makes things cooler, heading back to where we started.

A heart, by pumping blood, does something that explains why it's there. In the carbon cycle feedback case, an increase in temperature has effects that explain why, in the future, the higher temperature is *not* there. Some of the same shape is present—faintly and in a transformed version—in a different and larger system that involves the whole Earth. If we go back to Darwinian evolution, that process, too, is a kind of feedback, now using the term in a broader way. The useful effects of hearts (and adrenaline flows) help animals to stay alive, this leads to them having offspring who also have hearts, and so on.

The Darwinian process is a kind of grand feedback system that depends on organisms and reproduction, and this is one of the great engines of creation on Earth.

Here is one more borderline or faint case. Some kinds of learning, I said, are similar to Darwinian evolution. Trial and error is like mutation and selection. Tim Lenton (the Gaia-friendly Earth scientist I mentioned earlier), drawing on conversations with the evolutionary theorist William Hamilton, noted that although the Earth does not exist within a population of the sort needed for evolution by natural selection, there might be a scenario in which life started up on Earth, then crashed, then started up again a bit differently, and so on, until it found a way of doing things that was stable. There could have been a series of trial-and-error episodes in the history of the Earth. This could happen, in principle, and then one might say, with poetic license, that the Earth *learns*, rather than evolves, to maintain life well.

Has there ever been anything like this in Earth's actual history? Perhaps, very far back. There have been a couple of events in which the entire surface of the Earth, or much of it, was frozen over. A runaway global cooling led to a snowball, or ice slushy, on a planetary scale. Then Earth broke out of this and made its way back to a state friendlier to life.

Life wasn't completely extinguished during these snowball misadventures. What crashed and recovered was some sort of overall setup involving living activity, the atmosphere, ocean chemistry, and other factors. One can imagine a situation where this happened several times—a series of failures and resets—before things got onto a more even keel.

I was surprised by this idea when I learned about it from

Lenton. In principle it does make sense. This is a hint, a faint case, of a grand-scale selection process that the Earth could be part of. Whether the crash-and-rebuild sequence actually led to significant results is a further question. I wonder if the past events we have evidence for could have done much to shape the life-friendly processes we've been looking at in this chapter. The possible snowball Earth events were rare (two or three in total) and very far back. They were well before life on land, for example. But I don't want to dismiss the idea.

When I think about that picture in which the Earth system makes its way to a healthy state in fits and starts—getting going, collapsing, and having to stumble back—I am reminded of David Hume, the great Scottish philosopher of the Enlightenment, whose *Dialogues Concerning Natural Religion* (posthumously and anonymously published) include a conversation in which one character concedes that perhaps *some* sort of deity made the Earth, but—he asks—what sort? Perhaps, he says, this world "was only the first rude essay of some infant deity, who afterwards abandoned it, ashamed of his lame performance." Or, alternatively, our world "is the work only of some dependent, inferior deity; and is the object of derision to his superiors." Or, lastly, it is perhaps the product "of old age and dotage in some superannuated deity." That creator has now died, and since then his world has been left to go on its own way—"has run on at adventures."

However this life-covered Earth came to be, and whether or not there were fits and false starts before our current track was finally established, "running on at adventures" is exactly what has happened since.

3

THE FOREST

The Whole Huge Hill in the Small Pool's Stomach

The Blue Mountains, a little west of Sydney, Australia, don't owe their dramatic contours to the usual mountain formers—volcanoes, fault lines, the collision of subterranean plates. Despite their sheer cliffs, they are, strictly speaking, not mountains at all, but island-like remains of an older high plateau carved out by rivers and streams. They were sculpted by water.

The young Charles Darwin came through the area in the 1830s during the voyage of HMS *Beagle*, a five-year surveying expedition on which he was the moody captain's dining companion. He visited a particular spot, a waterfall:

> Following down a little valley and its tiny rill of water, an immense gulf unexpectedly opens through the trees which border the pathway, at the depth of perhaps 1,500 feet. Walking on a few yards, one stands on the brink of a vast precipice, and below one sees a grand bay or gulf, for I know not what other name to give it, thickly covered with forest.

> The point of view is situated as if at the head of a bay,
> the line of cliff diverging on each side, and showing
> headland behind headland, as on a bold sea-coast.

Darwin was moved by the valleys to oceanic imagery. He also wondered whether there was more to it—whether what looked like old coastal headlands actually *were* old headlands, left behind by a receding sea. He thought this because, first, water seemed likely to be involved in some way, but to attribute what he was seeing to "the present alluvial action"—to small streams of the sort he was wandering along—"would be preposterous." Something larger in scale was needed.

He came up with a rather elaborate scenario, with the sea carving out valley-like spaces, followed by an elevation of the land, and the retreating sea or river-flows putting on the finishing touches.

The power of slow, everyday processes in shaping the Earth was central to the work of Charles Lyell, a Scottish geologist whose work Darwin had studied on the *Beagle* (one volume a gift from the captain, Robert FitzRoy, a second arriving to meet him in South America). Lyell's insight, his realization of the immense power of small causes operating over vast spans of time, was a central influence on Darwin's thinking. But in a way, Darwin did not fully apply the possibilities of this picture when he considered the Blue Mountains. Later in the same century, the geologist Charles Wilkinson hypothesized that it was the streams themselves—"tiny rills" of the kind Darwin had followed—that had created the scene, by patiently cutting and washing. This was the view that Darwin had mentioned but dismissed as "preposterous." The innocuous streams now running deep in Blue Mountains valleys are a paradigm for Lyell's vision, as they were, and are, the creators of the canyons.

Ted Hughes, in his poem "Sugar Loaf," wrote about a trickle of water forming a pool, with a hint of inanimate menace, on an English hillside: "This will be serious for the hill. / It suspects nothing." Hughes, looking on, could see the possibility of slow consumption: "the whole huge hill in the small pool's stomach."

In the morning, the Blue Mountains' valleys are sometimes filled by clouds and fog, settling at an exact level on the cliffs like a cup. Remembering the water that made them.

The Bark-Palaces We Call Plants

All through a recent winter, I did a series of walks in those Blue Mountains valleys. Setting off usually from the same place, a small parking lot on the edge of a cliff, I would follow a path of steep stairs, ladders in places, for about forty minutes down. The drop starts immediately and one is quickly below the surface and the streets. Light dims, and green closes over your head. Following small cascades—one of those omnipotent streams—you arrive eventually on the valley floor, finding a forest with tall trees and an understory of ferns.

A forest of this kind is a product of a reconfiguration of life that began around 125 million years ago, in an event sometimes called the Cretaceous Terrestrial Revolution. The Cretaceous was the last part of the dinosaurs' time. This "revolution" (some would resist the term) was not associated with the dinosaurs' demise, which came later, but was a broad shift at the level of whole environments, and a later member of the list of big, usually controversial, named landmarks in the history of life (the Great Oxygenation, the Cambrian Explosion . . .). The Cretaceous gave us now-familiar forest landscapes, a new profusion of animals, and changed relations between land and sea.

Land plants arose from colonies of green algae. Ancestors of those algae, living as single-celled organisms in the sea, had engulfed some of the cyanobacteria we met in Shark Bay, bringing on board their photosynthetic power. Some of the algae came to live in collections and strands, with descendants that crept onto land sometime around 470 million years ago.

Small and inconspicuous at first, moss-like, staying close to streams and ponds, they branched and expanded into ferns, cycads, and conifers. They began a close and mutually beneficial association with fungi, in and around their roots. A new group, flowering plants, became visible about 135 million years ago—now we are in the Cretaceous—or a little before. Extraordinary success followed, with an intense radiation of forms. Around 90 percent of known plant species are in this group: grasses and lilies, aspen and oaks.

The form of the first flowering plants is unknown; there are various tentative, delicate candidates. To picture a fairly early flower, though, one can, perhaps surprisingly, picture a magnolia—a rather exuberant early effort, as if celebratory of the new way of living. Grasses, birches, and other more restrained forms came later, along with those geniuses of unrestraint, orchids.

In some settings, flowering plants replaced conifers. In other places, especially on mountains, stands of conifers continue on their own. Elsewhere the two can be seen together—a pine/birch forest. Forests are also full of deeper cousins—the tree ferns and eucalypts of Blue Mountains valleys. The eucalypts, flowering plants, are newer, but the ferns, an older form deriving from one of the earliest lines of land plants, are still there.

The rise of these forests was not a process in which new plants arose and conquered much of the Earth on their own. These forests coevolved with animals. The Cretaceous is within the time of dinosaurs, along with early mammals. In the formation of these forests, though, a bigger factor was insects.

Insects are sprinkled through the fossil record of life on land from about 410 million years ago, though they may have evolved a good deal earlier. The long years of insect evolution have seen a to-and-fro with plants of different kinds and eras, initially with insects acting just as consumers, among giant club mosses and ferns and then cycad and conifer forests. A further role began (or greatly ramped up) around the start of the Cretaceous. From here, insects were not just consumers of plants but also pollinators, enabling fertilization.

Pollination without insects or other animals is dependent on the wind or water (unless a plant pollinates itself). With the evolution of flowers, plants could now interact at a distance, in a way mediated by the perceptions, nervous systems, and actions of animals. Insects became, in a sense, instruments used by plants to span space.

Through the Cretaceous, both insects and plants radiated extensively, and this period also saw a reset of relations between land and sea. From here onward, the species on land are far more numerous than those in the sea—something like

85 percent of species are terrestrial today. A large proportion of those, and a majority of all animal species, are insects.

Birds also help to build forests, by spreading seeds from the fruit they eat and also by pollinating some plants. When picturing a forest expanding, one might start by imagining a process in which plants crawl over the landscape and animals follow. But especially in the case of flowering plants, it is the animal + plant combination that spreads across.

At the start of this chapter, we looked at how rivers shaped the Blue Mountains. Rivers, however, are not just inevitable consequences of rain or springs, along with the present shape of the land. They are different in the absence of plant life. Trees and other plants, especially with their root systems, hold a waterway's banks and stabilize them, creating definite channels. Water moving over land without much life tends to spread in sheets and braids. Rivers with definite shapes can still exist without plants; on Mars, which apparently has never had plants, the remains of meandering rivers can be seen. But when plants with extensive roots arose, in the Devonian period, rivers on Earth changed, growing twists, turns, and tighter bends.

Plants make riverbanks; riverbanks direct water; water carves canyons and mountains. Life shapes rivers, and rivers shape the land.

Forms of Action

In the early history of the transformation of environments by living organisms, effects were mostly achieved by producing and modifying chemicals. Sometimes, as with plants and rivers, organisms had effects through their growth and form. Another stage in this story is the evolution of action: behavior, controlled movement of the body.

When I talk about "action" from here onward, this will be what I mean. In a way, the releasing of chemicals (such as cyanobacteria releasing oxygen) is action, and so are some kinds of growth. But it will be action based on controlled movement— movement of parts of the body, and sometimes the whole— that I'll be looking at.

Controlled motion of this kind is a further transformation of energy from the sun. From the sun comes energy in the form of radiation. Some of this is transformed into chemical energy by photosynthesis, and some of this, in turn, is transformed into movement, especially in animals.

Here is a rough categorization of forms of action:

1. Moving around (migration, finding some shade)
2. Taking in food and other resources, feeding
3. Other interactions between organisms (mating, communicating, child care, contests)
4. Engineering the environment
5. Information gathering

This list is not supposed to cover everything an animal might do. That itself is a theme in this book—the open-endedness of behavior, the possibility of new things under the sun. All the categories also have vague borders and overlaps.

We might think about working with fewer categories. I have "feeding" as one category and, separately, "other interactions between organisms." Much feeding is an interaction between one organism and another (or at least an organism-part), so we could set things up with a big category of "interaction between organisms" that includes feeding within it. But not all feeding would be included, and my categories are set up in a way that is supposed to help us think about some particular kinds of action, especially the last ones on the list.

Each of these kinds of action can be a way of achieving other things on the same list. You might walk across the room (movement) with the goal of interacting with someone; you might interact with someone with the goal of transforming the environment (can you help me move this rock?). Each outcome can be a means to others. When there is a sequence of goals of this kind, my categorization will be based on the first one. If you talk to someone in order to get them to turn over a rock, or to find out where someone is, that is a case of communication, and it goes in the third category.

A complete list of "further" goals, or ulterior motives, would be a long one: getting some sun, applying for a job. When we are looking at evolutionary questions, questions about why behaviors of particular kinds have evolved, all these means-end relationships feed into the projects of survival and reproduction. In evolutionary terms, those are the outcomes that matter most. But they only "matter most" in this evolutionary context, and some animals, like us, pursue and value all sorts of things that don't have much relationship to reproduction or even, in some cases, survival. The fact that animals can value all sorts of unlikely things is itself a consequence of evolution; *wanting* is an evolutionary product, something that evolution brought into the world. But once wanting exists, it can take animals in all sorts of novel directions.

All of these forms of action are probably very old, and at least the first four (perhaps all of them) are seen in single-celled organisms. Bacteria in many cases can swim, can follow the trail of beneficial chemicals and avoid others. Bacteria signal to one another, though this is done chemically rather than with bodily motion. Controlled motion other than swimming is hard for bacteria, but this changed with the evolution of eukaryotic single-celled organisms, which are generally larger and more complex. Eukaryotes have several innovations, but what is especially relevant here is their elaboration of the *cytoskeleton*. This is a system of microscopic tubes inside a cell, organized to enable change in the body's shape. Now a cell can crawl, swim quickly, and engulf other cells.

My fourth category is engineering, remaking the environment. The term "niche construction" is also used in biology for this kind of action and its effects. In its early forms, this sort of effect, also, was often achieved with chemical secretions. The stromatolites of chapter 1 are partly made up of cyanobacteria and other organisms, and partly built by them. They trap and bind grains of sand into domes and columns.

All these early stages occurred before the evolution of animals, but animals, when they appeared on the scene, took all this up and ran with it. Literally so! They initiated a new kind of behavioral transformation of the Earth.

In animals, controlled movement was reinvented on the scale of large numbers of cells—trillions of them, in the case of animals like us—working together as a unit. In the very early history of animals, active movement has only been slowly uncovered. Fossils show the presence of some slow seafloor crawlers in animal life before the Cambrian explosion. Jellyfish may also have been swimming in the water column. And among the animals living fixed to surfaces, some may have fed by reaching fronds or tentacles to collect organic material.

Those early stages show little evidence of direct interaction between one animal and another. It may have been present, but it is hard to see. A few small worms may have hunted other animals. All this changes in the Cambrian, with its evolutionary "explosion" of animal forms and the beginning of a new regime of interaction.

Did very early animals engineer their environments? In one sense, they almost certainly did, but this brings us to an ambiguity in the idea of "engineering." As sponges feed, they filter the water. This action of very early sponges may have slowly cleared the seas, freeing them from a turbid, murky state and changing marine ecosystems for other animals. (This has been argued by the British biologist Nicholas Butterfield.) That is engineering in a way, but it is a byproduct of actions done for other reasons. Sponges draw water through their bodies and extract food. This achieves a filtering, but the goal of the activity is getting food, not clearing the seas. With cases like this in mind, it makes sense to distinguish the broad category of *transformation* of the environment from a more specific category of *engineering*. In this sense, engineering is a change an animal makes to its surroundings where that change made is the point, or part of the point, of the action. An example is building a den or nest that one can live in. This contrasts with cases where transformation is a mere byproduct of things done for other reasons, such as filter-feeding or grazing. I spent some time on the ideas of goal and purpose in the previous chapter, and we need those concepts to make this distinction. Some transformation of environments happens because that was the animal's goal, and some happens as a by-product of other activities.

From now on, I will use the term "engineering" (and "reengineering" and so on) for cases where the transformation does not arise as a mere byproduct. The cyanobacteria releasing oxygen transformed the Earth but did not reengineer it, in this sense. Another kind of transformation at an early stage that would not count as engineering is burrowing through dense organic mats while feeding. Animals began doing this in earnest at the start of the Cambrian. This behavior would have broken up and aerated the mats, but that was probably incidental to the project of feeding.

The distinction I am using here is easy enough to grasp in principle: Was transformation of the environment a goal, or a byproduct of other activities? But there will be a lot of unclear cases. This way of setting things up is also at odds with some terminology that is commonly used. The phrase "ecosystem engineer" is often applied to any organism that has significant effects on its environment, whether these effects are intended or byproducts. Earthworms, present-day descendants of some of those early marine burrowers, are said to be ecosystem engineers. In at least many cases, their effects are byproducts of feeding and other behaviors—earthworms live in an environment where just moving around will change things, and their waste products also have effects on the soil. In some cases, earthworms do make burrows to live in, long-term. From my point of view, that's different from merely cutting a swath through the world as you move and feed.

The fact that "engineering" is often used in this broader way is awkward, but we need *some* terminology to mark the distinction between transformation that is a goal of action and transformation that is a byproduct. We need this terminology in order to describe what is surely an important process in the history of the Earth. That is the transition from situations where transforming the environment was always, or almost always, a byproduct of what organisms were doing for other reasons (cyanobacteria releasing oxygen, sponges clearing the seas) to situations where evolution turns organisms into rebuilders and reshapers that have these effects by design. Eventually, evolution produces engineers who pursue these transformative goals in a deliberate, reflective, conscious way.

Again, these decisions about words do not matter much as long as the ideas are clear. The term "niche construction," which I mentioned above, is also often used in a way that includes both kinds of transformation of environments—fortuitous effects and those that happen by design.

In the previous chapter, we looked at coral reefs. Coral polyps can be seen as true engineers, in the sense I introduced here, but only if the boundaries of the animal are understood in a particular way. A coral polyp secretes material that forms a rock-like matrix around part of its body. Is this a home for the animal, or part of the animal itself? If the latter, it's not really engineering of the environment. The boundaries in cases like this can be vague, and the question might not have a definite answer.

Early animal engineering took place in the sea, as all animal life began there. Much becomes different—not only in the case of engineering, but with animal action in general—when animals move onto land. This move was made first by arthropods, the group that includes insects, and later by vertebrates and a couple of others.

Action is different on land and in the sea. This is not only because of the different animals found there, but because the scope for action differs in the two realms. Motion of some kinds is easy in water. One can drift, and also swim a little, nudge oneself along. With some marine organisms, it is hard to tell if they are actively moving or just going along with things passively. This is true not only of tiny plankton but of larger beings as well. Salps, animals not too far in genealogical terms from ourselves, can look, according to the species, like ghosts of packing material or luminous organic box kites, partly drifting and partly jetting, on their own or in connected colonies.

This kind of barely, faintly active movement is not really seen on land, or certainly not at the large (meter-long) scale of a salp colony. Terrestrial life is harder, in this as in other ways. Little movement comes for free, unless you are tiny (or in a patch of terrestrial water). Many scuba divers say that they initially became entranced with diving because it was like flying, or being weightless. The novelist Arthur C. Clarke, of *2001: A Space Odyssey*, said this. Flying, and especially hovering, in air are difficult; their analogues are easy in the sea.

If one of the delights of diving is effortless three-dimensional motion, people often find that trying to do other things under water is far from easy. Objects do not stay put. It is hard to exert force in rapid ways—to strike or hammer, for example. The medium is different in what it offers.

Early animals in the sea, and their actions, were probably radially organized—organized as discs, saucers, and rings. Action seems to be limited (at least so far) within this sort of body plan. The bilaterally symmetrical or *bilaterian* body plan, with front and back and left and right, that is seen in us, birds, insects, and octopuses is the basis for all the more complex animal actions. In the sea, animals have various body plans. On land, all animals are bilaterian. There are no terrestrial jellyfish.

Land/sea differences are especially marked in the category of engineering. Back at Shark Bay again, inland but not far from the stromatolites, are expanses of termite mounds. Shaped like towers or big abstract sculptures (chubby Brancusis), they are ten or more feet high. Termites don't usually live inside the towers but in the ground underneath, and the towers are for ventilation. These buildings reflect the demands of life on land, with its dry air and temperature changes, and also the fact that materials like soil and saliva, once shaped, will stay put, will harden and persist.

In the sea, most of the engineering is done by animals who "put their bodies on the line," such as the corals we looked at earlier. Bilaterian animals do not do much engineering there at all, as far as I can tell. (I treat beaver dams and lodges as terrestrial.) There are tube-building worms, and shrimp-like animals who build masts, like antenna masts, on which the animals crouch. These are made from secretions, too. Some stickleback fish build nests from plant material, and some male pufferfish build nests that also work as displays to females. The puffer-fish structures are impressive—flower-like, perfectly formed patterns with concentric circles in shaped sand, many times larger than the fish. Only one species is known to do this. It also appears (reports are cautious) that some "pistol shrimp" slowly blast cavities in sheer rock by snapping a huge claw.

Though they're not completely alone in these activities, octopuses stand out as the great manipulators of the underwater world. At "Octopolis" and "Octlantis," a pair of unusual sites in Australia, octopuses have been seen living together in quite large numbers—sometimes a dozen in a few square meters. At Octopolis, they have dug vertical shafts that are fifty centimeters or more deep (measured by putting down a rigid tape when no one is home). This is made possible by the fact that the site is a shell bed, and scallop shells are an excellent building material.* Spending time with octopuses in the sea, one encounters many dimensions of their dexterity. Banjo rays, medium-sized rays whose shape and body patterns do recall the musical instrument, hang out at Octopolis and carelessly drape their tails over dens. We saw an octopus repeatedly, almost resignedly, push an intrusive tail aside. This is quite an unusual motion in the sea, this deliberate rearranging of another animal's body. The famous documentary series *Blue Planet II* has a video sequence with a pair of clown fish bringing a coconut shell to an anemone, where the shell will be used as a place to lay eggs. This is no easy feat for the fish, as it involves

---

* Octopolis itself has been very quiet recently, with only a few animals present. The second site, Octlantis, was livelier on our last visit. Octopolis has declined and recovered before; I hope it recovers again.

flipping the shell with their mouths and pushing it in stages from behind. It takes a while. If an octopus was watching, it would think: "My God, you are making heavy weather of this. Just pick it up!"

Could there be a planet entirely covered by ocean, with no land surface, but where complex life evolves, proceeding all the way to advanced technology? On Earth, all the early stages of animal evolution took place in the sea. Could it continue there? Alternatively, might there be a planet that does have land and sea, like ours, but where marine animals dominate indefinitely? They make forays onto land, as we do into the sea, but maintain wholly marine societies?

Physical differences between land and sea become important again. The sea makes some things harder, others easier. Water is helpful to life at the start, and helpful to early animals, too, but in a technological context, water is a challenge. Water makes it hard to direct and contain electrical goings-on. Perhaps any sort of physical control that extends some distance over space becomes difficult in the sea.

Still, the last thing we should do is fail to be sufficiently imaginative. Possible technologies might use materials far from what we are used to. Earlier I mentioned shrimp-like animals (called amphipods) who build tiny tubes and masts. They crouch there, reaching for food in the water, like *Moby-Dick*'s Ishmael on his mast watching for whales. The material they build with is called amphipod silk. A tunicate or sea squirt called *Oikopleura* builds a balloon-like "house," also from secretions, with a fine mesh that catches tiny particles of plankton. Could these materials be taken further? Imagine an undersea technology without metals, an organic soft technology. It might all work much more slowly, but could this be another way of getting things done?

Perhaps, but the land-sea differences in what action achieves on Earth are probably no accident. It may be that the path leading to technology here—sea first, land later—is the only or the most feasible way for it all to happen.

This question links also to differences in social life. Sea animals can be very social, with schooling fish and shrimp. Dolphins became more social at sea after their ancestors returned from land. Dolphins, and also killer whales, engage in cooperative hunting of several kinds. But again there are differences. Collaboration in engineering is rare in the sea. Corals do build on the work of others when they make reefs, as described a few pages back, and their building is communal in some ways, but the closest thing I have seen to real collaborative engineering in the sea was a building project pursued by two fish. These were "sleeper gobies." The name apparently comes from the tendency of some species in the group to rest quietly on the bottom of the sea, but the pair I saw had different ideas.

I came across them nearly a decade ago now, at Cabbage Tree Bay, a dive site near Sydney. I watched them for several weeks as they worked steadily on the construction of several towers on the seafloor, along with a larger number of holes that seemed to be den openings. The whole complex was probably connected by underground tunnels.

The first tower was seventeen centimeters (a bit less than seven inches) high, and consisted of a pile of shells that had each

been carried individually to the site in one of their mouths, along with bits of smaller debris that were scooped up and placed similarly.

Both fish carried shells, sometimes staying close together, sometimes operating on their own. After building one tower, along with a series of fish-diameter holes in the seafloor at various distances from it, they moved on to build another tower, not quite as high, about six meters away. Some of the holes in the seafloor were augmented (decorated?) with small clumps of seaweed and also had shells laid around them. Holes seem to be opened and closed on different days.

Why do I think there were tunnels? Here I am relying on research into a closely related species of fish in Okinawa, Japan, where biologists introduced ink into the den openings and observed where it went. I didn't try this, and just watched as the two fish worked, day after day.

When fish build mounds, it is often thought to be a display, part of a competition for mates. In this case, the pairs are stable and apparently monogamous, both build the mounds together, and display does not seem to be involved. Although there is little research on these fish, it seems likely (drawing especially on the Japanese study) that these piscine engineers may be exploiting subtle features of the physics of water flow.

The overall goal of the building process is to make a den in which eggs can be kept safe. But an underground den can have bad water flow, and hence a problem of low oxygen for the eggs. If two openings to the den differ in height, as one is raised high by a mound, then slight differences in the rate of water flow across these two openings will lead to a pressure difference. This can produce a flow of water through the tunnel from the ground-floor opening where the fish enter to the shell mound itself, which doesn't have a hole at the top but has cracks where water can flow out. Quite a few other animals make use of the same physical principles to air-condition (or water-condition) their dens.

Collaborative building is a pretty unusual behavior in the sea. So is a related behavior: the use of tools.

Earlier in this chapter I distinguished five rough categories of action: movement, feeding, other interactions between animals, engineering, and information gathering. All of these can involve tool use; this is not another item that belongs in the same list, but something that can turn up in any of those, as a means. Tool use can be *how* you move, feed, engineer.

Suppose you are manipulating something. What makes it a tool? The feature that is basic to tool use is an *indirect* element: manipulating X to have an effect on Y, where X is not a part of your own body. Once again, the idea of goals can't be avoided here, as what is essential to a tool is that manipulating it is a means to some other end.

In addition to cases of tools used in engineering, gathering food, and so on, tools can have an information-gathering role. (I said a moment ago that in tool use, you manipulate X to have an effect on Y; you can't be the X, but you can be the Y.) Gorillas have been seen testing the depth of the water in a stream by probing with a stick. I learned of a wonderful case from David Scheel. An otter was filmed exhaling small air bubbles into the water from its nose and then sniffing them back in, as it could then sniff for traces of chemicals in the air. Air bubbles were used as a tool.

Chimps, bonobos, and crows are the most adept non-human tool users, usually with the goal of food extraction. New Caledonian Crows have made compound tools by combining smaller parts, and used tools to obtain other tools ("metatool" use). The list of seagoing tool users is short unless borderline cases are included, such as decorator crabs wearing anemones as protection from octopuses. (One small group of crabs is not so borderline a case: "pom-pom crabs" carry an anemone in each claw and use them as defensive weapons. They do look a bit like cheerleaders.) Dolphins use sponges to protect their noses as they probe the seafloor. Orcas hunt, in groups, by generating large waves to wash seals off ice floes. That process is lengthy and deliberate, rather awful to watch on video. I mentioned otters a moment ago (mammals again). There are some fish cases, but not many. Tools can be useful, but you have to be able to manipulate them, and fish and dolphins have limitations in that area. Octopuses—the magicians of marine manipulation—don't have those limitations, but there's not much they might do with tools that they can't do directly.

Land and Sea

Another feature of action, and also sensing, that marks a contrast between land and sea is the tension that can exist on a large territorial scale. Down behind our house a steep slope falls away, with some tall trees and an expanse of open air. For birds, this can become a field of discord, both within species and, more emphatically, across them. The main drama features parrots of various kinds, coming and going, skirmishing sometimes, watching and jostling. There are big white Sulfur-crested Cockatoos—noisy attempted enforcers—smaller lorikeets scared of no one, the more amiable Rose-breasted Cockatoos, and their huge relatives the Yellow-tailed Black Cockatoos. As well as parrots there are honey-eaters—occasionally pugnacious busybodies—along with kookaburras, which are large, carnivorous kingfishers (they eat snakes), and magpies. The whole place can feel like a Napoleonic site of tension and contest, made possible, I take it, by the long sightlines of air.

The arena doesn't always feel like this, but it fairly regularly erupts, and when it does, one has a sense of a very large terrain of action. I suspect that this is typical of land ecologies. On the Maasai Mara in Kenya, I remember our guide noting an antelope staring intently into the distance—into nothing, it seemed. But as the guide said, a lioness was out there (we eventually saw her), perhaps a full mile away, but very much part of the tactical scene. At least ostensibly, this is different from what one tends to see in the sea. Am I wrong to say this? Are large-scale Napoleonic fields present there also, just a bit less noticeable? Perhaps, but I doubt it—or doubt it outside of the special case of seals, orcas, and other mammals.

Starting out from those differences in sightlines, the neuroscientist and engineer Malcolm MacIver proposes an interesting idea. He thinks that these differences lead to greater complexity in behavior on land than in the sea, and also a different way that behaviors tend to be chosen. The transition to land saw a shift from *habit-based* to *plan-based* behaviors. He treats this as a transition made within vertebrate animals. Broadening his setup a little, I am going to think about more animals, and also include within the category of "habit" both behaviors established through trial-and-error learning and those that are more "instinctive" and do not need to be learned. In both cases, a behavior occurs because it has worked in the past. This might be the "past" of your own experience, or the evolutionary past. As we saw in chapter 2, learning by trial and error is quite a lot like Darwinian evolution (mutation and selection). In both cases, past successes feed future occurrences of the behavior.

In behavior based on plans, you need not rely on past success (though you can certainly take this into account); instead, you model or project the likely effects of one or more actions, given how you think the world is now, and choose based on the projected results. You might then do something you've never done before, such as taking a new route home. The distinction between these two is probably not sharp, but it's a real shift. Plans, in this sense, can lie behind action even when they're not conscious.

MacIver supposes that fish and other marine animals tend to respond to objects when they are very close at hand, because that is often as far as you can discern, and "planning" in this setting would not give you much benefit. On land, the complexity of a visual scene, with objects at many distances, makes it worthwhile to tailor your action, as best you can, to the specific situation before you. This requires a new kind of internal processing.

MacIver's version of this idea is perhaps too sharply drawn, particularly on the sightline question. Octopuses figure here once again. At Octopolis, the site I mentioned earlier in this chapter, I have seen octopuses respond to other octopuses coming in from some distance, and sometimes apparently choosing which of several incomers, or others, to respond to. I noticed this at the time especially because I'd read that octopuses are very nearsighted, but in these cases they seemed to be tracking others at a distance of at least three meters or so, which is quite a lot if you are on their scale.

I don't know if I did a real measurement; I have a vague memory of doing one, but I don't know if I recorded it if I did. This might have been one of the many deliberate actions that somehow get a bit lost under the sea. My collaborator David Scheel has the same impression that I do, and thinks it is pretty clear that octopuses at this site respond to one another at distances of four meters or so.

While diving in some waters you may also find yourself nipped by a territorial fish, such as a white-eared damselfish. These are small (and completely fearless), and their intention seems to be to dominate quite a decent-sized territory, very large in comparison to their bodies. Sightlines in a dense forest on land can also be little better than those in the sea. Still, I think MacIver might be onto something.

Zooming out, we can compare total scenes in a forest and

in the sea—on a reef, perhaps. The forest has its giant, ever-growing, solar-energy-collecting towers, along with plants of the dimmer understory. Among these are the buzzy, electrical centers of order and action that are animals. Those roles are more distinct on land than in the sea. On land, there are plants and animals, and not a lot of plant-like animals (in lifestyle, not appearance) or animal-like plants. Venus flytraps are exceptions, but there aren't many others. On a reef, the scene is composed largely of animals, but many of them are doing plant-like things. Every possible level of activity is seen. Animals sprawl and permanently drape themselves on others, who have sprawled and draped on someone else: corals, bryozoans (looking like lace or cotton candy), and ascidians (like stationary trumpets). These various languid marine body-drapers are only distantly related to one another; they are not close cousins.

On land, the plants stand and grow, while animals move through them and act. In the sea, the roles are more mixed up. Fungi, on land, are in-betweeners in some ways—we think of fungi as plant-like, but that is partly because all we usually see of them is their specialized reproductive structures, mushrooms, rather than the active, burrowing threads beneath. Those threads are the majority of fungal life.

Am I exaggerating the differences? Perhaps, and exceptions might be more numerous than I realize. My picture is no doubt shaped by what I've seen. Some of the time writing this book was spent in forests about seven hours' drive north of Sydney. Once I was coming back from some days in the rainforest, days walking beneath green parasols—tree ferns—a few feet above

my head, and the canopy a hundred feet higher. I'd been looking for birds (who had been elusive), drafting this chapter, and
thinking about life on land. On the way back I stopped for a
dive at Nelson Bay, on the same coast and an important dive
site for me over the last decade.

Up top it was blustery, messy, with waves rolling in. But below, in late-afternoon light, all was calm. Soft corals unfurled
their fingers, a few big fish roamed. I came across an octopus
perched in a mixture of soft corals, sponges, and trumpet-like
ascidians, holding a shell. A hermit crab was visible inside the
shell, and the shell itself had anemones attached. A few neon-
pink strands had been sprayed out by the anemone and fallen
back. The octopus probably intended to eat the hermit crab later;
anemones are placed by the crabs on their shells as anti-octopus
defenses, and those neon-pink strands are the anemone's own
armament. Those defenses had apparently failed, and this was
in some respects a scene of predation, but in others it showed the
commensal tendencies of reef life.

That word "commensal" means *sharing a table*. The bodies of ascidians, our relatives, were jumbled with the bodies of
corals, sponges, anemones. Fish wandered in occasionally, and
a little way off an impossibly elaborate nudibranch, an ornate
sea-slug, roamed over and between the bodies. The scene had a
profuse density, and also a jumbled peace.

The peace is in part deceptive. The octopus and hermit crab
looked like companions until one thought things through, and
noted the neon-pink ammunition lying around. And you do
see overt disruptors in the sea. Small sharks appear suddenly
and dive into every crevice, tearing things apart. Octopuses

rampage through the gardens, sending other animals scattering. But in among the ocean's near-empty spaces of blue, reefs often show this density, this jumbled animality, and a degree of commensal peace. This can be contrasted, again, with the forest, with its sharper separation of roles, and the Napoleonic avian tensions seen in the patch of bush behind my house.

The tensions on land also have exceptions. Up near the very top of Australia, on two mornings I made my way with a small group at dawn to a water hole in an expanse of dry. We waited as the light came up. Finches began to come in, first in small groups and then larger ones. They waited around, hesitated in the trees, and then came down in hundreds to drink at the edge of the water. Side by side, jostling a little and shoulder to shoulder, there were ten finch species by the end, along with some doves and others.

On the second of those mornings, Budgerigars—small parrots—appeared in large flocks. A few of these had shown up on the first day, but many more on the second. They gathered in trees, filled them, turned a dead tree from gray into a sparkling yellow-green. Occasionally they took flight together and came swooping and rocketing over the water hole, over our heads. We could hear and feel the thousands of small wingbeats. In the case of starlings, the term "murmuration" is used for their huge coordinated flocks that move like an amorphous animal. The term is sometimes extended by courtesy to other birds. The Budgerigar flocks were not as numerous or elaborate, but had some of that dazzling switching in direction, where leader becomes follower and follower becomes leader, as they came over.

A single sparrowhawk had been hanging around in a tall

tree. The Budgerigars were waiting, our guide said, working out whether it would be safe to come down and drink. At one point, small pale feathers fluttered down. The sparrowhawk had caught a finch, or some other small bird, nearby.

At its peak, with these flocks of beautiful small parrots going back and forth over our heads, it was like being under the ocean, looking up at the surface with waves above. Under a sea far from land, with waves breaking in all directions.

Another Stroll

All the forms of action explored in this chapter are guided by sensing. This is not a one-way, input-output relationship, though. Sensing guides action, and action also affects what you sense. This becomes explicit in the case of information-gathering actions, where an animal acts in order to perceive.

Once this acting-to-sensing connection is on the table, the possibility arises of seeing all these relationships differently. A framework sometimes called "perceptual control theory" holds that the purpose of action itself is to control the flow of experience. Rather than perception or experience having the task of controlling action, it's the other way around; action is in the service of perception. This picture has impressed a number of thinkers who have influenced my work (including Björn Brembs, György Buzsáki, and Fred Keijzer).

In reply: a lot of action is indeed like this. You turn the page, turn over the rock, rent the movie, click on the link. All those things are done to shape your perceptions. Some actions are done for probing and experimenting, or just to expose yourself to a chosen sensory flow because it's enjoyable. Animal life, human and nonhuman, has a great deal of this, but plenty of action is also *not* like this. Action has its own role. Action in general is for *getting things done*—getting food, finding shelter, caring for children. Many of those things, when you achieve them, will alter your perceptions, but this is often secondary. Suppose you are trying to get home—that is the point of your actions. You may sense the stages of the journey and also, if all goes well, the destination. But that can be incidental. What is important is *being* there (where it's safer, where your partner is).

A newer theoretical project, the "predictive processing" framework, stems from work on perception. It emphasizes the importance of prediction, and the ongoing correcting and updating of predictions, within ordinary seeing and hearing. In perception, we continually keep track of the differences between the stimuli we expect and what actually comes in. An extension of this view argues that action, too, is part of the project of prediction. When you predict, you anticipate; if all goes well, you are not taken aback. You minimize the discrepancy between what you expect and what you actually see. And you can often achieve this by acting, by changing what is around you so that it matches your expectations. One way to ensure your predictions come out well is to *make it so.*

According to the predictive processing framework, our brains are involved in a grand project, something seen in different forms in all living systems, and that project is smoothing the flow, anticipating what comes next.

I agree that prediction is important in how we track what is going on around us, but I don't agree with this prediction-based view of action. The main problem has been expressed in a well-known objection to the framework, which is usually called the "dark room objection." If you really wanted to smooth the flow and reduce surprise, you would stay in a dark room and never come out, or come out as little as possible. That's a choice that would *really* smooth things out. The limited appeal of this choice, and its dead-end status from a biological point of view, show that the point of perception and action is not just to reduce surprise. There's more to life than that.

This objection can be expressed explicitly in evolutionary terms—a Darwinian dark room objection. Suppose you are in a den, and have spent just about all of your life in there. You are a male funnel-web spider (a dangerous Australian spider). You, the spider, would quite like to mate. But if you go outside, who knows what will happen? You might meet all sorts of doom, including, perhaps, at the hands (or pedipalps) of a female you encounter. If you stay home—for one more day, then one more, and then forever—you can avoid surprises. But this choice is not a good one in Darwinian terms, as there is no chance of a female coming to you. If there are two kinds of male spiders in the population, one that always makes choices to reduce surprise and another that is willing to take some chances, we know which kind will do better. Animal life is full of interactions that are not very controllable, and sometimes you have to embrace this. Sometimes you have to take a chance. Animal life, especially in the context of mating and reproduction, often requires courting uncertainty.

During the process of action itself—as spider, person, or whatever—you will often be trying to get smoothness in delivery, smoothness in execution of the action. Predicting the consequences of your movements as you make them, and checking to see if things came out right, is a good way to handle that problem—the problem of actually doing the things you want to do. But in most cases, that is not the point of the action itself. More important things are usually at stake than seeing if your predictions come out right.

The way to think about perception-action loops, especially from an evolutionary point of view, is as another modification of our abilities as agents. Suppose you are trying to achieve something—a moment ago I used the example of trying to get home. When you are able to track the consequences of your actions, predict how things should look at various stages ("I should be seeing some lights by now"), and make adjustments if they don't look right, you're able to get home more reliably than if you can't do things like that. This is the kind of augmentation of agency that loops between perception and action make possible. You become able to adjust your plans, overcome obstacles, and deal with changing circumstances. Action is not *for* prediction or perception; it's the other way around. Action is central to the animal way of being. Perception, prediction, and "controlling the flow" are secondary.

Thinking about all this as I walk—acting, sensing, looping— I am reminded of one of my precursors, and a book with a long reach: Jakob von Uexküll's *A Stroll Through the Worlds of Animals and Men*.

Uexküll was a German-Estonian biologist working in the first part of the previous century. He did a wide range of work, but the idea that has floated consistently down to us is his concept of the *Umwelt*—"self-world," or "self-surrounding world"—inhabited by each organism. The stroll described in his 1934 book begins in a meadow—flower-strewn, humming with insects. Uexküll's interest was not the overall scene, though; he wanted to approach each organism and make his way *inside*:

> We no longer regard animals as mere machines, but as subjects whose essential activity consists of perceiving and acting. We thus unlock the gates that lead to other realms.

Those "realms" included the world of a tick and the world of a snail. No one, as far as I know, had done anything much like this before. Uexküll was trying to get inside other animals' point of view in a way that was not mere fantasy, but was guided by as much science as he could bring to bear, and he was doing this with a kind of philosophical affection for the most tiny and apparently insignificant creatures.

On his stroll, Uexküll saw each animal as confined within its own sphere, one made up of what that animal senses and acts upon. We may picture the animals around us, he said, "enclosed within soap bubbles." He introduces this image first with the idea of an animal's "visual space"—the soap bubble contains "all that is visible to them"—but he means all the senses, and often discusses the sense of smell. Further, an animal's realm is defined not only by what it senses, but also by what it acts on. Uexküll was one of the first to fully appreciate, in theoretical work of this kind, the fact that your actions affect what you sense, as well as the other way round. That enabled

Uexküll to reach his distinctive picture, with its bubble-like closure: "Perceptual and effector worlds together form a closed unit, the *Umwelt*."

His work had a wide influence in both biology and philosophy, commended by the philosophers Martin Heidegger and Maurice Merleau-Ponty, among others, and this influence continues. I was at a dinner party some years ago and was put next to an eminent professor of literature. When he heard what I work on, he immediately leaned across and asked: What do I think of the *Umwelt*?

Uexküll himself has an uneasy reputation now. Politically conservative and a German nationalist, he did not join the Nazis, as the philosopher Heidegger did, but he had ties to one of the Nazis' heroes, the racial and anti-Semitic theoretician Houston Chamberlain. Uexküll welcomed Hitler's rise, though he had limited involvement in what followed, and moved in retirement to the island of Capri in 1940. As with Heidegger, these bad political choices have not greatly affected his influence, and many of those who admire Uexküll now probably see themselves as progressive, if unorthodox, thinkers—people trying to look at the living world with a critical, philosophical eye. He also impresses a lot of scientists. Uexküll continues to strike a chord.

His image of animal life is a kind of biological solipsism— each animal with its own surrounding bubble, its own reality. How exactly we are supposed to think of the situation is a bit unclear. When Uexküll says "Perceptual and effector worlds together form a closed unit, the *Umwelt*," does he mean that the self-world contains all that one perceives *plus* all that one acts on? Or that the self-world only contains things that one can *both* perceive and act on? (Mathematically, is it the union, or the intersection, of the two sets?)

Some things one perceives but does not act on—distant stars—and there are others that one acts on but does not perceive—tiny specks of dust. Do you add the perceived and acted on together to close the loop? What is in the bubble? It's not really clear. In some ways this doesn't matter, though, as what is wrong here is the idea of closure itself, the "closed unit," the sealing of the bubble. That problem appears on either reading of how Uexküll defines the self-world.

Before resisting it, I do want to appreciate how Uexküll's picture can be felt as an advance. He was seeing some things right. He was seeing, first, the profound differences between the senses across different organisms, the differences between organisms in what they register and what they are oblivious to. He was also seeing some neglected features of the shape of action, the fact that there is not just an arrow from the senses to action, but also an arrow from action to the senses. You will often move in response to what you see, and as you move, this has effects on what you see at the next moment.

But this is not the whole story, in either case. Sensing has its looping aspect, the way it is fed by one's own actions, but there is also its openness to other things going on. Action, too, has its close-to-home aspect, where one aims to control one's perceptions, but it also has the ability to extend out, beyond anything one might sense. The living world is full of long pathways, and though many of them contain loops, they do not give rise to self-contained structures like soap bubbles. They extend, ramify, meander more than this.

Suppose we are investigating some unfamiliar animal,

perhaps an earthworm. If we initially assume that it perceives the world in a way roughly similar to the way we do, this would be a mistake. Here, the visual is almost irrelevant. A worm tastes or smells the environment around it, but perhaps in a fairly dim, muted way. It may also hear a little, but sensing for an earthworm seems to be predominantly a matter of touch, with sensors scattered over the body. The worm acts in response to what its body brushes against, also in response to chemical traces, and this motion affects what it senses next.

We might learn all this and imagine the worm's sensory envelope of touches and tastes. But we can also step back and, in a second stage, consider the worm's relationships to other organisms. We adopt the viewpoint of ecology. This is a viewpoint from which we consider the combined interactions of many organisms with different ways of life, different capacities to sense and act, and we recognize them all together in the same place. Then we have to think in terms of different shapes, different causal networks. The soap bubbles burst.

To see this, let's think about indirect influences, which the biological world is packed with. An earthworm acts on the soil, burrowing, in response to that sensed envelope of tastes and touches. As it moves, it leaves a path, aerating the soil like a subterranean plow, changing the soil for everyone within it, including fungi close by and trees that reach high into the air, entirely outside the earthworm's perceptual realm. The trees swarm with insects and provide homes for birds, and the actions of the birds have consequences, in turn, for the worms. If one was to draw a bubble-like shape around all the organisms whose activities *matter* to the earthworm, and all the organisms the earthworm affects, one's drawing hand would have to follow the intricate winding paths of these indirect effects, from A, to B, to C, and back to A again, extending far beyond what the earthworm itself can sense and act on. Ecologies form networks in which indirect connections are intricate and ubiquitous, and those networks do not resolve into bubble-like subworlds around each organism.

I can imagine Uexküll replying: Yes, those indirect connections do matter, but they are not part of the world *of each organism*. Those worlds are restricted, in each case, to what can be perceived and acted on. In response, I say that even if in sensing we were confined behind our own filmy veils (not something I do think, but even if we were), our actions extend out and ramify, forming vast networks with the actions of others. Uexküll made an advance by linking sensing and action, but perhaps he did not appreciate where this connection would lead.

When we encounter the world through our senses, the encounter *feels* as if it's "total," in a way. It feels as if the world is flooding into our minds, unmodified and unvarnished. The idea that we are responding to only a small sliver of what is going on—and other animals will respond to a different sliver and process it differently—is not an easy idea to take on board. Uexküll does help us do so. But if we go on to say that what we perceive is a world of our own, a private or subjective world, that is a mistake.

It is not easy to make sense of the relationships between our own idiosyncratic perspectives and a wider, common world—especially as any thinking one might do about that wider world is done from within one's own idiosyncratic perspective. And if the story told about the mind is centered just on perception, then our shared world can easily seem to fade. Recognition of the role of action helps with this. Our actions are poured, together, into a common arena. Each organism's actions affect the lives of many others, whether or not the actor has any inkling of it.

Actions emanate from points of view, from the peculiar angle that each animal has on things—yes. But those actions enter into a network with others. Subjectivity is important. In a way, it is inherent to life. But subjects inhabit ecologies containing other subjects.

Wings

Back near the start of this chapter, we looked at the Cretaceous Terrestrial Revolution—only controversially a revolution, but certainly an important time, as flowering plants crept over the globe and insects came with them. These two groups have been central to terrestrial life since then.

Right now, both groups are in the middle of a new, unwelcome set of changes. Across the tropics, forests are being felled and cleared at shocking rates. Many groups of insects, also, have gone into a disturbing retreat.

The insect situation is sometimes referred to as the "insect apocalypse," a wholesale breakdown of that part of our ecologies, caused primarily by pollution and pesticides. Whether the insect problem has quite that scale is presently unclear. Some groups in some places seem to be doing fine, but many are not.

The "apocalypse" was first discussed mostly in Europe. In butterflies, the losses have been massive. This loss, made visible by the good records kept of these beautiful animals, has occurred over something like a century, but the situation has become acute over the last few decades. In the United Kingdom, overall numbers declined by about 50 percent between 1976 and the present. The situation in the Netherlands is similar.

When I was young, the Australian bush in spring was alive with flies and other insects, bugs of countless kinds. A few years ago, my wife, Jane, and I walked in a rainforest in the spring, and she suddenly noticed the near-absence of bugs around us. Since her comment I have been watching, and on warm days I am continually unnerved by the relative buglessness of the forests. Again, when I was younger, if you drove for thirty minutes or so out in the countryside, your windshield would quickly become covered in a near-opaque mass of post-collision bug bodies. You had to stop every now and then to clear them (windshield wipers were nowhere near enough). That's not an issue anymore. Observations of this kind in Europe were among the first that led to talk of insect breakdown. Remember Uexküll on his stroll—"a flower-strewn meadow, humming with insects, fluttering with butterflies." Less so now.

In the case of forests themselves, not all the news is bad. In many countries, losses over the last few centuries are starting to quietly reverse. This seems to be happening for a number of reasons, mainly involving changed human uses. If we make a rough distinction between temperate and tropical forests, then temperate forest coverage seems to have been increasing recently, over the globe as a whole. But tropical forests are being cleared, burned, wrecked, at a faster rate, and their ecologies with them. Much of this is in the service of export products such as palm oil and beef. Those losses outweigh the temperate gains.

❀

A spring night with a full moon. Jane discovered them by hearing—a soft papery sound, a crumpling of paper, all around in the garden when she was outside for a moment. Cicadas, in the thousands, were emerging from the ground.

They would crawl out, make their way across the surface, and climb when they could. Australian cicadas of this kind are quite large, several inches long. A couple of trees seemed favored. They soon had many dozens visible. Each cicada would find a spot and hang suspended under a branch or on a vertical surface, and slowly extract itself from its shell. This took quite a few minutes. Then they'd hang for longer, getting their body sorted out, especially the wings.

Initially these wings were folded up, soft-looking, largely shapeless. We watched as they slowly stretched out to their full length and then became stiff. This is done hydraulically, with liquid slowly filling the veins. In twenty minutes or so, the wings were shiny and taut like airplane aluminum, extending some way off the end of each body. We did not see any of the cicadas fly, not yet. They ended up glistening in the moonlight, wings just minutes old—the newest wings in the world.

4

ORPHEUS

Cadences

At one point in the previous chapter we encountered a collection of birds in an arena of tall trees behind the house I live in. The tensions between these animals, extending through the long sightlines of air, were illustrative of life on land—out of the sea, anyway. Another conspicuous feature of the behavior of those birds, and many others, is the *noise*.

The sounds in this bowl-like aviary mostly come from parrots of various species, along with honey-eaters and a few others. From the Rose-breasted Cockatoos (or Galahs), a relatively gentle cheep; the Sulfur-crested Cockatoos issue a multi-frequency wrenching shriek. King Parrots emit single soprano notes of a half-second or so when they are sitting, and a great mixed-up blast of sound when flying. Among these come the pretty two- and three-note cadences of Crimson Rosellas, placed and repeated (forever auditioning for a Philip Glass opera), along with the laser-like cry of Rainbow Lorikeets, matching their neon riot of color, when visiting from lower altitudes. And sometimes present but elusive, in the background, sits a beautiful charcoal-gray parrot called a Gang-gang—gray except that the males' heads are coral-red. They have a call like the squeak of a rusted gate, or a cork being pulled from a bottle.

When all are going at once, the air fills with shrieks, cheeps, a few soprano cadences, and, as if in celebration, corks being pulled from wine bottles, over and over again.

Avian Life, Communication

Birds are an escape pod from—or for, rather—the dinosaurs. Their evolution began in the Jurassic, the middle part of the dinosaur reign, about 160 million years ago. A group branched off from other dinosaurs and slowly explored an unusual body plan—small, lightweight, feathered, warm-blooded, and with wings. Their evolutionary path included animals with much of a modern bird form, but claws on their wings and a snout with teeth. Feathers, including the modern "vaned" form as opposed to scrappy tufts, arose early, even before animals that looked in other ways much like birds. Early birds diversified in the Cretaceous, among the flowering plants of the previous chapter, and some of these small, high-energy, mobile dinosaurs then survived the mass extinction that wiped out their larger cousins, along with much else, about 66 million years ago.

It's not that the huge tyrannosauruses and their like died while birds all snuck through. In a chart representing this period, a lot of evolutionary lines within the birds end abruptly with the asteroid as well. But some birds did make it through, and these were the only dinosaurs that did. Once on the other side in the post-asteroid world, they embarked on a rapid, exuberant multiplication.

The evolutionary relationships for birds that are alive now look in some ways as you might guess them to be. A deep branching, very old, separates large flightless birds like ostriches and emus from just about all the rest. Then, within the bigger branch, a second split leads to ducks, geese, and other fowl on one side, and another diverse collection on the other side. We walk onward through a great cluster of branches (pelicans, hawks . . .), and then encounter a huge group called the *passerines*. This group contains more than half of all bird species, including robins, crows, and the like. Right alongside them, as a small branch of their own, are the parrots. Much of this cluster unfolded quite quickly after the asteroid, as birds took over a good part of the world they had inherited.

The diagram on the next page is the first of several "tree of life" diagrams in this book, each showing fragments of the network of genealogical relationships among living things. In each case, time runs up the page to the present day. Segments are not drawn to scale and many branches are omitted. Labeled branches sometimes represent just a few species (or one), and sometimes a larger group. This first drawing also includes the asteroid impact putting an end to *Tyrannosaurus rex* and the Enantiornithes, early birds who had claws on their wings, and teeth.

Back in the previous chapter we looked at the evolutionary history of action, especially in animals. I divided animal action into five rough categories: movement, feeding, interaction between individuals (other than feeding), engineering, and information gathering. A conspicuous behavior within the third of

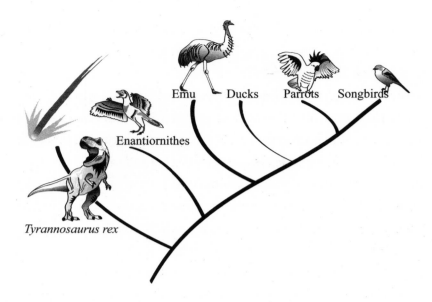

Tyrannosaurus rex

these is *communication*. Communication has borders that are hard to mark out, and it fades and merges into other forms of interaction. Communication is common throughout life; its role will become enormous, almost overwhelming, when we begin, in the next chapter, to consider humans.

We might initially say that an action is a case of communication when its goal is to get a message across, or convey information. But which interactions involve messages and which don't? We might try this: In communication, something is done by one organism to be perceived by another, and done with the aim (conscious or not) of affecting the other's actions or responses in some way. Yes, but some cases that would be included in that category seem distinct from communication—handing over food to share, for example, or physically blocking someone's path. Often, though, cases like that are mixtures, with a communicative aspect to them and other aspects as well. If so, what is the communicative aspect?

This question can be approached by looking more closely at the behaviors "on each side" of an action, display, or mark—the production side and the interpretation side. I'll start with one setup, which can be seen as central in some ways. In these cases, a conspicuous feature is that the behavior seen on the receiver or interpreter side is not much concerned with the intrinsic physical nature of whatever was perceived, but is directed onto something *else*, perhaps some distance away. Vervet monkeys, for example, give alarm calls to one another, and they have different alarm calls for different threats: eagles, leopards, snakes. If a receiver hears the eagle call, they look up; if they hear a snake call, they look down, and so on. This receiver-side behavior is directed on something else, the threat. The receiver's behavior only makes sense, though, if the behaviors on the sender side are set up the right way. It only makes sense to look up when you hear a particular sound if the senders make that sound when they've seen an eagle, not a snake. In a stable communication system, the habits on the sender side and the habits on the receiver side are aligned; they fit together. In this case, the different calls do not seem to be modeled on anything about snakes, leopards, or eagles themselves. You could do things that way, but it's not necessary, and the vervets apparently don't. If senders and receivers are "on the same page," then the particular sound or sign used to indicate something does not matter, and to be "on the same page" is to have that interlocking relationship between production and interpretation.

In that first case, the behavior on the receiver side that anchors the setup is a behavior directed on something else in the environment. In another group of cases, the interlocking behaviors on each side are different. Rather than coordinating behavior in relation to something else, they coordinate or initiate behavior between the animals themselves, as in a "Shall we dance?" signal, or something like that. Again, a "Shall we dance?" signal might be derived from something seen in actual dancing, but need not.

The idea that nearly anything could be used as a sign for nearly anything else in a communication system is described in linguistics and semiotics as the "arbitrariness" of signs. This is not always present; sometimes it does matter what a message is physically made of. The communicative side of a food-sharing action requires that what is handed over is food rather than something else, and a display made in a mating context might be chosen as a natural indicator of vigor or health. The medium can matter. But the core phenomenon is, I hope, starting to become clear. In communication, there is an interaction mediated by something produced by one party and seen (heard, smelled . . .) by another. What makes the interaction a communicative one is the fact that the behaviors on each side of the sign, sound, or mark are aligned, perhaps coordinating actions that are directed on some other object or situation, perhaps coordinating other actions of the sender or receiver themselves. (It might be both.)

There are mixed cases, where an interaction has some of this communicative flavor plus something else as well. Communication also extends outside the realm of action or behavior itself, as it includes colors, marks, and other permanent features of an animal's body. Bright feathers and long tails are designed to be seen, to get a message across and induce a response. The clear, recognizable phenomena of communication emerge from vaguer, partial forms—just as we saw, in previous chapters, in the cases of action, organisms, goals, and engineering.

Birds are enthusiastic participants in send-receive systems

of this kind, and their calls have a variety of roles—threats, alarms, advertisements. Many of the bird sounds in the fish-bowl aviary behind my house are probably "contact calls" between pairs or members of a group; they are staying in touch, registering one another's presence.

Communication, like other forms of action, is older than animals. Bacteria communicate by releasing and absorbing chemicals. Some of what they do may be faintly analogous to those contact calls in birds; bacteria use chemical communication to work out how many other cells of the same kind are around (this is called "quorum sensing"). The sea, home of early animal life, is not really as quiet as it can seem; shrimp click and fish croak, doing this to impress size and vigor on rivals or potential mates. But unless you are lucky enough to find yourself immersed in whale song, the sea's soundscape is nowhere near as dramatic as the choruses arising from birds, frogs, or insects such as cicadas. In fish, courtship often works through dances and visual displays.

Octopuses, who appeared in chapter 3 as maestros of manipulation, are not very social. But given their behavioral abilities, there is a lot they can do in this area if they want to. In the unusual circumstances of Octopolis and Octlantis, the high-density sites I mentioned a few times in that chapter, we have seen signals and displays. One we have called the Nosferatu— tall, dark, and cloaked, and, unlike its cinematic vampire name-sake, featuring the rear end of the animal raised over its head. This seems to be an indication of aggression: "I've seen you and I'm coming for you." We've become interested also in a less common behavior, informally christened the "arms to heaven" display. Two of the arms, not the front ones but the second pair, are raised over the head in a great arc and held there for a second or so. The body seems to be stabilized by having the front-most pair of arms held down so the next pair can reach high. The drawing on this page makes this clearer. This might look like an odd pose for an octopus, but the drawing is traced from a video frame—this is really how the behavior looks.

When we were working on a paper about the Nosferatu behavior, a critic said: "That is not a signal; that is just a preparation to jet toward another octopus, a gearing-up—and the other octopus can predict what is likely to follow, so it reacts." It is true that displays can arise from the "ritualization" of other behaviors, like preparation for an attack, and there won't be a sharp divide between displays and more "ordinary" behaviors. In the Nosferatu case, we do think it has become a display, at least in part. In any case, the arms-to-heaven gesture does not seem to have an alternative interpretation of the kind that was offered for Nosferatu. There's no other action that this sudden raising of the two second arms resembles, as far as we know. The closest might be a reaching-out, a probing—octopuses do a lot of that. But as the drawing shows, the arms-to-heaven is not much like a probe. The action is disarmingly (!) human, with arms skyward and curled slightly in. What does it mean? We are not sure, but it seems sometimes to be an "I've seen you!" or "Here I am!" signal, often done as another octopus makes its way closer, but without the aggression of Nosferatu. (I like David Scheel's suggested translation: "See me here!")

We can scour the seas for such cases, but—again with the mammalian exception of whale song—none of it is in the league of bird calls. I was sitting with some friends on a deck over the garden of Dave Pye, carpenter, musician, and cultivator of orchids. Suddenly there was a great racket. At least six or seven cockatoos began shrieking, and some other birds (bowerbirds) joined in with sounds of their own. Many or all of the cockatoos were close by each other, high in one tree. Dave said: There's probably a snake down there, or a goanna (a large Australian lizard); they are sounding an alarm. So we walked down under the birds, and, sure enough, a diamond python was curled up at the base of a bush—looking, I imagined, a little sheepish as the racket went on above him.

Display and Evaluation

Some actions are communicative; they exist within sender-receiver setups, and their goal is to affect the behaviors of those who perceive the communicative act or the mark it leaves. Within this category is another. Some actions and displays are made to be *evaluated* by the other side. Am I attracted? Am I impressed? Often I might not actually be impressed, but that can still be the goal that the behavior had. That is why the other animal spoke, sang, wrote, painted, or danced in the way they did.

I mean this category of "evaluation" broadly, to cover all sorts of responses that include some assessment of good or bad, attractive or repulsive. Evaluation or appreciation is a special kind of receiver-side behavior. I say it is "receiver-side" although some of what we evaluate was not produced for that purpose. A lot of what we evaluate *was* produced for a reason of that kind, though, and a huge amount of effort by animals is aimed at getting particular evaluative responses to occur.

Song is a case in point. In human life, the Orpheus myth, coming down to us in different versions from the ancient world, has encapsulated the power of music. Orpheus, who could charm not only people but animals and stones themselves with his lyre, failed to rescue his lover Eurydice from the Underworld after she was bitten by a snake (perhaps not heeding the cockatoos' warning). After his rescue attempt, Orpheus wandered, spurning others, until his mourning prompted his murder by the maenads, female followers of Dionysus. The earliest two operas that have survived were both written about Orpheus. In different versions of the myth, the preoccupations of local social contexts, especially sexual concerns, are layered onto the old story. But through all this, a central thread is the uncanny and sometimes uncontrollable power of music.

The power of this combination of behaviors—display, evaluation, attraction—is not restricted to human life. It is a life-shaping, and hence Earth-shaping, combination. Evaluation is subjective; it is tied to the goals and values of a receiver, and how something appears to them—how it strikes them, whether it is found attractive. Though it is subjective in this way, evaluation has wide-ranging effects on what is around us. The ornithologist Richard Prum uses the phrase "aesthetic evolution" for evolution that is driven by displays and evaluative responses to those displays.

Birds, the focus of Prum's book *The Evolution of Beauty*, show us what aesthetic evolution can do, with their plumage, displays, songs, and body forms. Flowers are another example. Flowers are made to be seen or smelled, made to be drunk from, made to attract insects and other animals. They are not just made to be perceived, but made to *appeal*. Attracting insects, birds, and bats allows flowering plants to interact, plant to plant, over long distances. The previous chapter noted how these plant-plant interactions are routed through the behaviors and nervous systems of animals; they are also routed through those animals' values and goals. Forests of flowering plants depend on the interaction of displays and evaluation. Thor Hanson, in his book *Buzz*, contrasts forest scenes of a typical kind with the vegetation on the Juan Fernández Islands off the coast of Chile. These islands are, and have long been, almost completely without bees. As a result, the flowers are mostly small, greenish-white, and lacking the symmetrical displays of petals that bee-visited flowers tend to have. I said back in chapter 3 that to imagine an early flower, one might picture a magnolia. We should picture it also as white. Magnolias evolved before bees did, and they evolved to be fertilized by beetles. Multicolor clusters of flowers, especially blue and yellow, came with bees. (According to Hanson, most bees can't see the color red; that is a bird-attracting color.)

At this stage, it is worth taking a moment to ask a basic question: What *are* colors? Whether colors are real features of the "external world" or exist merely in our minds has been debated by philosophers for centuries. I think that the habits we have of talking about colors as features that have to be *located* somewhere, inside or out, are a bit at odds with what is actually going on.

The full story about color, in outline, looks like this. Visible light is a form of electromagnetic radiation. That radiation exists on a wide spectrum, from radio waves to gamma waves, with color in the middle. The differences along this spectrum involve the wavelength, the distance between peaks in the wave. This to me is such a surprise—that radio waves, visible light with its colors, X-rays, and gamma rays are all essentially the "same stuff," differing just in wavelength (and with definite scare quotes around "stuff"). In the range that is visible to us, finer wavelength differences are associated with colors. The surfaces of objects around us, as a result of their makeup, reflect some wavelengths of light and absorb others, and our eyes then absorb what reaches us. (Jackie Higgins comments in her book *Sentient* that a "red" flower is, in a sense, not red but anti-red, rejecting red and absorbing the rest.) The phenomenon of color, then, involves objects reflecting and radiating light, the radiation itself, and the responses in the eyes and brains of animals, which can differ between us, other mammals, insects, and so on. *That whole* is what the coloring of the world involves, where it lives.

In any behavior, preferences of some kind must be in the picture. Having detected something nearby, do you approach or avoid it? Here is sugar: Is that a good thing or a bad thing? Any behavioral choice reflects an agenda and goals, but these may be implicit, or "wired in," and not felt by the organism. Even bacteria prefer some chemical environments to others. Especially in cases with insects and some other animals, we might wonder whether attraction and preference are experienced at all—whether the insect finds the flower pleasing or exciting, as opposed to just fitting a specification or a search image. The question perhaps has two sides. First, we can ask whether an assessment is experienced in any way at all (remember the bacteria), and a further question is whether the response is felt in something like an emotional way, or more dispassionately ("Hmm, very suitable"). Prum, in *The Evolution of Beauty*, tends to press ahead, assuming that evaluations are indeed felt. His book is mostly about birds and mammals, where the question of feeling is not too vexed. Once we put insects, and their all-important relation to flowering plants, into the picture, the question does press.

Even if an evaluation is not emotionally felt, it is still tied to the values and point of view of some agent, and subjectivity in this sense can be a powerful force. Back near the start of this chapter, I sketched the evolutionary history of birds and said that their most distinctive feature—feathers—arose even before the dinosaurs in question looked very bird-like. Why did feathers appear so early? Their most conspicuous function now is flight, but feathers, it is thought, appeared initially in animals that had no chance of flying. They must have had some other role. Insulation, the control of temperature, used to be the standard hypothesis on this matter. When I was a student, this was often used as an example of change in function in evolution; feathers first had the function of insulation, and then flight. They initially had one sensible, practical role, and then another. But now it is thought likely that the initial role of feathers, at least in part, was something more extravagant: display. Prum supports this view, and so do others.

Nature has a mix of happenstance beauty and designed, crafted beauty. Some things are made to be appreciated, even if they were not made for us. Others ended up in a form that we humans, or some of us, or us plus perhaps some nonhumans, find beautiful even though they were not made to be seen at all. I once posted a photo of an intense sunset, up in the far north of Australia, on social media and a person commented, "Beauty for its own sake." It would be more accurate to say: beauty for no sake.

On the "beauty for no sake" side of the divide we find not only sunsets, but that marine analogue of a flower-filled forest, a coral reef. Healthy reefs have an abundance of colors—dark greens, cornflower and neon blues, turquoise, orange, and pink. Why are reefs colored? I had always thought the colors, and their diversity, came from the light-collecting symbionts living inside the coral polyps. Light-gatherers of this kind do not have to be green. But in this case, all the symbionts in corals are fairly closely related and their own color is a green or brown-green, not much different from plants in a forest. The colors in a coral reef—the blues and pinks, the turquoises—instead tend to be largely, at least, a result of chemicals made by the coral animals themselves. These chemicals seem to be provided by the polyps as a kind of sunscreen for their symbionts, to prevent them from being overloaded, and also to organize their light-collecting activities.

When I was young, we were given brightly colored zinc sunscreen to stripe on our faces. The colors, other than white, were not functional; they were added to encourage us to wear it. Sunscreen now tends to be transparent; the fashion has not persisted. So with a layer of protection over photosynthetic cells, a coral reef is a bit like a forest covered in brightly colored sunscreen.

In relation to the mix of designed and undesigned beauty (beauty for no sake) in nature, seahorses are an interesting case. They are beautiful animals, at least to many people, with their implausible, delicate bodies. They form long-lasting bonds, and pairs in some species engage in elaborate dance-like greetings each morning. These dances are meant to be seen and recognized, and perhaps appreciated. Their role, expressed in human terms, might be some approximation to, "Yes, we're still here, still together, still glad to be."* Seahorses can change color on both rapid and slower timescales, and some of their color choices may figure in those morning dances (they do have color vision).

Those implausible bodies look like they were designed on a whim by a jeweler—until you see them in their milieu, in their element. I was once diving at Nelson Bay, the site described in the forest-and-reef section of the previous chapter, and spent a little too long in the calm water with an especially beautiful radiant yellow seahorse, when the tide turned and the water began rushing out. Both the seahorse and I started to twist, and

* Here is one description: "Both seahorses brightened in colour from a dark brown or grey to a pale yellow or off-white. They then turned parallel to one another, aligned head to head and tail to tail. Their tails grasped a *Posidonia* shoot, and they began to circle in the same direction, as if in a maypole dance, with the male on the outside. The pair intermittently released the holdfast and swam slowly in parallel across the bottom, with the male grasping the female's tail. These two behaviour patterns, circling and parallel swimming, alternated until one of the seahorses darkened and ceased to respond to the other. The female then moved away, but the male sometimes pursued her, and she might briefly resume greeting before finally departing." From Amanda Vincent and Laila Sadler, "Faithful Pair Bonds in Wild Seahorses, *Hippocampus whitei*."

in a moment it was clear who was at home there and who was not. I soon had trouble keeping any kind of position and control at all. As I was battling, a swarm of stingrays came past. They were high in the water, managing to swim against the tide, but doing so by swimming very hard. These were cow-nosed rays, a name that does no justice at all to their diamond-like form. They looked like a flock of gigantic starlings. (I noted in the previous chapter that a flock of starlings is called a "murmuration"; a collection of stingrays is called a "fever," and that is very much how they looked.) Then they were gone, up toward the river whose tidal release was sending all this water down on us.

Soon it was not possible for me to retain any sort of position. I let myself go, and went off like a balloon with the rushing tide. As I went, I passed a tiny and even more delicate yellow seahorse on a sponge—this one can't have been more than an inch and a half long. With her slender tail, curled like a lock of hair, she was hanging on calmly, effortlessly, and doing just fine as I careened past toward the exit.

Song

Many birds, such as the parrots of the opening of this chapter, can make calls but not *song*—not something sustained and organized. Most of the elaborate avian singers belong to a particular group called songbirds (or oscines) within the passerine birds, the large group I mentioned earlier that makes up a majority of all bird species. Not all of the oscines actually sing, but they share a distinctive vocal organ that enables some to reach remarkable sonic heights.

At the moment, it appears that the whole enormous branch of passerines, and the songbirds themselves, originated in Australia (though it was a larger version of Australia, with other, now separate landmasses attached). Debates about bird classification and origins can be quite fraught. As Tim Low notes in his book *Where Song Began*, the idea that Australia might be the birthplace of so much of the splendor of bird life faced considerable resistance (including from Ernst Mayr, a bird-resembling evolutionist who perched astride much of twentieth-century ornithology), as if Australia was too scruffy and disreputable a place to be the first home of the group that produced nightingales and larks. In belated recognition, a huge branch of the bird tree, one containing a majority of all bird species, including songbirds, has recently been designated the *Australaves*.

Australia today includes living representatives of the earliest known branchings in the genealogical tree of songbirds. Some products of those branchings are my next topic.

The first split within the songbird tree gave rise, on one side, to just a handful of birds alive now, the lyrebirds and scrub-birds, and to a huge collection of birds on the other side. That spindly lyrebird/scrubbird branch has just four species living today. The tree diagram on the next page shows some of these relationships. We are zooming in on the right-hand side of the first tree diagram for birds on page 92.

It's often said that lyrebirds are "ancient" birds—the most ancient songbirds. This way of talking is confused in some respects; a lyrebird today is the product of as many years of evolution as any other living bird—or you, for that matter. Lyrebirds are distant cousins of other songbirds, but your more distant

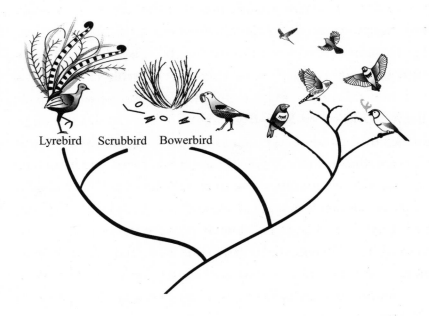

Lyrebird   Scrubbird   Bowerbird

human cousins are not more "ancient" than your nearer ones. Lyrebirds are also products of a branching that led to very few survivors today. That also does not make them ancient; it makes them distant cousins of other birds, off by themselves without a lot of close living relatives of their own.

Still, lyrebirds do look old. They have a dinosaur-like appearance, at least to me. Their fossil record also goes back a fair way, and they have at least one feature that is probably genuinely old: Lyrebirds and scrubbirds have a different kind of syrinx, or voice box, than other songbirds.

Lyrebirds are quite large, around the size of a pheasant, with dark feathers and, especially on males, long tails. They have a prominent forehead that can look a bit Mesozoic. Lyrebirds spend most of their time on the ground but can fly when they want to—although it often looks like an approximation of flight, as if an early attempt. They are agile, moving quickly with flappy strides and leaps through thick forest. Their long legs have large claws, used to rip up the ground as they rummage for food.

Lyrebirds are fairly common in the forest that introduced chapter 3, the forest reached by descending stairs and ladders into a valley in Australia's Blue Mountains (the species is the Superb Lyrebird, the only one I've seen). I was sitting quietly down there once, in a clearing around ten in the morning, when I heard a couple of sudden, unexpected sounds. Turning, I found a lyrebird. I didn't see her arrival, but there she was, quite close. The lyrebird had descended noisily from a tree—they sleep there at night—and this one was keeping impressively relaxed hours.

Standing up, she made exactly the sound you would make if you were a smallish dinosaur who had woken up, jumped out of a high tree, landed awkwardly, and were trying to pull yourself together: a deepish grunt and suppressed squawk.

A few minutes later, another appeared suddenly, though I again did not see the fall. Thump. And a third.

I have followed lyrebirds for some time through the forest, once they are on the ground. They rove around tearing things up. Sometimes much smaller birds follow closely, evidently looking for stray bits of food kicked up by those big claws. I saw one of these little wrens get so close underfoot that it was thrown out the back in a great tumble, head over heels. It reminded me of octopuses hunting and small fish following them to see what gets unearthed.

I saw one lyrebird in the early evening, after a several-course and very messy dinner, go and clean herself off in a stream. First she cleaned her legs, then nearly her whole body, splashing around. She then went and sat on a branch above the ground. There, she appeared to dry off and preen. A bath after dinner.

Lyrebirds are also, many agree, the most spectacular song-birds of all. Their mimicry is astounding. Males produce a cascade of near-perfect copies of the calls of other species, in quick succession. These are concatenated, sometimes jumbled, and mixed in also with some mechanical-sounding calls that are not mimicking anyone. Females mimic also, and seem to mimic different species than males.

One study found that even other *birds* can't always tell lyrebird counterfeits from genuine calls of their own species. Sometimes you can tell; sometimes the mimicry seems too "formal"—like an operatic soprano too carefully singing a folk song. Their sound also projects more, sometimes, than the original might. But that is a rather fussy review! They are just so impressive. At least in males, it appears that much or most of their repertoire is picked up from other lyrebirds, although they can add new sounds on their own. Males are calling to impress and attract mates. The function of female songs is less clear; some singing appears to involve competition with other females for territory.

In the next chapter, we'll encounter some ideas about human behavior and evolution that were developed by Kim Sterelny, a philosopher. He and his partner, Melanie, a historian, have a house in an Australian forest with a large population of lyrebirds. This can engender a fair amount of sonic confusion. A flock of cockatoos found their calls answered unexpectedly, and seemed to lapse into an irritated silence. Melanie is a committed gardener, continually planting and restoring, and often hammering large metal stakes into the ground to make protective cages around new plants. One day, Kim had been imploring her to take a break. She agreed that she might have been overdoing it and went inside. A little later, Kim heard a telltale ringing sound, metal on metal, of more hammering of stakes. He went outside to berate, or at least plead. It was a lyrebird. This sound, Kim said, was distinct from the abrupt mechanical sounds that lyrebirds also make, though perhaps it was a modification of such a sound.

Bowers

In songbird evolution, the lyrebirds branch off early. Then there's another early split, leading on one side to another small cluster of species alive today, and on the other side to thousands. The smaller cluster includes another group of birds that are notable for their actions, especially in the light of the classification of actions I gave in the previous chapter. These are the bowerbirds.

Lyrebirds have that slightly dinosaurian look, but bowerbirds just look like birds. They do move with an awkward hop, as if (on analogy with lyrebird flight) *walking* is the project that evolution is still working on here. Their great forte is collecting and engineering. Male bowerbirds build a nest-like structure on the ground, but it is just for display. Constructed from plant stems, it has, in many species, two gracefully arched walls, meeting at the top or not quite, forming a tunnel. Other species build what look like huts or maypoles. A collection of objects will be placed out front.

Different species of bowerbirds often prefer different colors. Where I live, the Satin Bowerbird is the local species, and it collects bright blue objects. To find a bower in the undergrowth, look for those objects. (It's like finding an octopus—look for what the animal has done.) The blue objects, which often now tend to be human-made, such as plastic pegs and bottle lids, will be mixed in with some bright yellow ones. That combination seems to have a special role, and a male will sometimes hold, in its beak, a blue object plus the petal of a small yellow flower. These, or just a yellow petal, are presented to any interested female.

Males don't just add continually to their bower. There's a lot of rearranging, and what looks like some careful subtraction. The collections of colored objects are also tended and modified. The best collection I've seen had a regular array of slender yellow grass strands and feathers underneath, dozens of blue objects on top, plus—in a Gothic touch—a single, small white skull.

Why do they choose blue? Color choices vary across species, and do so in intriguing ways. The blue-collecting Satin Bowerbird has intense blue eyes, and blue-black feathers on mature males. The Great Bowerbird, up in the north of Australia, ignores blue objects and collects white and other pale-colored ones, with a few other colors, including red and green, sprinkled in. That species has pale gray feathers, and in the only individual I've seen, its silver-gray-white feathers were quite close in color to its ornaments. Males of that species also have a lilac-pink crest. The Spotted Bowerbird, which I've never seen, is said to have no particular color preference in its collections, and its body, also, is mixed colors—browns, grays, green, and again a lilac crest. As you can see, I am curious about resemblances between the ornaments and the bodies; although the principle seems far from firm, matches in some cases seem unlikely to be coincidental.

In the case of preferences for blue, rarity has been conjectured as an important factor. Before all that plastic was available, blue objects would have been rare in many bowerbird environments. Far from civilization, the blue objects seen in bowers tend to be parrot feathers and flowers. An interest in rare colors makes sense—until humans degrade the currency. Studies of some other species have suggested that rare objects are not preferred in those cases. However, there's no need to assume that the various bowerbird species are all doing the same thing; each species has a system of its own, and they could have evolved in different directions. In the case of Satin Bowerbirds, I keep coming back to that match with the birds' brilliant blue eyes.

What about those combinations of blue and yellow that figure in the Satin Bowerbird displays? As the botanist Katherine Preston noted to me, yellow and blue are "complementary" colors, at least in some color schemes, and their contrast might be especially strong. Yellow also matches the Satin Bowerbird's beak color in adult males, and several things might be going on here at once. Jared Diamond, in the course of some intrepid work on a spectacular bower-building species in the mountains of New Guinea, saw hints of local "cultural traditions"—different preferences and styles in different nearby locations, probably due to the copying of older birds by younger ones. This is now looking possible in several species.

Whatever account is given of their color choices, the bottle caps, petals, and other collected objects here are *tools*, in the sense introduced in the previous chapter of this book. They are tools not for building, but for social interaction. This is not usually how they're described, but I think that's because of our habitual association of tools with more utilitarian projects. The

bowerbird's objects fit the requirement that the animal is manipulating one object with the goal of having an effect on something else, in this case another bowerbird.

The effect these tools are aimed at—the bowerbird's collection of objects, and the bower itself—is evaluation and appreciation. They are intended to impress. A bird guide I traveled with, Laurie Ross, watched a bowerbird laboriously construct what looked like a fine bower. The bird then saw his product fail to get any response from several females in a short period, and he tore it down to build another.

Bowerbirds are not just collectors and builders, but in all ways tremendous displayers and advertisers. They hold out their objects, dance, and sing in a low, sliding *coo*. Like lyrebirds, they do some vocal mimicry. Their courting behaviors seem to employ every possible means to make an impression: body, sounds, found objects, built artifacts—everything.

Bowerbirds are an extreme illustration of the way birds have been shaped by the linked activities of display and evaluation, and they have taken these activities in an unusual direction.

It's surprising to me that just this one small group of birds, out of all the species, engages in this kind of collecting and building. A few other birds use tools in their displays. The Palm Cockatoo of far north Australia drums rhythmically with a branch—a drumstick that has been cut and shaped by the bird—on dry wood to attract a mate. But there seems to be nothing else like these elaborate structures built by bowerbirds. Gerald Borgia, after studying the birds extensively, has suggested that bowers themselves originated as places where females could view male displays and ornament collections while avoiding the possibility of being subjected to an unwanted copulation. To initiate a mating, the male has to leave his main display area, at the front of the bower, and go around behind it; this gives the female a chance to make an exit. From there, bowers were elaborated. In addition to evaluating displays and the rest, females began to assess a male's quality by the bower itself. In this view, the close inspection of ornaments and displays came first, the first bowers arose as a protected area like an opera box, and only later became something the females assessed aesthetically as well. All this still leaves open the question of why collecting ornaments is itself so rare.

When they are elaborate, bowers are reminiscent of peacock tails and other expensive-looking aids to display in some male birds. Biology has seen a long-running and sometimes tense debate about features of this kind. One view has it that these features are used by males to advertise health and vigor, in a way that is hard to fake. Only healthy males can afford to produce such extravagant features. An alternative is that these features are the result of a "runaway" process where a bodily feature in males, and an initially somewhat arbitrary prefer-ence for that feature in females, become genetically associated with each other. As this association becomes established, each feature becomes more and more extreme. These much-debated differences don't affect my larger themes here: the sheer im-portance of display, evaluation, and attraction as elements of the living world, especially of animal life. Thinking specifically about birds, it's also appealing to think that all this elaborate communication and display was in place, in such extravagant styles and in a separate evolutionary line, well before humans started doing any of these things.

Orpheus in the Undergrowth

Orpheus, the mythological figure who could charm all who heard him, including stones, and later prompted the first op-eras, played the lyre. That the world's most accomplished song-bird carries a lyre on its body is a glorious, lyrical fact, a true piece of evolutionary alchemy.

That name—lyrebird—comes from the feathers on the tails of males. A lyre, the musical instrument, usually has curved, bow-like wooden arms that connect the main body of the in-strument to a crossbar, and strings run between the crossbar and body. A male lyrebird's tail has two long curved and banded feathers (the "lyrates") that sit on the outside and are extended outward when displaying, with many finer and pale feathers between them.

On one of the first occasions when I spent any time with

a lyrebird, I was walking a rainforest path and heard what sounded like a whipbird. These are small and elusive birds, with a call-and-response between pairs that includes a sharp, impressive whip sound—a sizzling, ascending snap. The call I heard was very much like a whipbird's, but a bit too clear, too well projected (as in my earlier comment about some lyrebird mimicry being overly operatic). I left the track and started walking up into the bush.

The path I'd been on was a standard and well-traveled one. A minute or so off it, I was in a completely different place. The walk became dense and steep. About half the things I touched seem to prick or slightly sting me. I found Orpheus standing on a low stump. In quick succession, he was a whipbird, a black cockatoo, a Laughing Kookaburra, a magpie, and many I didn't know. I moved a little toward but also around him, trying to give him space. Initially he edged away, but after a while he seemed not to mind and I was able to get quite close. I stayed there for about half an hour.

In a campground parking lot in the same area (Dorrigo Rainforest), I locked the car, which beeped, and heard an immediate echo. I unlocked and did it again—the same echo, not matching the car exactly, but close. I never saw the imitator, but suspect it was a lyrebird. The scientific literature is somewhat skeptical about claims of mimicry of human-made sounds, at least in the wild. This may be partly because of some exaggerated early tales. If lyrebirds living in captivity count, then the case is clear. A lyrebird in Sydney's zoo has been recorded producing various human-origin sounds. Its rendition of a baby crying is amazing; at least to me, it's indistinguishable from a human cry.

I also said earlier that male lyrebirds acquire their repertoires not, primarily, by directly copying the calls of other species and combining their sounds, but by copying the organized songs of other lyrebirds. The initial copying of a whipbird or parrot has to happen at some stage among the birds in some region, but the sound then stays in place through copying. Other birds are good mimics, especially some parrots and starlings, but do any others pass sounds from bird to bird in this way? If this capacity of lyrebirds is old, then this is, I suppose, the oldest recording medium on Earth.

This system can preserve a sound for a considerable time, too. A whipbird had attracted me to Orpheus, the lyrebird I'd watched in the undergrowth. Whipbirds are not found in Tasmania, the island at the very bottom of Australia, but lyrebirds were introduced there in the 1930s, and they brought with them the sizzling snap of the whipbirds. In 1964, the lyrebirds down there were clearly reproducing that call. A (human) recording made in 1984 still had a "barely recognizable" remnant of the sound. For thirty years the lyrebirds' mental record remained intact, and faded a few decades on. Lyrebirds can live for twenty years, so this preservation need only have covered a couple of generations, though it might have been more. If another, younger lyrebird was listening to Orpheus along with me, somewhere nearby, then his song, though not preserved in its particular details, might live on as a contribution to others, carried forward through time.

WHO WE ARE

5

HUMAN BEING

Another Forest

On another continent, halfway round the world, a forest emerges from farmland in Rwanda, central Africa. You walk in through a mix of broad green leaves, which gives way soon to dense bamboo. Stands of tall stems all lean one way, then another.

The walk is a climb. The bamboo gets skinnier, accompanied by stinging nettles. Soon the path is winding through vague, overgrown green shapes. Eventually, our guides point them out: mountain gorillas. Huge animals, black against the forest's green.

These first ones we saw were part of a large family group, named Igisha, of nearly three dozen. Mountain gorilla groups often have several related adult males, "silverbacks," with one of them dominant. Together with them will be various adult females who won't be closely related to one another, some number of younger males and females, along with children of various ages. A group has its own home range, with a rough core area and a periphery. These territories are not strict and can overlap, but different groups avoid each other.

The adults are massive. When a male stretches out a single

arm, it is truly, eye-wideningly, huge. But when all is well in the group, the atmosphere seems to be one of gentle, low-key affection.

The group we visited on this first encounter was scattered, with some on the ground and others wandering in suspended patches of the low canopy. On our second trip up the mountain, we came upon a group of about five sitting together, quite close. A male on the ground kept an eye, quite carefully it seemed, on youngsters climbing overhead.

There we are, a small, quiet clump of humans and a similar-sized group of gorillas. We are all primates, apes. We share a great deal of history and a lot of DNA, but are obviously different, with clothes and cameras on our side, and journeys that brought us here from all over the world.

The gorillas want nothing from us. They show occasional interest, sometimes move past us very close. But we hardly matter. They steadily strip leaves, take apart stems and branches as we watch—a continual stream of fresh green food. On each visit we are allowed to be with the gorillas for an hour, exactly, and then we say something like a silent goodbye and walk back down the hill.

Looking back up into the mountains from below, near the end of the walk, I see great humped forms. Some of those overgrown green-canopy shapes now look like huge gorilla bodies bent over, as if the whole forest is expressing their presence.

Culture

Mammals arose back in dinosaur-dominated times. But most of the great mammalian enterprises unrolled after the mass extinction that ended the dinosaurs' reign on land. During our time with songbirds in the previous chapter, we looked at some groups that branched off from the rest of their part of the genealogical tree quite early, wound tenuously through the epochs, and led to just a few surviving species today. The same is seen with mammals. The monotremes—egg-laying mammals, the platypus and echidnas—are an early-splitting group with just five species (or fewer, on some counts) alive now. Another early branching led to marsupials, such as kangaroos, on one side and the much larger collection of *eutherian* (or placental) mammals on the other. As with songbirds, Australia is where many of the present survivors of these ancient offshoots have their home.

Within eutherian mammals, primates are one of the groups that appear in the fossil record soon after the mass extinction, though they might have been around a while before that, living inconspicuously in the last days of the big dinosaurs.

One branch within primates is the great apes, or hominids, dating from some 15 million years ago. The term "hominid" has changed its meaning; it used to refer just to us and a few very close relatives, not to gorillas and the like. Now it is used for a larger cluster, which includes gorillas, chimps,

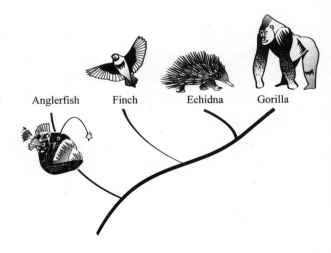

Anglerfish   Finch   Echidna   Gorilla

bonobos, orangutans, and us, along with extinct species on the same branch. Within this cluster, our closest living relatives are chimps and bonobos, followed by gorillas, with orangutans a little further away.

These relatives of ours, the other great apes, are forest animals. They are generally quite social (with orangutans much less so). But sometime over 5 million years ago, a primate line made its way out of the forests onto the African savanna. There, these adventurous apes began to form more complicated, integrated societies.

The human form of social living is special among animals, as it includes collaboration among large numbers of unrelated members of the same species. Even the tolerance seen in humans is unusual, at least among primates. The primatologist Sarah Hrdy offers a memorable thought experiment in which, on a crowded commercial flight with hundreds of unrelated people crammed together into a metal tube, she imagines how things would go if the passengers morphed into a collection of chimps. "Any one of us would be lucky to disembark with all ten fingers and toes still attached." Not every human flight goes smoothly, but body parts tend to remain with their owners. Many fish would probably do better than chimps. Don't try it with octopuses. Human getting-along is a step outside the ways that close-up living works in many animals, especially our nearer relatives.

Our tolerance of strangers (such as it is) and willingness to collaborate with others required changes at the level of individual psychology, but the feature of human life that I want to emphasize more than any other in this chapter is the role, and rise, of *culture*. I intend that term in the broad sense that is used in biology and anthropology—culture is not just Beethoven, though we get there eventually. Culture in this sense refers to the establishment and development of ways of behaving that are passed from generation to generation, and sideways within a generation, not through genes but through watching and imitating, learning and leading, and (sometimes) deliberate instruction. Cooking food, wearing clothes, rules that prescribe who you can and can't marry—these are all aspects of culture in this broad sense.

The cultural spread of behavior can begin with just one individual watching and imitating another who is doing something that seems to work. But this passing on and passing around of habits, rules, and techniques can become more organized, based on communication and ritual. It comes to include "material" culture—the fashioning and use of tools that become standardized, and the deliberate transformation of the local environment. Eventually, societies produce objects, marks, and social behaviors whose overt role is to consolidate and carry patterns of behavior forward: "This is how we live."

Culture not only consolidates behaviors but also gives rise to a new kind of change. As behaviors recur—are imitated, encouraged, and taught—they can also be slowly improved. Details can be refined, and one technique or habit can be combined with others into a useful sequence or chain. If a small innovation spreads (a better way of weaving, for example), it becomes a platform for more experimentation. Human behavior becomes a mix of individual tinkering and persistent cultural tides.

Within these culturally embedded forms of learning, a special form is what Kim Sterelny (the philosopher deceived by a lyrebird in the previous chapter) calls "scaffolded" learning.

Individuals of one generation, through their actions, encourage the learning of particular skills or ways of thinking in the next generation. This is not just learning by imitation, but learning that is actively aided by others. For Sterelny, human societies continually rebuild the social and material scaffolding that children rely on as they grow up. This creates a "looping" pattern within a culture, a loop between the actions of those who are already present and the experiences of new arrivals, who then continue the practice. An example of scaffolded learning is apprenticeship, acquiring skills by watching, helping, being taught by someone who knows them well. Human upbringing involves a lot of apprenticeship, even where it's not obvious. Sterelny's book on these topics is called *The Evolved Apprentice*—the title summarizes the picture. Scaffolded learning is not common in animals. There are a few species whose mothers teach some skills, but this is an area where humans have become different.

When did culture start to take on this role in our ancestors? The anthropologist Joseph Henrich, whose work I draw on often in this chapter, thinks that it happened gradually, but included a transition he describes as "crossing the Rubicon"— reaching a point of no return. At this stage, it becomes hard or impossible to get by *without* culture, and from here its role only increases. (The Rubicon is a river that Julius Caesar crossed in 49 BCE during the early stages of his revolt against the Roman republic; after this crossing, turning back would be pointless, and the only sensible choice was to march on to Rome.)

The picture to have in mind here is not one with a single species, our species, taking the step. Henrich suggests a date of around 2 million years ago for the point of no return. That is early in the history of our genus, *Homo*, and before the appearance of our species, *Homo sapiens*.

Until recently, researchers tended to think in terms of a pretty sharp divide between humans and all other living animals with respect to this feature. Social living of various kinds is common, but the kind of information sharing seen within culture was regarded as almost nonexistent in nonhuman animals. Now this looks wrong, with a growing list of culturally learned behaviors in other animals, especially chimps but also many others. The lyrebirds and bowerbirds of chapter 4 are both examples—lyrebirds with their song repertoires, and (probably) the bowerbirds with their decorative styles. Even bees show simple forms of cultural learning. The question of why other animals lack culture has now been replaced by a different question: Why did it take off and become so elaborate in humans, while remaining a minor element (hardly noticed at all for a long time) in other species? Is it due to brainpower, or perhaps a more cooperative style of social living that was already in place in our lineage, a style of living that made culture especially useful and encouraged its early sparks?

That last question is unresolved, though I'd put some stock in the idea about cooperation. More generally, we can see culture as bringing together several of the forms of action that we looked at in the last few chapters. Culture nearly always involves social interaction (though you might watch, and copy, secretly). Once we get beyond its simpler forms, it tends to involve engineering—making and reshaping, "material culture" as I called it a moment ago. Before long, some parts of material culture are made *for* purposes of social interaction; they are made to aid ritual, and cultural memory. And though we can imagine a narrowly practical way this all might go, in fact it seems to have involved a great deal of display and evaluation. Culture brings those older forms of action together, and it augments them, makes them more powerful.

Living in social situations of this kind leaves a mark on our psychology. One example of this involves a very interesting behavior, also perhaps a disconcerting one. The example involves the awareness of norms—awareness of how people should behave—in young children.

Children often seem to have an eye out for transgressions and violations in everyday behavior. This tendency seems a likely case of something that would need to be learned, probably through a fair bit of experience of social life. But a surprising series of results show that very young children appear primed to interpret various behaviors they see in terms of norms, and experiments keep pushing earlier and earlier the age at which this is seen.

One of the first papers looked at two- and three-year-olds. The children would watch someone do something that was new to them, playing a simple game with toys, and the demonstrator would do this new thing in a deliberate sort of way. When the children afterward saw a puppet do the new thing differently, they would spontaneously protest and correct the puppet. Two-year-olds issued commands: "Don't!" Three-year-olds did this and also made normative protests: "It does not go like this!" They seemed primed to look for norms, and also to enforce them.

A moment ago I said I find this behavior disconcerting, but the way some of the experiments played out, with very young kids taking umbrage at the most arbitrary violations by others, does have a certain charm. Findings of this kind continued; even eighteen-month-olds do the same sort of thing. As some of the experimenters noted, it's not surprising that very young children want to follow local norms and watch out for them in new situations; what's surprising is that a three-year-old would want to enforce these norms in others. It had been known before this that children do have their eyes out for norms in contexts that involve helping. In the newer work, we see this extending to settings where there's no helping in the picture. It's all arbitrary—do you have to make the yellow block move by pushing it *this* way?

Does this mean that we've learned that looking for and enforcing norms are "in the genes"? No; just about everything in human development involves a combination of genetic and environmental factors, tangled together from the start. But we've learned that an ordinary developmental pathway for a human tends to give rise to this behavior without anything like the amount of instruction we might have thought necessary, and it appears very early. The behavior appears only in a particular kind of social context, and the kids do have to learn what is proper in their circumstances—do you push the yellow block with this thing or that one? But they will be inclined, without much prompting, to make a normative distinction of this kind and act on it.

In a case like this, we can also see the possibility of a sequence in which learning starts out heavily involved in some behavior and then its role gets reduced. In highly organized social setups, where it really matters that you get a sense of the right ways to behave, some things might start out being just about entirely learned, but if a genetic mutation pops up that can nudge the newcomer along, make the task easier, then that genetic change could spread. An attentiveness to distinctions between okay and not-okay behaviors, a tendency to interpret what you see around you in this way, could well be advantageous in a situation like this. As my language "nudge along" indicates, all this is liable to be a matter of degree; we might end up with a *little* bit of initial attentiveness to this feature of situations, and then a little more. Behaviors and habits that initially require learning can become more firmly set in the human developmental pathway. This is a way in which culture can infuse nature, and a way that human life tends to frustrate both sides of old "blank slate" versus "all in the genes" dichotomies.

In my sketch of the role of culture in human life so far, I have followed Henrich's account quite closely. He emphasizes the development of useful knowledge, habits, and techniques. In fact, just about the entire story, as he tells it in his book *The Secret of Our Success*, is a story about the accumulation of devices and tricks, adaptation to difficult circumstances. Henrich seems in awe, and rightly so, of the knowledge seen in traditional societies throughout the world. He marvels at their ability to develop complicated methods for processing and detoxifying foods, methods that reliably work even though no one really understands why. People in traditional societies survived easily in environments that turned out to be impossible for well-equipped European explorers, who perished or turned back in despair, leaving a trail of well-attired bodies behind them as they retreated. When I talked a moment ago about a cultural

"Rubicon" that was crossed, this difference between locals and intruders illustrates what Henrich has in mind. His Rubicon is a stage at which typical individuals being born into a society could not possibly learn on their own all the techniques and habits they need to stay alive, even if they wanted to. They have no real choice but to become part of the culture they find themselves in, and continue the process of absorption, transmission, and occasional improvement.

Not everything that becomes entrenched in a culture in this way is so beneficial. Mixed in with the accumulation of solutions to problems and fine-grained knowledge of conditions can be more destructive practices. Quite a few traditional societies invest a lot in practices involving the detection and punishment of sorcery. This can become a significant part of life and one with heavy costs. That is an extreme example, and other cases have more of an appearance of unhelpful arbitrariness. Given the nature of cultural transmission, it makes sense that any culture, traditional or modern, would end up with some practices that work well and others that have just gotten "stuck."

In Henrich's treatment of the growth of culture in human evolution, this unhelpful side is so far in the background that you wonder whether he thinks it exists much at all—or whether, perhaps, he thinks that cultures are so tightly knitted together that the highly effective parts cannot be pulled away from the elements that appear more costly or at least arbitrary. Some of the cases here are so intriguing. Tierra del Fuegians, living at the very tip of South America, traditionally made arrows by choosing wood from a tree whose branches are crooked, and laboriously straightening it. Each shaft was then pressed into a grooved stone and rubbed with fox skin. When feathers were added, right-handed archers should use arrow feathers from the left wing of a goose, and vice versa . . . We might read an account like this and think we can sort through which elements are useful and which are arbitrary preferences that became entrenched even if they did no good. Henrich's message is that if we think we can do this, we are probably fooling ourselves.

Communication Again

Some of the cultural patterns that took root in early human societies would not require language. But language, when it arose, would have transformed just about everything.

The age of language, in evolutionary terms, is still unclear. It is probably older than our species, arising in at least some form back in the lives of earlier kinds of *Homo*. Many linguists through the twentieth century saw language as completely different from everything else that we and other animals do. This view was championed by the American linguist Noam Chomsky. He argued that language, in its central features, could not be something that came into being in small steps and slow improvements within social life, but must have arisen through a decisive shift on the internal side, a change within our minds.

This has come to seem unlikely in the light of work in a variety of fields, including anthropology, psychology, and animal behavior. This work has made a pathway to language that moves through gradual steps seem plausible. Gesture, rather than vocalization, may have been the main medium during some early stages. Gesture in some nonhuman primates is rich and complex even when vocalization is simple and inflexible. Language could become vocal after it had already achieved some of its distinctive features. The freeing-up of hands that vocalization enables certainly seems advantageous, and the transition might also relate to what was being *said* back then. In thinking about language origins, people sometimes imagine a sort of focused, one-on-one communicative exchange, but the paradigms of early human communication might instead have been more broadcast, exhortative, group-level: "HEY everyone! We're going to do *this*, and then *this . . . Let's do it!*"

In the previous chapter, I looked at communication in a general way, with the birds chattering away before us. I set out a framework based on sender-receiver interaction, the interlocking of behaviors "on each side" of signs and symbols. Communication is an interplay between production and reception, speaking and hearing, gesture and interpretation. Human language fits this pattern, but it has special features. I'll discuss two, both of which are seen in faint forms in some nonhuman communication.

The feature of language that motivated the language-is-special view defended by Chomsky is syntax, or grammar. A language has rules by which basic elements can be combined, recombined, and recombined again, yielding an endless stream of new sentences, expressing things that have never been said before. Rather than a fixed collection of signals (*eagle approaching*), a language contains a collection of words from which new combinations can be continually formed. This open-endedness is central to the power of language, to its creative role both in social life and in our minds.

A simple version of this feature is seen in the dances of honeybees. These dances are built on rules by which both the distance and direction of food can be communicated when a foraging bee returns to the hive. This system is not creative in the way that language is, but it does have principles by which elements are spliced together. This is also seen in some kinds of primate communication, including more complicated alarm calls than the vervet ones in the previous chapter.

The second feature of language I want to highlight is one that bridges the social and psychological. Human language is based on a back-and-forth between senders and receivers, as usual. But the point of language, at least some of the time, is to connect the *thoughts*, the private inner states, of speaker and hearer.

Some very old views of language offered by philosophers emphasized this side. John Locke, in the late 1600s, saw language as a medium by which the privacy of our mental lives can be bridged. Each of us comes up with all sorts of thoughts from which others, as well as ourselves, might "receive profit and delight; yet they are all within his own breast, invisible and hidden from others." Language, he said, arose to enable our invisible ideas to become publicly available.

From an evolutionary point of view, there has to be another step in the story. Speaking and listening can only arise and spread if they have practical benefits of some kind, if they help individuals make their way through life, help societies function, or both—it will probably be both. This means that language has to guide action as well as thought: that is where the rubber hits the road, in evolutionary terms. But it does seem that the *way* that language earns its keep in human life, the way it manages to call forth the effects that keep it around, often does involve its ability to connect the impressions, reflections, and musings of different individuals. Language use is, in a phrase from the philosopher Josh Armstrong, a form of "minded communication." This is communication in which the linking of minds, as well as behaviors, is part of the story of how it works.

Some other primates show glimpses of minded communication. The use of calls and gestures can be guided, in some cases, by one animal's sense of what has been seen or heard by another. These "audience effects," where a speaker or sender does things differently according to their assumptions about the knowledge or preferences of the audience, is a first step down a road that leads from sender-receiver coordination to the revelation of our minds' hidden contents.

Construction, Convention, Imagination

Some primates build platforms in trees to sleep on, but they are simple and temporary. Birds' nests, in contrast, can be very elaborate. Weaverbirds, in Africa, are especially impressive. In Kenya I saw a city-like collection of intricate, globe-like nests suspended from branches over a stream. We don't know much about shelters used in the earlier stages of the human evolutionary path. The artifacts whose history we do know well are stone tools.

The first evidence of stone tools dates from about 3.4 million years ago, though at this stage the tools may not have been actively shaped, just put to use if they started out suitable for cutting and scraping. Deliberately shaped tools follow, from perhaps around 2.6 million years ago, and toolkits had bone and horn added. From about 1 million years ago, fire was used as well. Earlier in this chapter, when I was introducing the cultural passing-on of behaviors, I mentioned the example of cooking. Cooking, as a behavior, is definitely not "in the genes"; it is learned and reproduced in the social environments that humans grow up in. However, in another sense, cooking *is* in our genes—it has left its mark there. The use of fire to cook food changed the evolution of our guts—they became smaller, for a start—and also our teeth. In a social environment where cooking is common, the genes that are favored differ from the ones that do well if food is always eaten raw. The fact that cooking is kept around by way of culture is beside the point.

The same is likely to be true of stone tools and our hands. The "precision grip" between fingers and thumb formed over 3 million years ago, before *Homo*, perhaps because manipulation had become important to our lives through the use of tools. Behaviors based in culture can feed back and affect genetic evolution.

The building of shelters during our early days might have been common, but if so, this practice didn't leave much trace behind. There's good evidence of the building of enduring structures from about 500,000 years ago (and scattered evidence from earlier), but I will jump ahead to a landmark, the oldest known group-level building projects that used stone on a large scale. These are found in present-day Turkey, the Göbekli Tepe buildings. They were occupied from about 9500 to 8000 BCE. The dates are important because, at least in the European and

Middle Eastern context, this is a date before, or right around, the start of agriculture and settled communities.

The scale of Göbekli Tepe is substantial—hectares of stone columns that probably once supported roofs, decorated with carvings that endure. This large-scale building project did not, apparently, arise *from* settled society. That had been the usual assumption—that agriculture and food storage might prompt the first permanent buildings. The Göbekli Tepe buildings are old enough to raise the possibility of things going the other way round. They mark a major investment in religious and ritual practice, it seems, and would have required a lot of people. Perhaps a strong development of ritual life motivated a settling-down, in this case, and the beginnings of an agricultural society.

Much early settling-down probably did not involve buildings on anything like the Göbekli Tepe scale. A transition from a nomadic existence to agriculture and a settled life once seemed a natural example of human progress. Recent discussions have questioned this. Early farming would have been a precarious existence and, quite possibly, less appealing for the average person than a hunter-gatherer life. But a settled life with farming brings with it larger population numbers, also specialized soldiers and other enforcers, and this meant that agricultural communities could often dominate the environments where they settled.

Our picture of this transition—from a hunter-gatherer life to farming—has often been populated by stereotypes. The hunter-gatherer life has been portrayed as simple, also—on the positive side—as very egalitarian, while settling down brought with it a more complex and structured life. In fact, life without farming was diverse, sometimes settled and prosperous (especially on coasts), and saw a kaleidoscopic variety of social organizations.

Discussion in Australia, where stereotypes about indigenous societies have been especially marked and also harmful, has seen a new appreciation of the rich complexity of these cultures in the millennia before European contact. It still appears true that the process of settling down and the growth of surpluses, whether achieved through farming or in other ways, makes new levels of inequality possible. Hierarchy and enforcement grow within everyday life.

The political scientist James Scott's book on this topic has a chapter called "The Golden Age of the Barbarians"—a deliberately incongruous phrase, as we think of barbarians as unkempt, brutish types. What Scott means by "barbarians" is just people living outside of a settled state. (This was an old meaning of the term.) The passage to statehood runs, in each locality, through the twilight of a life that gradually becomes impossible as it is edged out by more organized, higher-density, more unequal living. (Here I assume that the transition is local and does not involve outright invasion, which is another way for things to go.)

Though there would be much diversity across places, and all this does depend on what you like, it may well be that the first time the average state dweller was better off than the average non–state dweller, or "barbarian," in a lot of locales was many, many centuries later. I remember being amazed when I first learned that, in old hunter-gatherer skeletons, when an adult died, their teeth were often in pretty good shape, by modern standards, despite never having seen a toothbrush or a dentist for the whole of their lives. The teeth of people from early agricultural societies tend to be much worse. The average early farmer, living in a world of steadily accumulating sewage and tax collectors, dealing also with the first of countless waves of disease coming in from their domesticated animals, might have had good reason to look wistfully at the lives of the last barbarians, retreating from the fringes of their newly settled lands.

A medieval coronation ceremony is performed, and suddenly an individual acquires the ability to direct the movements of huge numbers of people. Whole states are set in motion, in one direction or another. If a different young person had been under the hands lowering the crown, masses of people would have taken a different path.

The phenomenon seen in the coronation is an extraordinary extension of a trend we have been following for a few chapters, a shift toward longer lines of control of nature, achieved through deliberate action. In human life, this trend is taken very far. The way this works is dependent on the details of particular circumstances and cultures, but a couple of general features of the human animal give it this capacity.

One is enormous social coordination, made possible especially by language. Another is psychological: the imaginative generation of plans, consideration of possibilities, the formulation of distant and novel goals. With this, action acquires a new kind of directedness, directedness on the merely possible, as represented in thought and language.

Back in chapter 3, I looked at a shift in the history of action from habit-based to plan-based choices. Rather than just going with actions that have worked before, a planner tries to model their situation, assess options, and choose the one that looks best. This will tend to be slower than relying on habit, but sometimes it is worth it. When it begins, this is a shift in the causal processes by which things get done in the world.

In the first discussion of goals and purposes in this book, in chapter 2, I distinguished two ways in which things can be brought about because of their likely effects. One way is through feedback from past cases; past outcomes, successes and failures, can affect what is done now. A number of different but analogous mechanisms can support this. I discussed two back then, Darwinian evolution and learning by trial and error—continuing to do things that have worked, avoiding those that have not. Another kind of learning, introduced just now in this chapter, can also have this role. This is learning by imitating others who are successful (and avoiding the imitation of failure). This has a mix of features of Darwinian evolution (as it is on the scale of a population) and ordinary individual learning. It's a culture-sized version of trial and error in the individual.

All this is in the first broad category of ways in which things can happen because of their effects, the category involving feedback from past cases. The other category is the one where a future outcome is represented and sought, even if all this is new: I am doing X because I think it will lead to Y, though this has never happened before. It might be that X has never before been used to get to Y, though Y is familiar (perhaps X is a shortcut), or Y itself might be completely novel.

The distinction between plan and habit might be somewhat vague, and actions can have some of both. A bit of planning, some use of novel methods, might be laid on top of a habit that is more established. Habit-based behavior almost always has to include some fine-tuning for the circumstances, and this might be the beginning of the transition. At some point, though, we do see a new kind of choice. This is not found just in humans; rats engage in an imaginative "pre-play" of behaviors that involve navigation in space, using internal maps in their brains to try out possible paths. Eventually, we reach the situation where humans can consciously plan, using language to formulate what they want to do and how it might be done, and pursue goals that are arrived at through imagining, with little or no precedent in history at all.

Play that involves explicit pretense—I am the king!—arises early in young children. This starts as young as eighteen months (around the same time as those norm-enforcement behaviors I mentioned earlier in this chapter). It doesn't seem completely unique to humans, though nonhuman cases, in a few other primates, seem rare.

My emphasis on the role of the imagined brings to mind a view developed in a bestselling book by Yuval Noah Harari. In *Sapiens*, Harari says that a key advance seen in human action, especially social action, is guidance by fictions. Fictions in his sense include religions, companies (like Peugeot), and money. I think that there is some role for fictions in such cases, but it is not the main thing going on. Many behaviors that Harari understands in terms of fictions are better understood with the idea of *convention*. In these cases, we have interlocking behaviors and expectations within a community that can be used to coordinate action that has large effects. Language itself is like this; it is a pattern of behavior sustained purely by convention, by people's expectations that speaking and hearing will continue to align, more or less—align well enough to keep things going.

This is true of a lot of what Harari describes as fictions or myths. They don't rest on something that is putatively real but actually not so (a fiction); they rest on convention-based patterns of behavior that have been reasonably stable, and that we, who are part of the pattern, have some reason to believe will continue.

A case Harari discusses that does sometimes look as if it involves fiction is money. Objects of no intrinsic usefulness—bits of paper, shells, records in computer files—become the focus of a huge fraction of our activities. In some cases, behaviors around currency might be guided by fictional beliefs about intrinsic value, but in general the practice is sustained by mutual expectations—the expectation that what I work for and receive (dollars, as indicated in bank accounts) will be seen as valuable by others. Often, expectations and actions that involve a government play a special role; tax payments are demanded in the form of dollars or euros. But this is not essential, and can't always have been in play when early currencies arose.

The fiction view can seem exciting because it makes the whole enterprise, the edifice of coordinated human action, look precarious and fragile. And it is fragile. Conventions are inherently fragile. If we give up enough of the interlocking behaviors, it all falls apart. But human social actions in most cases are not held together by fictions. They are, in a way, more freestanding than that.

Writing and Time

These words—marks on a page, or images on a screen—bridge us. They bridge two people. So does spoken language, but writing is distinctive in its relationship to time. Written marks persist, bridging time as well as the differences between people.

When you write just for yourself—notes, reminders, diaries—you are both sender and receiver, over a temporal gap.

The anthropologist Claude Lévi-Strauss, in his wry, moody memoir *Tristes Tropiques* (a book that begins, "I hate traveling and explorers"), discussed this aspect of writing: "Writing is a strange invention. One might suppose that its emergence could not fail to bring about profound changes in the conditions of human existence . . . It can be thought of as an artificial memory, the development of which ought to lead to a clearer awareness of the past, and hence to a greater ability to organize both the present and the future." Perhaps literacy might be seen as a plausible marker of the transition from primitive life to civilization? But then: "Yet nothing we know about writing and the part it has played in man's evolution justifies this view." As Lévi-Strauss notes, most of the major transitions in human living occurred without and before writing, and the period after writing was invented included long periods of cultural stagnation. What writing *is* good for, he says, is controlling people: "the integration of large numbers of individuals into a political system, and their grading into castes or classes." Tight social control is possible without writing, but writing firms it up.*

The outlines of Lévi-Strauss's sketch correspond, at least

---

* Here are some comments from the political scientist James C. Scott: "Early colonial history is rife with indigenous resistance to the first colonial census; peasants and tribesmen alike understood perfectly well that a census was the necessary prelude to taxes and corvée labor. A similar attitude toward writing and record keeping permeates the history of colonial peasant rebellions against the state. The first target of peasant wrath was often not so much the colonial officials themselves as the paper documents—land titles, tax lists, population records—through which the officials seemed to rule." (*The Art of Not Being Governed*, 2009)

roughly, to what is now believed about the origins of writing. Writing is thought to have appeared independently three or four times, first in Mesopotamia, perhaps around 3200 BCE, in Egypt soon after (probably independently), and later in China and Central America. Writing did not arise as an attempt to make permanent the transitory sounds of speech. Instead, its main initial roles were recordkeeping and administration. It was not a general-purpose system, but specialized for these roles. Many "graphic codes" are not based on the sounds of words at all, and the transition in a few cases to sound-based codes may have been prompted by the need to keep track of individual people—to write down proper names. Later, writing took on a wider range of roles. In Sumer (Mesopotamia), tablets with hymns, poems, myths, and allegories are seen from about 2600 BCE. (Does that seem a long wait, or a short one? To me it seems long—many hundreds of years.)

According to the French cognitive scientist Olivier Morin, the feature that Lévi-Strauss and I emphasized at the start of this section—the creation of a flexible, widely applicable new form of memory—might have been especially late to take hold. Outside of those narrow recordkeeping roles, the bridging achieved by writing was, in earlier stages, mostly an adjunct to other ways of carrying information forward.

Morin notes that in much of the ancient world, memorization was a highly prized skill. It was often an essential part of the curriculum in literate societies (in Mesopotamian, Jewish, and Hellenistic traditions). In ancient Greece and Rome, the "memory palace" or "method of loci" mental technology was widely taught and used. Here, a person memorizes a large collection of items by imagining a palace or other building (which might be real or made-up), and placing the items at particular locations within it. The items can then be encountered, "retrieved," in those places later, on an imaginary path taken through the building. An older tradition of memorization used in Aboriginal Australian cultures combines the use of places, actual rather than imagined, with stories—a narrative is built that sets items to be remembered into a landscape, one that can then be physically traversed or mentally recalled. On a larger and more permanent scale, "songlines" or "singing tracks" tie songs to landscapes in a way that integrates navigation, ritual, and the maintenance of ecological knowledge.

Related to the primacy of mental memory even in literate ancient societies was a valuation of recitation—saying things out loud. In the formation of a treaty or alliance (Morin's examples are from ancient Mesopotamia), spoken oaths were what mattered, even if a text served to help people remember. In other settings, shamans might use pictorial, writing-like codes to jog their memory during incantations. An inscription was an aid to speech, and only usable alongside other remembered knowledge. These uses of writing contrast with uses in which the aim is to get a message to someone at a different, perhaps distant time, someone to whom the information can be quite new. The transition to this modern role requires that texts become more self-contained. You need to know the language or code, but the text has to make sense without a lot of context and stage-setting that require memory or some other way of carrying information forward. Aboriginal Australian "message sticks" are an intriguing intermediate case. These carved sticks were used to send messages over long distances. The message was delivered orally by its bearer, and the artifact was, in its normal uses, an aid to recall and recitation (as in those Mesopo-tamian treaties). It also had a passport-like role. But at least in some cases, the meaning of a message could be read from the stick when the bearer was missing.

Morin and Lévi-Strauss emphasize the unobviousness of what seems obvious to us now—the boundless possibilities, in relation to time, that writing enables. But this broader use for writing did eventually take off, and writing become a general-purpose, long-term, highly precise memory for just about everything. External representations also lend themselves to manipulation and transformation. Mathematical symbolism, especially, is like this; knowing how to use a symbolism is knowing how to pro-duce new formulas that take things further. A technology that started as a device for social control could also become central to the history of subversion and revolution—*The Rights of Man* (Thomas Paine, 1791), *The Communist Manifesto* (Marx and Engels, 1848). The internet continues the trend.

This side of writing—the time-bridging side, and to some extent the whole phenomenon—is a version or manifestation of something more general. This is a "looping" pattern. An action is done at one time to affect perception later. The shape of the ac-tivity doesn't look much like a loop if you write something to be read immediately by another person. There's a role for writing that is quite speech-like—achieving near-immediate contact, as with a phone text message. But writing also has that other role, where permanence matters, and if we zoom out our view a bit, a culture as a whole is continually laying down marks, meant to be read, that carry its way of living through time.

In cognitive science, when a person makes marks of some kind to read or make use of again later, this behavior is described as "offloading." Information is offloaded from the brain to the wider world, and then taken up again. The practice is often more transformative than that term suggests. Through actions of this kind, an idea is not just externalized but also given a new form that can be worked with in different ways— the example of mathematical symbolism is again a good one. Drawing and painting can have the same role, along with other ancient ways of making marks, such as carving. All this is a combination of several kinds of action we've looked at in other chapters. Making a mark is a small piece of engineering, transformation of the environment (chapter 3). This is also a sender-receiver behavior (chapter 4), even if the receiver is the same person as the sender, at a later time.

Written language is not just a combination of sender-receiver interaction and engineering; it is a practice that embodies the power of each of these in a unique way. There are various practices of making marks to be seen, many pictorial traditions and "graphic codes." In written language, speech itself, which has been shaped in social life to have great expressive power and flexibility, is carried over into the realm of inscription, where it can endure, and can be worked on in new ways.

Stepping back from writing, and looking at all the forms of action discussed in this chapter, a good part of the story of how we came to be *us* is the story of these patterns of action. We're beings with a certain kind of evolved body and brain, but who we *are* is dependent to a particularly high degree on what we've *done*. It is a result of what we've built and continue to build, how we teach and imitate, which behaviors we encourage, and the ways we transform our surroundings. The twentieth-century biologist Richard Lewontin wrote a number of philosophically minded papers. One is called "The Organism as the Subject and Object of Evolution." It claims that organisms are not passive recipients of evolutionary forces, but active in their own development and evolution. Lewontin meant this generally, and in his account of organisms as subjects he made use of many of the phenomena described in the first chapters of this book—niche construction, the chemical effects of life, and so on. This idea of an active role for all organisms in evolution is true to some extent, but it's not a message that applies the same way all over. Humans have been active in our evolution to a particular degree, through culture and technology, and the loops discussed in this section are part of this. Our offloading, perception-feeding practices are part of our characteristic place in the world.

The Greek philosopher Socrates, back around 400 BCE, advised against a reliance on reading and writing, as he thought they led to shallow forms of understanding. People's memories would dim. He imagined an Egyptian king addressing writing's inventor: "You provide your students with the appearance of wisdom, not with its reality."

At least, this is what we're told about Socrates's views by Plato, his student. Socrates did not write his philosophical ideas down. Plato did, and many he presented as the words of Socrates. Historians debate how much Plato's Socrates has to do with Socrates himself. When there's no written record, retellings serve the purposes of the tellers. Even when ideas *are* written, there's still a good deal of this—people select, edit, and translate. But inscriptions can provide a very different degree of stability.

It's possible to see anxieties about new technology as conservative and shortsighted. (The development of the printing press led some to concern about overload, as well as misinformation.) But neuroscience and psychology tell us that there are genuine questions here. "Cognitive technologies" change our minds as well as our social lives. Literacy, in particular, has significant effects on our brains. It increases the size of the *corpus callosum*, the main connector between our left and right hemispheres. This change is not genetic, but driven by individual experience. It also changes the way objects other than words—faces and houses—are processed visually, shifting literate people from a more holistic approach to one based on the tracking of specific features. A scanned literate brain looks different from one that's not—an area of the brain lights up so reliably when literate people look at words that it's known as the "visual word form area." These changes don't only occur when a person learns to read in childhood; if someone learns to read much later, the brain can be affected in these ways as well. The main concern of this kind today relates to the effects of smartphone technology, especially its effects on attention and memory, but the shifts in how our minds work started much earlier.

For each transition of this kind we can ask: Are we better off? We might make generalizations that contrast two ways of handling information. In one way, ideas are offloaded and marked down in an external, potentially public space. They are available to be worked on in new ways, and are potentially stable over long periods. In the other, retention is more psychologically active, relying on "onboard" memory and speech, and ideas are transformed differently.

In the case of music, traditions that use or reject inscription can flourish alongside each other without conflict. I marvel at notated music, at its stability and portability. The French composer Olivier Messiaen wrote "Quartet for the End of Time" in a German prisoner-of-war camp during World War II. Now it can be sent intact, note for note, to ensembles for new performances across the world. Musical traditions that rely on oral memory, with its more active re-creation, live on with their own greatness. (Music that relies closely on audio recordings is in some ways in between, but more akin to the unwritten traditions.) Some other parts of culture feature the same kind of coexistence, but in many contexts there seems to have been an ongoing choice, a series of forks in the road, between the two ways of handling information that I sketched above.

The next round of choices we encounter may have a different shape, though, if they involve internal cognitive aids, neurally implanted, whose use does not run through the channel of ordinary sensing and action. Might they move us toward restoration of some of an earlier cognitive style, strengthening our capacities for freewheeling internal manipulation? They would not take us all the way back if a strong role for text remains, and I don't want this section to seem nostalgic for a Socratic, less literate way of being. I'm reminded of a quote from an interview with the Australian novelist Richard Flanagan, some of whose grandparents were illiterate and whose father was the only one in his family to value reading: "He never ceased to marvel till the end of his days that you can divine the universe with these

26 symbols. People who come from generations of literacy might have lost that sense of its transcendent and liberating power."

Why Us?

It's natural to ask one more question to finish this chapter. Why did animals of our kind go down this road, when and where we did?

This is more like two questions. Why was it animals like us (primates, mammals) rather than someone else, and how likely or inevitable was it that someone would do it? I'll look at the first question here, and return to the other one later.

Biologists tend to emphasize contingency—the role of accident, the winding and easily deflected paths that took us to where we find ourselves now. Stephen Jay Gould imagined a "replaying of the tape" of evolution, from around the time of the Cambrian, and argued that we'd probably not get anything like the same sort of history a second time. Biologists looking just at the later stages have said similar things. Jared Diamond's book *The Third Chimpanzee* casts us as an initially unremarkable species that did a remarkable thing. Others resist the message of contingency. Simon Conway Morris, a paleontologist who worked on some of the Cambrian fossils that led Gould to think in terms of accident, suspects that the general path we saw from back then is not surprising, and we might see something quite like it if the tape was wound back and the sequence began again.

People thinking about alternatives to the human evolutionary path often ask the question in terms of intelligence. Which other animals might have gotten very clever, or might do so if we leave the scene? My emphasis in this chapter has not been on intelligence as the human specialty, but on culture. If we imagine a species in which everyone is a lone genius, in an entirely non-cultural way, we are not imagining a species with anything like the role in the world played by humans. (Such a species would probably also be hard to evolve; the reflective, intense intelligence seen in humans might be something only likely to appear in a cultural species, even when that intelligence can be manifested in lone-genius form.)

The anthropologist Joseph Henrich, whose work I have used a lot in this chapter, has a story about the "Why us?" side of things. Primates (land-dwelling, warm-blooded mammals) evolved in the forests for arboreal life. This life gave them strong, grasping hands. They came down from the trees, in the story sketched at the start of this chapter, and these hands, especially after the primates began to stand somewhat upright, were freed for manipulation—for open-ended, exploratory manipulation of the objects around them.

I was reminded of this while watching the gorillas described at the start of this chapter. One male I watched for a while sat and—with those colossal, tree-trunk arms—fiddled patiently, intently, with some slender branches and stems.

As Henrich continues the story, once on the African savanna, these primates encountered many more predators, big cats and others. Imagine, for example, trying to sleep in such a setting. A general primate strategy in response to these kinds of threats is to form bigger groups. (In a variant of this story, Sterelny sees the formation of bigger groups after leaving the trees as a response to an opportunity—collaborative hunting—rather than

a threat. It could be some of both.) In this enlarged social setting, the patterns of family life and child-rearing then changed,
with longer childhoods, larger networks of relatives caring for
infants, the formation of stable pairs, and other social shifts.
With language on board at some stage, the rest is history.

Another biologist, Antone Martinho-Truswell, tells his own
story about the evolutionary road to braininess and culture, and
does so with an eye on a comparison between ourselves and
birds.

Humans in many ways are atypical mammals, and this goes
beyond obvious differences such as writing and making coffee.
We are also different in our long lifespans and reproductive habits, including the way we look after children. Humans are fairly
monogamous, at least compared to other mammals, and our
children are helpless when young. These features are unusual in
mammals, but similar to what is seen in many birds, especially
parrots. With his eye on those similarities, Martinho-Truswell
identifies an unusual evolutionary path that birds went down
first, and that we discovered, in a modified form, later.

In Martinho-Truswell's story, the birds' version of this path
begins with their unusual longevity, which was enabled by
flight (very useful for escaping predators). A number of features
stem from this, but Martinho-Truswell emphasizes especially
some traits surrounding reproduction and the raising of young.
Biologists distinguish between *precocial* and *altricial* offspring.
Precocial offspring become independent quickly—they can
move around and feed themselves soon after hatching or birth.
Altricial offspring are helpless and need a lot of care. Most birds
are altricial. Birds also tend toward monogamy, or at least a
situation where both parents are involved in the raising of the

young. I say they "tend toward" monogamy; there are plenty of exceptions, and even when a species appears monogamous, often the females engage in a lot of matings outside the relationship. The term "socially monogamous" is sometimes used in these cases, and that arrangement seems very common in passerine birds (the big group that includes more than half of all bird species). Parrots, who are next door to passerines on the tree, appear in many cases to be more genuinely monogamous, and parrots often show intense pair-bonding.

For Martinho-Truswell, long lives and close family ties lead to an intensely communicative intelligence in parrots and some other birds. This package of features also tends to be self-reinforcing—smartness, sociality, long childhood, and so on. Put it all together, and you get an evolutionary "rocket," a path to a life of extremes.

Martinho-Truswell thinks we did something similar, tens of millions of years later. In our case, some initial braininess got the process rolling. This also made us long-lived, and the same package of traits surrounding reproduction and child care could then take hold. We ended up, as parrots did, with a highly social and communicative form of intelligence, and culture and technology followed.

In Martinho-Truswell's story, our highly social way of living is "downstream" of those characteristics involving child care and reproduction. For Henrich, the move toward more social living is "upstream" of those characteristics; as we encountered the problems of life out of the forest, we became more social and developed new patterns of family life.

Animals can end up very social and brainy despite living differently from both humans and birds. Dolphins are large-

brained animals, and full of human-like quirks such as mirror self-recognition and play. They are not helpless when they
are young (I guess that would be very difficult in the sea), and
also not at all monogamous, with no care of young by fathers.
They are very social and communicative, though. Sociality itself
seems to drive the story of their high intelligence.

Given all this, could dolphins have taken off in a human-like
way, and achieved a technologically complex, dominating role on
Earth of the kind that we have? Might they still do so if we leave
the scene? Dolphins do have glimmers of culture. Once we ask
about technology, manipulation becomes an issue, though. Like
fish, dolphins have bodies built for swimming and can't do a lot
of manipulation of objects. This is also harder in the sea than on
land, as we saw in chapter 3. They might become more amphib-
ious in a takeover scenario, but they'd need some bodily changes.
Dolphins as they are now do show some tool use; they appear
in the rather short lists of tool-using marine animals. They use
sponges to protect their noses when probing for food in the seafloor. While working on this chapter I learned that some dolphins wear long strands or clumps of grass draped over their
dorsal fins, apparently to attract attention from other dolphins
in social settings. But all this is limited, and they are highly social animals without being invested in technology, tools, or niche
construction. When one imagines their possible futures, it would
take them a long way off their current path to get them into a
more human-like life in those respects.

In a comedic but often insightful series of books (The
Hitchhiker's Guide to the Galaxy), Douglas Adams imagines
that dolphins are actually the smartest animals on Earth, but
prefer to live as they do, with none of the fuss and clutter of

human life. If that was all true, the fact that they are better off living as they do now would not stop dolphins from going down an evolutionary path toward a more technological way of living if there was some advantage to those who took the first steps, then an advantage to those who took the next step, and so on. The relevant kind of advantage here involves survival and reproduction, in comparison to other individuals in the same species. Humans may have been happier as hunter-gatherers than in early farming societies, but if they were, that would not have been enough to stop them from being outcompeted by people living in larger, settled groups. In the dolphin case, it's not easy to see an evolutionary road toward technology and a state-based life in any case. Our primate ancestors on the savanna had grasping hands and lived in an environment where niche construction and technology came readily, with the aid of the stable, handier materials of dry land. This led humans not just to an evolutionary rocket (to use Martinho-Truswell's term), but eventually to literal rockets as well.

While we are in the sea, what about octopuses? They have great manipulative ability, also a willingness to engage with novel objects, and some species put much effort into the construction and tending of dens. But with respect to the kind of path we are talking about here, they face other obstacles. Again, it is not just a matter of being clever; it is a matter of becoming cultural.

Some animals are well set up for culture, even if they are not there now, and some are not. Octopuses are not. They are not very social, engage in no parental care at all once their eggs are hatched, and have very short lives. The high-density octopus sites that I discussed in chapter 3, Octopolis and Octlantis, seem quite special. There's no teaching of children and no other cultural transmission in the wild (as far as we know). A bit earlier in this chapter, I talked about the evolution of new systems of memory—imitation, apprenticeship, writing things down. These are all ways of accumulating knowledge and skills. Octopuses have trouble with these sorts of things on nearly every scale or, more accurately, little interest in them.

In his book *Built by Animals*, which was helpful to me back in chapter 3, the biologist Mike Hansell imagines a conversation between a Martian space traveler and a Venusian time traveler who meet in a hyperspace bar several million years before the present. The time traveler, who has returned from a trip into the future, surprises the space traveler, who has been spending some time visiting Earth, by saying that in a few million years some of Earth's animal life would have complex technology, including the beginning of space travel. He adds that it will be primates who achieve it.

The Martian who has just returned from Earth says: "What, from that lot? You're kidding me . . . I have had a stick waved at me once or twice and I've heard they can shape stones a bit but I would have put my money on the birds."

Yes, for a long time, birds were far more elaborate builders and engineers. I am not sure about the Martian's bet, though. We should be mindful of the costs of the miracle of terrestrial flight—the difficulty of having a body and limbs that can manage that, and the limitations in other areas that result. Earlier in this chapter, I described the impressive nests of weaverbirds.

Hansell says at one point that these might be just about the summit, not only in fact but in principle, for avian engineering. Contrast all this with our primate-style life—grounded, grasping, grubbing around at the roots of things.

In Greek myths and later reflection on them, especially in writers like Nietzsche, a distinction between the Apollonian and Dionysian is sometimes seen as a big divide. The division is named after the Greek god of light, sun, music and dance (Apollo), and the god of wine, vegetation and fruit, intoxication and ritual madness (Dionysus). The procession of socially complicated animals in the years after the asteroid-caused extinction strikes me the same way, with birds as Apollonian, creatures of the air and music, and primates as Dionysian denizens of vegetation, pushed into big and integrated groups, and thence into culture, by the perils of life out of the trees.

6

CONSCIOUSNESS

Experience and Animal Life

The previous chapter described an animal, a primate, whose living patterns and mind have been permeated by culture. This has many consequences for what those animals can do, for their role in the world. Another side of all this is how it *feels*—what it feels like to be the outcome of an evolutionary and historical process of that kind. That is the topic of this chapter: human experience, our form of consciousness. Human conscious experience is a joint product of our animal nature and the infusion of our lives with culture.

The starting point is the fact that there's a way the events of our lives, or some of them anyway, feel from the inside. There's something it feels like to be us. This feature is now often referred to as "consciousness." That is a broad use of that term, where consciousness does not require a reflective, "here I am" kind of awareness, or anything like that. The term "consciousness" now tends to be applied to even the simplest kinds of feeling; you are conscious if it feels like anything at all to be you. The same phenomenon can be called "felt experience," "subjective experience," or "sentience" (though that word brings with it particular connotations of pleasure and pain). Future work in this area will probably develop new and better ways of describing and categorizing what is going on, so I won't worry much about the terms. I'll generally use "felt experience" for the broad phenomenon, although most of the chapter is about experience in us, where the word "consciousness" is more clearly apt.

Much is unknown here and speculation is unavoidable. I won't give arguments for my basic picture (those can be found in my other work), but will outline and apply it.

I see felt experience as widespread in animal life. Some of the features responsible for it have entered the scene in earlier chapters of this book. I looked at the evolution of action and its control by sensing. An animal is a nexus in which sensing and action meet, with a mass of causal lines coming in and radiating out. That feature of animal life is important for this book's theme of action and transformation, and it also creates a system with a point of view. It creates a system to whom things seem a certain way—a system that *is* a "whom," in fact, rather than just an object in the world.

The history of such systems starts with single-celled organisms, moves through the evolution of controlled movement, and on through the rise of animals. In animals, large numbers of cells work together to create movement, sensory systems become organized arrays of cells, and coordination of these new wholes is made possible by nervous systems. Nervous systems may have first arisen largely as a means to "pull bodies together," to make action possible in these unwieldy new objects. When animals became more active, during the Cambrian period half a billion years ago, nervous systems together with richer senses achieved an opening-up to the world. This was a time of the *focusing of subjectivity*, resulting from the demands of a life featuring more engagement with other animals, and a need for decision-making in real time.

This feature that I call the "focusing of subjectivity" arises from the integrating of information from different senses, the use of these senses alongside traces of the past in memory, and, in addition, the establishment of loops between sensing and action of the kind that have been encountered in several chapters of this book. Mobile animals have to process information they get from the senses in a way that takes account of the consequences of their own actions for what they sense. In this way, a tacit "self-other" distinction is embedded in a mobile animal's dealing with the world.

Some aspects of felt experience arise as natural consequences of the animal way of being, consequences of the fact that in animals, evolution built systems that are very much "whoms," as I said a moment ago. All this is the first element of my picture of the biology of experience. A second element is a view about those internal controllers, nervous systems, themselves. People often think of a nervous system as a network a bit like an old-fashioned telephone exchange, with connections and relays. It's a collection of discrete units, neurons, whose activity is firing and making others fire: neuron A's firing affects neuron B, which affects C, and so on. In this view, a nervous system's job could faithfully be done, at least in principle, with a very different sort of device, one not made of living cells, as long as it formed a network with the same connections between its parts.

More of what goes on in our brains matters than that, most likely. A nervous system is a physically unusual object, and those peculiarities are probably important to the explanation of how felt experience comes to exist. As well as containing those node-to-node connections I mentioned a moment ago, brains contain rhythms and patterns of electrical oscillation that span the whole system, or large parts of it. I'll refer to these as "large-scale dynamic patterns."

An example is the oscillation in electrical activity in our brains that is picked up with an EEG (electroencephalogram) device, a mesh of electrical detectors that sits on the head. Some of what an EEG reading tracks is a great mass of those familiar neuron-to-neuron effects, the "spiking" or "firing" of cells, but it's also picking up slower, less localized patterns in the brain's electrical activity.

Why might large-scale patterns of this kind matter to felt experience? I want to approach this question by looking at the evolutionary side, and at several different kinds of animals. Some decades ago, Francis Crick (of DNA fame), Christof Koch, and others began to argue that some of these large-scale dynamic patterns have a role in human visual experience, because they help us to integrate the various features that we perceive—matching colors to shapes in the objects we see, for example. The large-scale rhythmic patterns that Crick and Koch wrote about are not human peculiarities, though; they are all over the animal kingdom, including in animals that can't see at all. They don't appear in the same form everywhere, and they have different speeds, with different triggers, and so on. But they are found all over the animal world. Why are they there?

Back in the 1960s, the neurobiologist L. M. "Mac" Passano (often working with C. B. McCullough) described large-scale electrical rhythms in simple jellyfish-like animals called *Hydra*.

Passano conjectured that spontaneous rhythmic activity might be a feature of very early nervous systems, and might figure in behaviors such as feeding. Once a spontaneous pattern of activity of this kind has been established, that pattern can be modulated by sensory events and other goings-on. It becomes a platform on which events can be registered and responses can be coordinated. Passano suggested that these ancient rhythms could have evolved into the more elaborate electrical patterns seen in other animals. The picture is one where rhythmic activity starts up early in animal evolution. This activity recurs, restarts, in each individual as their nervous system comes into existence, and also continues on, species to species, over the millennia. The rhythms continually change in the individual (as they sleep and wake, for example) and also change on an evolutionary timescale, reaching new forms in larger nervous systems like ours.

The first thing this picture does, in the project of explaining how felt experience can be a biological phenomenon, is change our view of what nervous systems are like, and what kind of activity goes on in them. Brain processes include network-like, unit-to-unit flows of information, and they also include these more diffuse, large-scale patterns of electrical activity, continually shifting and being modulated by the events the animal encounters. The idea that all this feels like something "from the inside," to the animal itself, is not at all surprising to me. It's not that these rhythms and other large-scale patterns are all that matter, but they are part of what makes nervous systems into special physical objects, objects that organize nature's energies in a unique way.

Connections can also be drawn between this picture of

nervous systems and the feel of experience itself. Again stepping back in time a little, Passano gestured toward a kind of
power that comes from organizing the activity of a nervous system in this manner. It can make the system responsive to very
subtle signals, such as tiny glimpses in vision. When a large-
scale pattern of activity is set up and then modulated by events
as they happen, this can also give rise to a kind of natural integration, a bringing-together, of processing. I said a moment ago
that the brain's large-scale electrical patterns will be affected by
what is coming in through the senses—by sight, by touch—
and they will also be affected by other things going on inside
the animal: Is it running low on food? When a total state of activity is being perturbed in this way, many different influences
can have effects together, in concert, on that whole. This may
be useful for the animal in working out what to do, and it also
has links to the nature of felt experience itself. A feature of ordinary experience that is sometimes underplayed, even denied,
in recent scientific discussions is the fact that at each moment,
our experience has many facets that are present together. Even
if you are focusing pretty intently on one thing—this book, the
road you're driving on, or a person you're talking with—the
total "feel" of experience is affected by hints from much else.
It's affected by other things you are sensing, by your mood, by
how your body is arranged, your energy level, and more. All
these are part of that moment's *gestalt*, even if their influence is
very slight. This feature of experience is just what we'd expect
to find, given the view of brain activity I've been outlining over
the last page or two, in which large-scale patterns of activity are
being modulated by many different influences at once.

This oscillatory activity in the brain might be something

that arises almost automatically when a nervous system comes to exist—at least when those nervous systems are made out of the materials in animals on Earth—or it might be something that had to be built and installed, to help animals do what they do. It could be some of both of these; there's an unknown interplay here between the tasks or functions of early nervous systems and the inherent tendencies of the materials that came to hand.

Think back for a moment to the first part of my sketch of the biology of felt experience, and the idea of a "focusing of subjectivity" as animals became more active. Some animals acted more, sensed more, and developed richer links between the two. When we initially picture this, it can sometimes seem that a simple robot could do it all just as well as an animal: all it needs is good sensors (such as eyes), a memory, a way to integrate processing, and so on. I suggest that the role played by our animal natures is greater than this. Not just any set of control devices could give rise to experience, and not just any set of control devices could enable animals to do what they do. I am making a bet here about a link between what animals do and what is inside them, the internal resources by which the animal way of being becomes possible.

That is my picture of the biology of experience. A lot is missing, and it's more of a sketch than a worked-out theory. But it is different from other such sketches, and it makes contact with what we know about animal life, with what experience actually feels like, and with some surprising features of nervous systems across the animal kingdom. This is a view in which felt experience is not restricted to brains like ours (those of primates, or mammals). Instead, it is probably found in a great many animals, including some who are far from us in evolutionary terms: octopuses, crabs, bees. The list of sentient animals is probably long. In addition, the presence of felt experience is probably a "graded" phenomenon, with a lot of gray-area cases, rather than always being a yes-or-no matter. The history of animal life probably won't contain sharp lines separating the animals that have experience from the ones that don't. Animals like earthworms, scallops, and anemones may end up in a liminal region, where experience is neither fully present nor fully absent.

If this view is right, then although artificial minds may be possible in the future, they would have to be different in their physical makeup from computers of the kind we have now. It won't be possible to build a new conscious being just by devising a very complicated program that might run on a present-day computer. The situation is different with another technology that is developing very quickly; this is the technique of building "neural organoids" by growing colonies of animal (sometimes human) stem cells that self-organize into a small living model brain. This is not a road to a wholly artificial mind, because the system is grown from cells, but those living parts could be combined with nonliving parts, and the prospect of a new kind of sentient being opens before us. If they do become sentient, then especially in the earlier stages of this work, what might experience be like for these creatures? Does their experience seem likely to be positive?

I gave a talk about biology and AI once, and ended the discussion saying that parts of my talk could be seen as an invitation to build new kinds of hardware. The next day I woke up and thought: Is that such a good idea? Perhaps a natural barrier exists between the "I" side of AI—intelligence—and felt experience, at least within the sorts of machines that exist now, and that are relatively easy to build. We might try to overcome the barrier with new hardware, but should we? A barrier of this kind might not stop AI systems from causing us all sorts of trouble in the future, but if they are not sentient, it will simplify the ethical questions about how we should deal with them. Perhaps the barrier is a blessing.

In any case, all this gives us a picture of the biology of felt experience, one we can hold in our minds as we start to think about a special case—us.

Human Minds

Part of the story of human consciousness is the story of animal experience in general. Another part involves the side of our lives described in the previous chapter of this book: culture, language, technology, and sociality. Our minds have been drenched in culture. What difference does this make to an experiencing brain?

The biggest factor is perhaps language itself. Technology of many kinds is important, but the role of language is broader, older, more ubiquitous. That is what I will look at here.

Language starts as a pattern of social interaction, and it becomes a tool for thought. There's still a good deal of uncertainty about how deep its role is. Language has sometimes been seen as *the* medium for complex processing, but views like this underestimate what nonlinguistic animals can do. Rats make use of map-like representations that enable them to not only remember paths they've traveled, but also consider possible new ones. A 2022 paper found that crows could learn to generate "recursive" patterns, in which one structure is embedded within another, in the way also seen in mathematical systems and language. In our own case, Stanislas Dehaene, a French neuroscientist who has influenced many of my discussions of the mind, recently argued, together with a group of colleagues, that human minds make use of a number of "inner codes" that are quite distinct from the languages we speak.

Nonetheless, language seems to have a cluster of important roles in our minds, some overt, some more subtle. I'll start with some of the subtle ones, where we find that the *way* language has become physically part of us has left us with some clues about its role, and about what we'd be like without it.

Language, especially speech, is lateralized in our brains; it is among the skills and abilities that differ across the left and right sides. Many parts of our brains are duplicated across left and right, including the large cerebral hemispheres. The consequences of this duplication are seen especially in individuals who have had the main connector between the two hemispheres cut, to treat severe epilepsy. These are the so-called "split-brain" patients. I have used these remarkable cases to work through some puzzles about animal and human minds in earlier books. Much of what we'll be looking at here is less exotic; ordinary people who've not had separations imposed between the two sides can still give us information about differences between left and right.

In most humans, language—or at least speech—is mainly controlled by the left hemisphere. The left side of the brain also controls the right hand and receives sensory information mostly from the right side, and vice versa. Most humans (around

TOP: Dorrigo Rainforest, Australia, looking up.

BOTTOM: The stromatolites of Shark Bay.

TOP: A Satin Bowerbird works on his bower in the Blue Mountains, Australia.

BOTTOM: A Great Bowerbird in the Northern Territory, Australia.

TOP: A pair of Rose-breasted Cockatoos (Galahs) work on a nest in a tree hollow. Blue Mountains, Australia.

BOTTOM: A mountain gorilla, from the Kwitonda group. Volcanoes National Park, Rwanda.

TOP: Insect prowess: an Australian "bull ant" of the *Myrmecia* genus.

BOTTOM: Octopuses at their dens at various Australian sites. These are all the "gloomy octopus" (*Octopus tetricus*).

TOP: A lioness in the Maasai Mara National Reserve, Kenya.

BOTTOM: Finches at a water hole in the Northern Territory, Australia. The four with green and mauve are Gouldian Finches; the watchful one on the right is a Yellow-rumped Mannikin. (See the online notes for the others.)

TOP: Yellow-tailed Black Cockatoos—a flight collage. The photos were taken in the same encounter, but I am not sure if they're all of the same individual.

BOTTOM: An air/sea traveler, a Pied Cormorant.

A Superb Lyrebird in Blue Mountains National Park, Australia.

TOP: A male lyrebird's courting display. His head is behind the fourth large feather from the left.

BOTTOM: The giant cuttlefish of "End and Beginning."

90 percent) are also right-handed, which means the left side of the brain has a "dominant" role. That idea of a "dominant" side should not be overinterpreted, as suggesting something about overall control and personality; for now, it involves just how different limbs and especially hands are chosen to do things, such as grasping and pointing.

Are left-handers using the right side of their brain for speech? Mainly no, it seems. Seventy percent or more use the left side, as right-handers do. The reason is not known.

The left hemisphere not only controls language but also specializes in the production of sequence-based behaviors of other kinds. The left also seems to be associated with what is known as "executive function"—top-down control, overcoming impulses, thinking things through.

What does the right hemisphere specialize in? One example is the processing of melodies. That's interesting; we might have expected that a melody is a bit like a sentence. An important case is touch, which features a strong role for the right hemisphere and left hand. Suppose you are asked to detect (perhaps compare) shapes that are put in your hand, doing so just by touch. Are two shapes the same or not? This is done better in the left hand. The right hemisphere seems generally better with spatial tasks. And in case you were thinking the right brain is a bit primitive, it is better with numbers. That makes some sense of the question about melody that I mused about a moment ago—music is not like language, to the brain, but like mathematics.

Face recognition is more a right-hemisphere skill, and the recognition of emotions is, too. Some simple but striking work has been done in which people are shown manipulated photographs or drawings of a face where one side has an emotional expression and the other side is neutral. How much emotion is seen? Again, the right hemisphere processes visual stimuli from the left side of the visual field, and if the left side of a face, as seen by the viewer, is the emotional one (happy, surprised, angry, whatever), then the face tends to look more emotional than if it's the other side. This page has an illustration of the effect, in which the top row of faces all show emotion on the left but not the right (in sequence: happiness, sadness, anger), while the faces in the bottom row have the two sides reversed. In experiments, the faces are usually shown in pairs rather than all at once, with an emotion on just the left or the right—this is an illustration, not an image used in a study. Positive emotions seem to have a stronger bias than negative emotions, at least for some viewers. In my own case, the effect is pretty strong, especially for happiness, even when the faces are shown together like this.

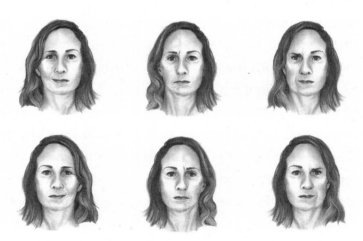

A setup with these differences between the two hemispheres does make sense, as advantages can often be gained from handling different tasks with specialized mechanisms that work in a partly self-contained manner. That is fine as long as you can bring everything together when you need to, and that can be done by the corpus callosum, the highway between the hemispheres. This highway is found only in mammals, and not all mammals (not marsupials, or egg-laying monotremes like the platypus). The presence of this highway seems to allow specialization of the two sides to become more elaborate, as Michael Gazzaniga, one of the main split-brain researchers, has argued.

If the corpus callosum has been cut, then we see left-right differences in starker form, and one thing we see is a distinctive style of cognition on the left. The left, verbal hemisphere is then the one most readily interacted with, and as Gazzaniga observes, it makes up stories about things it does not and cannot know. The left looks for narratives, for patterns and unity, and tries to get things to make sense even when they don't. In experiments, the left hand (controlled by the right hemisphere) sometimes acts on information that the left side of the brain does not have access to, and when the person is asked to comment on a behavior of that kind, they will make up an explanation. In one experiment, a patient had the word "bell" shown to his right hemisphere and the word "music" to his left. When he pointed with his left hand at a picture of a bell, the patient then explained this by saying that the last time he'd heard music it was from some bells nearby. (Gazzaniga adds that there were in fact bells nearby, but still . . .)

As well as engaging in this made-up storytelling, the left hemisphere tends to make other interesting mistakes. In some further experiments, split-brain patients were shown pictures representing everyday events and hours later were asked to say whether any of a second collection of pictures had also appeared in the earlier one. Both hemispheres were equally accurate in recognizing previously viewed pictures and rejecting others that were not shown earlier—as long as the new pictures, the ones not previously shown, were not thematically related to any of the earlier ones. The left hemisphere would incorrectly "remember" seeing pictures that had not been shown before if the pictures were thematically related to an earlier one. For example, the left hemisphere might see a picture of a man looking at his alarm clock in the first stage of the experiment and later see a new picture of the man brushing his teeth, and he'd be pretty likely to misremember having seen the teeth-brushing picture earlier, whereas the right hemisphere would not.

Gazzaniga's view is that our left brains contain an "interpreter," a side of the mind, or almost a sub-mind, that has a particular style: inquisitive, a seeker of patterns, a lover of narrative. The interpreter is so invested in unity and narrative that it makes things up when it has to. At least in a case where the person is intact, treating this as a "sub-mind" (this is my term, not his) may go too far, but the idea that the left hemisphere has a particular cognitive style, and sends us down this unity-seeking road when it can, seems a powerful one.

People have come up with a number of evolutionary sequences (narratives!) that could unify (!) and make sense (!) of all of this. Here, I make use of several of these, adding some ideas of my own.

The bilaterally symmetrical body form appeared early in animal evolution. This body form, which enabled new kinds of action, also brought with it the duplication of many parts, including parts of the brain. Along with vertebrates, many other animals seem to show some specialization or a difference in "style" across the two sides of their brain. Not all the same things end up on the same side in all animals (especially as vertebrates are the only ones with those crossed wires, with the left hand controlled by the right side of the brain, and so on). In vertebrates, the right brain seems more attuned to relations, especially social relations and relations in space, while the left side looks for categorizations. An intriguing difference that bears on conscious experience is mentioned by the lateralization expert Lesley Rogers. She writes that the left side tends to operate with "focused" attention on particular things, while the right's attentional span is broader, more open. This left/right difference is seen in nonhuman species as well as us.

Then, in our own ancestors, language arises. It gets housed in the left (in a large majority, even most left-handers). Once installed, language has cascading effects, not only on social behavior but also on thinking. It becomes a means by which that left-side style—the storytelling, theory-seeking style—becomes strongly established.

The right side is not antisocial; as we saw, the right is better at recognizing faces and tracking emotions. The left/right difference does not map to a difference between a more solitary mind and a socially embedded one. But in those narrative-seeking, storytelling, left-side tendencies, we see something about what language and culture have done to our thinking. This is not a situation where the left and right process things the same way, but only the left can tell stories about it; as we saw in those memory experiments, the two sides don't process things the same way.

In the memory experiments I mentioned a moment ago, we saw different tendencies across left and right. The left tends to misremember events when this serves a narrative, and the right does not. It's natural then to ask: Which side is closer to how normal humans (those with an intact corpus callosum) behave? This is an easier question to investigate, and in some later work, Gazzaniga found that a normal, intact person shows those patterns peculiar to the left hemisphere. It is easy to induce people to make errors of falsely remembering that they've already seen items that are "thematically related" to ones they have seen earlier. At least in this kind of task, the unity-seeking style of thought prevails.

There's a side of our minds that can sometimes get a bit lost in subtle psychological experiments on sensing, remembering, and so on. What I have in mind is conscious thought, especially where one pauses and reflects. This is particularly important in human projects with large effects: making plans, embarking on new ventures, and so on. Those decisions are often social—deliberation and choice are tied up with defense and discussion—but they also have a psychological side, and a role for conscious reflection.

In this sort of thinking, language is a tool with a unique combination of properties. By means of language we can engage in mental *quasi-acts*, internal sayings and rehearsings. These can help us assess, remember, and affirm ideas. With the aid of language you can also connect just about any idea with any other. The power for free recombination of ideas that gives language much of its social importance gives it power in our minds as well. The internal version of language can go further, in some ways, than an external version. You can run along a verbalized soliloquy and introduce a remembered image or smell as if it was another word. Inner speech can orchestrate an internal multimedia event.

Some of what I'm talking about here falls into the category of *reasoning*. In their book *The Enigma of Reason*, the French cognitive scientists Hugo Mercier and Dan Sperber argue that although philosophers and others have tended to see reasoning as a paradigm of self-contained, individual thought, its evolutionary origins are probably more social. These origins lie in projects of coordinating social life and, especially, trying to convince others of what to think and do. For Mercier and Sperber, we don't reason to *find* conclusions, but to get others to *agree* with our conclusions. They allow that our brains have many processes of "inference" going on inside them that we use to work out what to do and think. These processes are usually unconscious. Reasoning, as they see it, is something more specific. This is the process where one idea is explicitly brought in as support for another: you should think *this* because of *that*. Language is then pretty much essential, as it enables you to bring ideas together in the right form, putting one idea in place as the justification for another.

Mercier and Sperber argue that the essentially social role of reasoning shows up in our strengths and weaknesses, including the logical mistakes we tend to make. These "errors" don't show that reasoning is a bad tool for its purpose; instead, we've mistaken where reason came from and what that purpose is. An example of an error we all tend to make is confirmation bias—looking for things that support our present view, and not seeing evidence that pushes the other way. In a project of trying to convince others to follow us, this is no error at all.

Mercier and Sperber's idea about origins seems pretty reasonable (!) to me. A difference between their picture and mine is the extent to which these origins hang over the activity today. Even if reasoning has its origin in trying to persuade, this skill can operate in a new way inside an individual. There, it can become a means to find new conclusions, to probe ahead and uncover what is hidden.

A category that tends to recede in their story is deliberation—by an individual, rather than a group such as a jury. For Mercier and Sperber, there are inferences, which are mostly unconscious, and there's reasoning in the sense of reason-giving— "here is why this is the right conclusion . . ." Deliberation is not the same: "Something has gone wrong; what should I do next?" This activity is akin to reasoning in the role that language has, at least much of the time, but it's more open, more exploratory. And this feeling of "openness" need not be a mere rationalizing illusion. Old tools can be given new roles. We can step back and reflect, using this socially derived tool. We can ask, "What sort of food should I really be eating, when I factor in everything I can think of?"

A related way in which language and culture affect our minds involves the nature of the *self*. This theme takes us back to the ideas about narrative that were emphasized a few pages back. Part of what gives us a sense of having a definite self is the feeling that we are a subject in a coherent story that extends over time. Some aspects of selfhood do not depend on any of this. There is a selfhood that comes from the physical unity that animals of our kind have as a result of evolution, and also from the memories we have of past events. But as well as the memories themselves, there's the role of our narrative urge. We tie old memories into a story and try to make sense of continuity through change. This probably depends on language, our narrative tool. When we do this, some of what we arrive at is "cooked up," to various degrees—it introduces fictions, and smooths over rough patches. But the inner narrator is not just a commentator who comes along after the fact; it can also shape how one handles the next choices and challenges that arise. *This is who I am.* As you interpret your past, you affect your present and what you might do and become in the future.

Let's follow these paths a little further. When I've talked about "language" so far in this section, I've meant spoken language. Literacy has its own role, though. As we saw in the previous chapter, reading and writing are relatively recent cultural inventions, and most humans have not been literate. But when literacy comes on board, it has effects on the brain. As I said in the previous chapter, it increases the size of the corpus callosum and changes patterns of activity seen in brain scans, with a left-brain area becoming very active when recognizing words. This appears to reorganize our face recognition skill, pushing it more to the right than before. I said some pages back that emotion recognition is stronger in the right hemisphere, and that was written as a claim about people—everyone. But we should wonder: Were all the people who were tested on emotion recognition able to read? Might their brains have been rewired by reading in a way that makes the result less applicable, or not applicable at all, to non-readers? We might also give some thought to the *language* they were reading. Over thirty years ago, Jyotsna Vaid and

Maharaj Singh wondered whether the usual results showing left visual field processing of facial emotions might be due in part to the left-to-right reading habits of the subjects; this might make a left-to-right scan "come naturally." They compared how those artificial composite faces I mentioned earlier were interpreted by readers of several different languages—Hindi, Arabic, Urdu— including some people who read both left-to-right (Hindi) and right-to-left (Urdu) scripts. It was quite hard to interpret the results they found, but there did seem to be an effect of reading background, where the left visual field bias for emotion processing was more marked in people who read left-to-right. On the other hand, a leftward bias in looking at faces has been seen in some other animals—rhesus monkeys and domestic dogs— though the dogs had it when looking at us, not at other dogs. Human-like responses to chimeric faces (with emotion on the left seen as stronger) have also been found in chimps. The situation seems to be a real tangle, with a role for features of our brains that are shared across other animals, and a role for the details of culture as well.

Giorgio Vallortigara, writing about animals with deeper divides between the left and right sides, such as fish, reptiles, and birds, wondered where the felt experience of these animals ends up. The question is especially acute when an animal's eyes are on the sides of its head, as in fish, but not only then. Might such an animal have two different sensory perspectives on the world, each with a different feel? Or might the animal retain a single point of view, but find the two sides of the world have a different "coloring," with the experienced-left side more socially loaded and more relationally connected?

That second option would be an extreme case of something

that seems to be present also in us, with our right hemispheres picking up emotions better than the left. Those artificial faces with emotion on one side and not the other are very striking. I have become so curious about this that I keep trying to attend to the left of my visual field, and that doesn't work, as it just brings the "left" into the center. (Closing an eye doesn't work, as each of our eyes sends information to both left and right hemispheres.) This point about movement is an important one, too, because one way animals deal with the quirks of their left-right separation is by continually moving their head—you see a lot of this in birds. A unity of subjectivity is achieved in part through action.

Do filmmakers make use of any of this? In film, motion from left to right is often seen as having a different feel from right to left. Left to right movement is seen as progressive and natural. Exactly the same sequence reversed by flipping each frame, so the motion starts on the right, can look disconcerting. This has gone from being semi-implicit lore, and perhaps something that early filmmakers made use of without realizing it, to being a topic of scientific work. A famous essay by the critic Roger Ebert, written before the scientific work started, listed a left-to-right preference for movement among a number of other generalizations, including the idea that "right is more positive, left more negative." People have tended to explain left-right phenomena in movies in terms of explicit cultural ideas in the West about left and right (an old word for left being "sinister"). But all this might also have to do with perceptual effects that stem from lateralization of the brain.

If that is so, the causal relationships here might form quite a thicket. I said a page or so back that, when looking again at how we process faces for signs of emotion, language differences seem to have a role—people who read a right-to-left language are different from those who read a left-to-right one. A similar effect has been found with action sequences in video clips. In a study of how soccer goals were interpreted (as stronger, faster, more beautiful), native speakers of Italian and Arabic differed quite a lot in how the direction of the action affected their judgment. Arabic, unlike Italian, is a right-to-left language on the page, and the Arabic speakers interpreted right-to-left goals as stronger, faster, and more beautiful than left-to-right ones. Some of those ideas about filmmaking I just mentioned could be more specific to particular cultures than they initially seemed.

Here is one more thought about the psychological role of language. Our minds have a side that is intensely private—mind-wandering, reminiscence, disconnected free reverie. Until the watchers in a dystopian future start scanning us all the time, no one need know what you are imagining or remembering. Some of this is present in nonhuman animals; mental exploration of space is visible in the rat's brain, as a result of the inner maps mentioned earlier. A rat can be quite physically still, asleep or awake, while activating a series of "place cells" in its brain that normally register its actual location. Whether this mental exploration is felt or not by the rat, it is a kind of offline rehearsal of action. This is related to dreaming, for which the evidence is now strong in quite a number of nonhuman animals.

This side of the mind, full of quirks and the unrepeatable, is the home of a pure kind of individuality. But the social tool of language, once internalized, gives special power and reach to what we do here. Again, this side of the mind is not wholly dependent on language, as seen in the mentally meandering rats.

But with language on board, it flowers. It makes possible a form of private creative thought—or private at first, made public if we choose—that is immensely rich. Reverie can be steered and magnified by letting the narrative side of the mind run on, calling on traces of images and sounds as it does so. You can, as the philosopher John Dewey said a century ago, tell tales to yourself that no one else would believe, and do so with good reason, to your benefit. Language expands the power of free combination, of contemplation of the merely possible and impossible. An enlargement of the private is made possible by the internalization of a social tool. This distinctively human combination of the private (offline, whimsical) side of the mind and its basis in a social and cultural set of skills seems incongruous, almost ironic. It is a great gift from the public to the private.

Hyperscan

My sketch of the biological basis of felt experience at the start of this chapter had two elements. The first involves the role of sensing and acting in the animal way of being—the origin of subjectivity—and the other makes much of some physical peculiarities of brains and nervous systems, with their mixture of cell-to-cell influences and large-scale dynamic patterns. The ideas we were looking at just now, concerning language, the different hemispheres, and the role of culture, relate pretty clearly to the first of those two—to sensing, point of view, and so on. If we turn to the other part of my sketch, it might seem unlikely that much will be added to this story about consciousness and human life. The electrical rhythms that I discussed earlier are found across many animals, including species with brains very unlike ours. If we're interested in consciousness and culture, it initially seems that those features shouldn't make a lot of difference . . . Not so fast.

The last few decades have seen advances in brain-scanning techniques. I sketched some basics earlier in this chapter. The EEG method dates from around 1929, and a lot has happened since then. A 2002 paper set a lot of work in motion; it was called "Hyperscanning: Simultaneous fMRI During Linked Social Interactions," by a team led by Read Montague. The paper explores the idea of scanning the brains of two or more people at a time, when they are engaged in social interactions.

They used the fMRI method (functional magnetic resonance imaging). This is a scan of the brain, from outside, that is not looking directly at neurons and their electrical activity, but at changes in the oxygen supply, through the blood, to different parts of the brain. The social interaction used in the study was a simple game of deception, where one person sends a message and the other has to guess whether they lied. The two people were not face-to-face, but in separate scanning machines. The main idea of the paper was to introduce the method, and they don't go through detailed results, but it showed some correlations between brain activity on each side. The paper introduced the term "hyperscanning," and the method took off.

That is the conventional opening of the story. In fact, there was an earlier experiment, published in 1965. This one used not fMRI (which had not been invented) but EEG, a more direct pickup of overall electrical activity in the brain. The paper, by two ophthalmologists, T. D. Duane and Thomas Behrendt, came out in *Science* magazine on a single page. It was an ESP study of "identical" (single-zygote) twins.

This is an appealing replay of history. The EEG method itself was introduced by Hans Berger as part of a search for telepathy. Decades later, the first known study of real-time relationships between two people's EEG rhythms was another telepathy study. The ophthalmologists were interested in communication across unknown channels. In the test, one twin would close their eyes in a lit room. Closing the eyes tends to initiate a particular kind of rhythm (alpha rhythms) in the brain. Might the other twin, in a separate room, enter the same brain wave pattern also? They reported that in some cases, the answer was yes.

This study was done very informally, with no statistics. A few other studies of this kind followed, including a much more technically sophisticated one, not using twins, led by a Mexican researcher whose career bridged scientific and shamanistic approaches, Jacobo Grinberg-Zylberbaum. This 1992 experiment, using EEG scans, reported success in transmission across nearby but shielded rooms. Grinberg-Zylberbaum disappeared, in a still-unsolved mystery, two years later.

I am not as instantly dismissive of this sort of work as many people are. I'm open to the possibility of unexpected channels, but skeptical on balance. Anyway, as with EEG's discovery by Berger, the double-scanning method became mainstream, in this case after the 2002 paper that introduced the term "hyperscanning." A lot of papers about hyperscanning that include a quick history at the start do not mention the adventurous ophthalmologists' paper at all.

The usual goal of hyperscanning work is to look at the relationship between the brain activity in two different people during a social interaction, and make comparisons to other situations. Several different kinds of scanning are used: fMRI, EEG, and a couple of others. The EEG work is especially relevant for the themes of this chapter, as it looks directly at large-scale electrical patterns in the brain while allowing people in the experiment to interact naturally. The other methods contribute to our picture in different ways.

The picture emerging is a surprising one. In some social settings, especially those featuring cooperation and teamwork, there's a lot of correlation between the large-scale dynamic patterns in one brain and the patterns in another. This is called "interbrain synchrony." In measuring the correlations we reach some technical topics that I understand very imperfectly. You are looking at a pair of rhythms, or a series of events over two brains, and seeing if they match up to some extent. This might be done by looking at their frequencies, or at the "power" of the oscillations (are both rhythms strong when one is strong?). You might look at the phase (are the peaks lined up to some degree?), or at combinations of these. You also have to try to work out whether any synchronization is just due to some external cause affecting both people, rather than mutual influence between them. Many studies find that the patterns do show associations of some kind when the people are socially engaged, to a degree that is often surprising, given the physical separateness of the two brains. The brain rhythms don't fall exactly into sync, and all this is a matter of degree. But it's still, surely, a surprise.

The synchronization doesn't just happen when people are looking at the same thing or performing exactly the same actions. Two people playing a guitar duet do synchronize, but so do two people who have to cooperate to perform a task and have different roles—for example, one person might have to locate a target in a scene and use their eye gaze to send information to another person who hits a button, or two pilots might be working together in a flight simulator. When people are in a situation where they can choose to be more cooperative or less so (in a computer game), synchronization is greater when they are being cooperative, and a researcher can even predict cooperative interactions from whether people's brains are in sync. In a more purely cooperative task that two people had to do together, pairs with higher levels of synchronization performed better than pairs with less. Synchronization of brain rhythms also seems to be part of the explanation for the "cocktail party effect," where a listener can pick one voice out from several that are going at once, and follow what is being said by that person despite noise and competition.

This whole phenomenon is especially puzzling when the brain rhythms that are matched are very fast. In work using the EEG scan, synchrony of brain rhythms can occur in the "gamma" band. This is a speed of oscillation above twenty-five cycles per second, sometimes much faster. That seems too fast for the synchronization to be controlled by anything visible in a person's behavior.

I'll come back to those questions about how the contact is achieved, but let's first ask something else. What might all this *do*, when it is real? What difference might be made by the syncing, whether it's those surprising cases with very fast cycles or something else? Reports made in these studies sometimes include a feeling of contact between people, a sense of being—and now the old metaphors take on a new meaning—attuned, in sync, with someone. This is seen as one of the things that synchronization might explain. How could this be possible, though? How could you tell that someone's invisible super-fast rhythms are in sync with yours, or are not? What difference could it make?

The most radical option (outside of the telepathic camp) that I know of is a view outlined by the cognitive scientists Ana Lucía Valencia and Tom Froese. They suggest that there is a partial merging of the physical basis for the experience in one person and the experience in another. Part of the physical basis for "your" experience is activity in the other person's brain, and part of the basis of their experience is in your brain. The sense of sharing and contact with another that we sometimes find and often value might have a more substantial physical reality than we had supposed. As Froese put it in another paper, "when we become aware that 'we' are sharing a moment with someone else, it is no longer necessarily the case that we are fundamentally separated by our distinct heads—we could really be two distinct individuals sharing in one and the same unfolding experience."

This goes against the usual view, one that otherwise seems entirely adequate, that each of us is an individual subject, perhaps having *similar* experiences to someone else, but each having our *own*, with no literal merging between them. If that is wrong, it is truly a massive change.

I want to be open-minded about these possibilities. I accept a materialist view of the mind. This means that there are some physical processes in nature that are, themselves, also mental processes, and this includes sensations. It's not that these physical processes *cause* the mental ones; they *are* them. Every sensation has a physical basis of some kind, a basis that exists in some particular place. In addition, other physical goings-on might cause the sensation while not being part of it. The thing that I am calling (and that Valencia and Froese also call) the "basis" of the sensation or experience might always be entirely inside one person's head, or not always so. Are there reasons to expect things to be one way or the other?

If minds and brains are for controlling actions, and those actions animate individual animal bodies, this gives us some initial reason to think that the physical basis for experience will always be localized inside an animal. Valencia and Froese also discuss an argument that was given by the cognitive scientist Andy Clark, where he says that conscious experience will require very fast and intricate activity in whatever physical basis it has, and this probably can't take place *across* two different brains because the interface between them, their separate bodies, would be too slow. The bodies of the two people would act as a kind of filter (a "low pass filter") between them, so that all the rapid and high-frequency activity that consciousness relies on would have to take place separately in one person and the other, not in a unit that is spread across them. Valencia and Froese respond that although this argument about the body as a filter initially looks completely reasonable, the evidence from hyperscanning suggests it might not be right. Somehow, two brains *can* become coupled together in surprising ways, and that opens up the question of whether the physical basis of an experience, and hence the experience itself, might be literally shared across them.

An alternative view is that the hyperscanning experiments are picking up not a merging, but a connection between two minds that stay distinct from each other. If this is offered as an explanation of the feeling of togetherness or contact across people, it is less directly an explanation than the more radical view. In the radical view, a feeling of contact comes from a partial unity between minds, a partial blending. In the alternative view, it's a meeting without being a merging; the feelings on each side are separate, but are affected in subtle ways by what is happening on the other, and that shows up as an experience of contact. What would those effects be, and how might they arise?

The main possibility to look at seems to be that subtle cues in the behaviors on each side are picked up and lead to a degree of synchronization in some internal processes. This feeling of alignment might have effects on the two people's experience, as is more overtly seen in the case of dancing.

A problem to grapple with is how this could work in the case of the faster neural rhythms. It's not hard to see how similar rhythms across two people could be switched *on* at roughly the same time. But it would be hard for this to be very exact, I assume, and it wouldn't explain ongoing synchronization across the two people, in any case. What might bring about the tight connections? I will offer a few ideas (making use of other discussions).

In an old experiment done first by chance in the seventeenth century, the Dutch physicist and inventor Christiaan Huygens noted that two pendulum clocks near each other will become synchronized (though they end up swinging in opposing directions—out of phase) if their rhythms start out fairly similar and the clocks are also physically similar. Their motions come into alignment. This also works with metronomes. The effect is pretty puzzling, and it has now been studied quite a lot. The picture we have is that the effect does work by physical influences that go through whatever the clocks or metronomes are fixed onto (no metronome ESP), and the nature of the influence— I think!—is generally like this. Each device as it moves tends to nudge the other—gives it a little "kick," as some writers say—

that perturbs it from its current pattern, whatever that might be. The mutual nudges or kicks go on and on, but if the two clocks happen to fall into a state where they are closely synchronized, then the kicks cancel and neither affects the other. They are in an equilibrium.

In the physics cases, with clocks and metronomes, this is all pretty exact. In the brain, nothing will be so neat. But there might be a situation in which tiny visible movements and other cues in a social setting act to nudge and perturb two people's brain activity, and when this happens, some arrangements across the two people are more stable than others—they don't get pushed away from, or not as much. Then the two people's brain patterns might be brought closer and closer together, even with respect to those very fast patterns of activity. Perhaps what people can track in each other is a complicated combination of movements spread across the whole body. The way a person produces many tiny actions together might have, without them realizing it, a subtle rhythmic signature. These rhythmic signatures in small ordinary motions might play a role in explaining the feelings of contact between people that I mentioned earlier.

All this is very much on the edge—it is scientifically controversial, attracts critical papers with titles like "Beyond the Hype," and so on, and its importance is hard to interpret. But I am struck by this work. The hidden lining-up of activity seems to me remarkable, even without any argument for a literal merging of minds. This work has already changed my intuitive sense of how some everyday interactions go. An actual cocktail party now seems different; it is, among other things, a sea of interacting brain rhythms, going in and out of sync. Feelings of attunement or contact between people, whether stable or fleeting, might be taken more seriously as physical realities than they have been before. They are not just unconscious judgments (hmm, this person is okay), but reflect something deeper in the links between us.

I'll mention one other idea relating to the social role of interbrain synchrony, linking to the previous chapter. This idea is usually discussed independently of any exotic neural ideas. The idea is that a distinctive part of human life is the formation of shared intentions, which are sometimes called "we-intentions." In some cooperative situations, it's not just that I want to get something done and I know that you might be inclined to help me; more than this, we get to a stage where the intention is something that exists across both of us, a we-intention. *We intend* to move this big log over there. I've not seen this idea as pivotal in the way some others do. In part, that is because I've thought that we can understand collaboration quite well in a more individualist way. I have beliefs (or at least assumptions) about what you are up to, and you have beliefs about what I am up to, and so on. Valencia and Froese, as you might expect, think there might be more reality to these special mental states, we-intentions, and think that interbrain coupling might be part of how they are achieved. They even wonder whether the we-perspective might be primary for us in some sense, fundamental in human life, so that *I*-thinking comes later. I doubt that. The acting *I* is more basic than the acting *we*, potent though the latter may be.

Brothers

That is human consciousness as I see it, a combination of features of felt experience that come from the animal way of being and a powerful cultural overlay. That is what happened to a group of primates, initially just another skinny branch of the evolutionary tree, over a few million years.

Alongside us all through this book and the two that preceded it, *Other Minds* and *Metazoa*, has been the genealogical tree of animals, the animal part of the tree of life. Our branch is the mammals. In Africa and Australia, one gets a strong sense of this part of the tree. In Australia, we see traces of the lower branchings heading off to a few distant cousins—echidnas and platypuses, and then marsupials. In Africa, we encounter the great thicket of branchings within eutherian mammals, the group on the other side of the split from marsupials.

That evolutionary thicket has proved hard to fully resolve, but it includes one early split leading to elephants and a few others, including hyraxes (like outsized, scrambling guinea pigs) and aardvarks. In the branch on the other side of that split, we find a

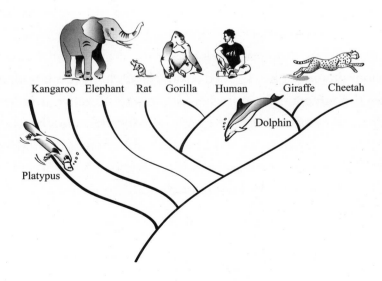

divide that shapes two big collections of familiar mammals. On one side are horses, deer, dogs; on the other, primates, with a collection of rodents and rabbits. (The previous page has one more "tree of life" drawing, simplified as usual, that illustrates some of this.) If we look across from our home with the rodents, we see giraffes walking, as Karen Blixen said, like long-stemmed flowers, along with antelope, jackals, and whales.

Dolphins and other whales are in that group. Manatees, on the other hand, are with the elephants. A return to the water happened several times in different groups of mammals.

In that big cluster of mammals along with the deer and the whales are also cats. In the Maasai Mara, Kenya, I saw cheetahs in the wild. Out on grasslands in the sun, two of similar size were jogging along together. They were radiant, almost glowing, it seemed. I thought, right away and unexpectedly, that these were the most beautiful animals I had ever seen.

Afterward, I asked one of our guides, Collins, about them. One was male, I saw. The other? He said that both were male, young brothers. They had formed a coalition, a bond, and would stay within it permanently.

One turned his head back, glancing at the other, to check without slowing. They seemed a miracle of animal evolution, but more fundamentally, a miracle of self-organization, a miracle on the part of matter itself, that it had come together into that form.

The combination of wild beauty and companionship was overwhelming. I expect never to forget them. Those radiant animals, with their bond, jogging together through my dreams.

LIVING ON EARTH

OTHER LIVES

Ethical Decisions

With the minds that evolution and human history have given us, we can reflect, criticize, and look ahead. We can make choices on the basis of debate. We can discuss how we want to live on Earth, as well as trying to understand what goes on.

That ability is one consequence of the path our species took through sociality and culture, as described in chapter 5. Also as a result of that path, our species began to have effects on the natural world that no other species has had. In this chapter and the next, I look at some of those effects. Now that we can see what we're doing, what should we do next? Should we change course, and if so, how?

In this chapter, the main topic will be our relations with other animals that have come under our close control, especially in farming and food production, and also in scientific experiments. The next chapter will range more widely, looking at climate change, extinction, and the loss of wild nature.

❖

Human action has dramatically changed the overall shape that life has on Earth. We've had a huge effect on the distribution of animals, in particular. I'm going to begin by thinking about this in terms of the *biomass*, the amount of living matter that exists in organisms of various kinds. In a later chapter I'll talk about the relationship between biomass and the number of individual animals, as some questions depend more on one and some depend more on the other.

About half of animal life is made up of arthropods, the group that includes insects. I'm going to set them and other invertebrates aside here, and also set aside fish, which, despite our depredations, still seem very numerous (the oceans are huge). The rest of animal life is dominated by livestock. As you can imagine, making estimates is difficult and the numbers should be seen as rough, but it appears that fourteen times more biomass is in farmed mammals than in wild mammals, and farmed birds make up over twice as much as wild birds. Livestock as a whole makes up more than ten times the biomass of wild mammals and birds. Humans themselves are a large component in the system; about nine times more biomass is in *us* than in all wild mammals. The startling level of domination that we've achieved raises many questions, and it surely seems that something might have gone awry. But if we've done something *wrong* here, what kind of wrongness is it? And how might we put things right?

Rather than just diving in, I'm going to approach all this by way of a general discussion of ethical questions. Philosophy has a standard menu of options for understanding what we might really be up to when we offer ethical claims. One position has it that we can describe "moral facts," real features of the world, values that are inherent in events and actions themselves. Another suggests that moral claims are not descriptions at all, but commands. They might instead be expressions of an emotional response. Perhaps the moral claims we make are attempted descriptions of moral facts, but attempts that always fail because such facts don't exist. (I am going to use "ethical" and "moral" nearly interchangeably here, as many philosophers now do, though in this context I prefer the term "ethical.")

Behind many of these debates lies a deeper division, between a picture in which we are discovering what is right or good and a picture in which our role, inevitably, is one of construction or invention. Are moral values found or made? Do we learn what's right, or decide on it? Both pictures have appeal. We create value systems in order to live together—in that sense, we are constructing them. But at least part of the time, this creative act feels constrained, not arbitrary. Ethical thought and debate can feel like an attempt to understand hidden relationships; we can discover that we were wrong, admit this, and improve our choices. If we don't think that we are in touch with something beyond ourselves when we do this, it seems to throw the project of moral reasoning away. But it's hard to make sense of what this "something beyond ourselves" might be. It's easier if God is in the picture, and other views of the universe can also be friendly to objective moral knowledge, but a modern scientific outlook makes the problem acute.

Those traditional options I listed for understanding moral language are stark and simple. Perhaps we need a more mixed, more complicated view of what is going on? I'll outline a view of that kind, and will approach it by looking, in a schematic way, at how we came to be where we are.

Chapter 5 looked at human social life, and at how it might

have acquired its unusual features. Human societies include a lot of cooperation, and within these arrangements, temptations arise to exploit others, dominate, or free-ride. Norms or principles of behavior, whether implicit or explicit, arise to keep the group functioning. That seems to be the beginning of ethical thinking. A picture like this is seen in historical sketches that have been developed by many writers, including Philip Kitcher, Kim Sterelny, and others: norms arise to protect cooperative social projects from exploitation and collapse.

Work from psychology and anthropology suggests that these cooperation-smoothing roles are not the whole story. There can be a tendency to read back into history *some* kinds of norms, the ones that secular liberal societies have separated out from more of a tangle. The social psychologist Jonathan Haidt and others have developed a framework that recognizes roughly five distinct psychological responses that are part of an "intuitive ethics" seen in different forms across cultures. The features that these intuitive responses track are *harm*, *fairness*, *loyalty*, *respect*, and *purity*, where that last one tends also to be related to notions of *sanctity*. Each culture will turn some of these "up" and others "down," and factions within a culture may want to make their own adjustments. Traditional religious societies often regard harm as below purity/sanctity in importance; secular liberalism does not trust purity intuitions and would like them out of the picture. A "live and let live" attitude toward homosexuality, for example, has often required a tamping-down of concern over purity, and so has a willingness to let women choose their own paths in relationships and social life. The big questions I mentioned above arise here again: If you *don't* suppress the illiberal moral intuitions, if your society emphasizes loyalty and purity over fairness and harm prevention, are you making a mistake, or just making your own choices?

Somewhere in this mix, on the psychological side, are other phenomena that we encountered back in chapter 5. In social life, a lot of weight is carried by a sense of sheer propriety—*this is how things are done.* This might be related to loyalty and respect, occasionally also to purity, but it seems to have its own role. (Remember, from that chapter, those young children primed to look for norms, and to enforce them.)

Norms that guide behavior may start out implicit but then take the form of principles and rules. Eventually, they include written legal and religious codes.

The norms that guide social life eventually also come into greater contact with reasoning and reflection. I don't think of this as happening only in societies with written codes, but also in settings with storytellers, interpreters, and others who hold and express traditional law. Once norms are explicit, and once decisions can be questioned and defended, consistency starts to become a constraint. Even if the response to a challenge is just *This is how we have always done things*, to say that is still to offer an explicit defense, and it can be challenged in turn: *Have we really? What about that time when* . . . Especially because existing principles must always be adapted to new settings, the idea of *parity* takes on an important role: cases that are similar should be handled in similar ways (treated on a par). If you did *this* in earlier cases of some infraction, then you should respond in a similar way now, unless you can say why not. Priests, chiefs, and the like might obfuscate, deflect, or ignore such appeals. But once we can reason, this spotlight gets directed on everything.

Especially when parity questions are on the table, norms also become more answerable to factual matters. If you have been told to make a sharp moral distinction between your group and others, and it becomes clear that the "others" are not much different from you, it is still possible to keep in place the sharp distinction in how you treat people, but now it's under pressure. (This can be seen as a clash between loyalty and fairness, two of those intuitive modes of thinking I mentioned earlier.) "That is how we do things" can have power, but it doesn't stick indefinitely. All this brings an essentially practical, forward-looking activity into the realm of argument and evidence. Those five components of intuitive morality (purity, loyalty, etc.) might be where we start out, but there's nothing stopping us from re-shaping our ethical thinking in radical ways, if we choose to.

That is a schematic sketch of normative thinking and its history, especially in social life. Suppose it is roughly right. Where do we end up? I noted a moment ago the simplicity and starkness of the traditional philosophical options for understanding ethical language: it is describing facts *or* making commands *or* expressing emotions . . . I suggest now that the habits of ethical thought and discussion we have ended up with are almost *designed to defy* those standard options. What we find ourselves with is the result of bringing the prescriptive, evaluative, choosing side of life into the realm of explicit statement, defense, and reason, especially in areas that deal with social relations and behavior. Ethical claims are a kind of valuation, and valuation in some form is just about inescapable. It is putting options in order, working out what to do. The valuations we make are reflected in various behaviors, including choosing, criticizing, and so on. In some situations where we make valuations, we are not much worried about disagreement—if you prefer jazz to classical music, no one needs to argue with you. In other situations, disagreement is a problem. If we're working out how people ought to behave, or how social life should be organized, then different possible answers do tend to clash, and the conflict has to be resolved. Resolution might be achieved through force, legal authority, or reasoned arguments.

That is my view of what we are up to. Ethical choice is forward-looking in its function. We're working out what to do, how to live, what choices we will encourage and discourage. The point of the practice is forward-looking, but its "inputs" are diverse, including factual matters, our sense of similarity between cases, and more. Though the point of the practice is forward-looking in this way, the format in which we make ethical claims also allows us to direct them backward, to criticize things done in the past. Ethical claims are not equivalent to commands or expressions of an emotional response. They don't fall into one of these other categories of things we say. Valuations, including ethical valuations, are "their own thing."

This view is closer to the *made* side than the *found* side of the divide that I mentioned earlier. But there is plenty we can find, or discover, when we try to defend one decision or judgment in the light of others, when we encounter new factual information, or when we apply an old value to a new situation.

I say this view is closer to the made side than to the found side, but perhaps it is a blend, living in a balance between them? I'm tempted to say that, but it might mislead a little. The possibility of "finding things out" in this area comes from the fact that, due to language and reflection, just about everything we know about can be brought to bear on our valuations. But a lot of flexibility remains. Suppose a person makes no commitment to giving reasons, respecting parity arguments, and so on. If a person just ignores all that, and determines what they value in a more chaotic way, I don't think they need to have made a factual or logical mistake. They might, but might not. A person can choose how well integrated with the rest of their thinking they want their ethical orientation to be. And even if someone does take parity arguments seriously, these claims are dependent on which similarities between cases are seen as important and which are not; they depend on our rather flexible sense of what is similar to what. There's an inherent freedom in the situation that should not be sidestepped or obscured.

To say that is not to downgrade the activity itself. The practices and their transitions that I've been describing in this section are a central part of the human enterprise. We are taking the basic, ancient activity of valuation and trying to integrate it with rational reflection, especially in our choices of how to live and how to organize social life. We are trying not only to get a factual picture of the world, one that reaches into the galaxies and the distant past, but also trying to shape our goals and living patterns in a rational way.

Food and Farming

Now let's consider, in this light, our relationships with other animals. I'll first look at the largest problem in sheer scale. That is farming, especially modern industrialized farming.

Early forms of domestication of animals for human use probably included a mixture of coercion and mutual benefit, where animals such as goats and sheep benefited from our protection. Through selective breeding, they often became less able to survive on their own. The most momentous changes occurred in the twentieth century. The level of control exerted over the lives of farmed animals greatly increased. Their living conditions moved further from those of their ancestors and, in many cases, became more and more brutal. The shape of animal life on Earth was changed by human farming, and then again by industrialized agriculture.

Huge numbers of mammals and birds now live in continual, lifelong confinement in factory farms, or CAFOs (concentrated animal feeding operations). About 73 million pigs are alive at any time in the United States alone, for example, with a large majority confined indoors for their entire lives. Cattle are something of a special case, as their lives in modern farming are often a mix of an initial period on pasture and confinement in outdoor "feedlots" later.

As an ethical problem, the situation of intensively farmed pigs and chickens is perhaps the most alarming; the only good thing that can be said about their lives is that they are short. The lives of mother pigs, the breeding "sows," are perhaps the worst, with most of their life spent in various metal crates that are barely bigger than the animal's body. The raising of mother pigs in these tiny prisons now generates enough outcry that some practices are changing in this area, but at the time of writing, most sows in the United States still experience this. Setting aside the full-time mothers, pigs in modern operations are removed from the mother after a couple of weeks (traumatic for both), may be subjected to various no-anesthesia operations (castration, tail cutting), and then spend the rest of their life before slaughter in crowded indoor pens. That life might total around six months.

Chickens raised for meat live a much shorter time, six weeks or so, also in extreme crowding. The demands of rapid growth have led to these chickens having distorted, ungainly bodies. Life as a battery hen raised for eggs might be worse. Much more could be said, but I think the picture is clear.

Should we stop doing these things? And if we set out on a path of large-scale change, where does this end? The questions do not only concern cruelty. Industrialized farming is environmentally harmful in many ways, and encourages the emergence of dangerous diseases. Those are serious concerns, but in this chapter I am going to focus on the welfare side.

On questions about intensive farming of these kinds, the major ethical theories in the modern Western philosophical tradition tend to converge, at least at first. The *utilitarian* approach to ethics is based on a direct accounting of the total amount of good and harm done by an action, where "good" and "harm" are usually understood in an experience-based way. From a utilitarian point of view, once we recognize the enormous suffering present in factory farming, and the fact that the only good it does is to give us cheaper food, it's clear that factory farming is a great evil. Peter Singer's landmark *Animal Liberation* (1975) was written within that approach. The *Kantian* ethical framework, named after the eighteenth-century philosopher Immanuel Kant, is a rival to utilitarianism, and perhaps the approach that professional philosophers have been most attracted to in recent decades. A Kantian thinks that our goal should not be getting better things to happen by any available means (as in utilitarianism), but acting in ways that respect the preferences and projects of others. We should not treat other agents as mere means to our own ends, but as "ends in themselves."

Kant had little interest in the lives of animals, but his view has been revised in this respect, especially by the American philosopher Christine Korsgaard. In this framework, what is bad about factory farming is not so much the sheer suffering, but our imposing control and so completely thwarting the preferences of other animals. The change to the Kantian framework that brings nonhuman animals into the picture is recognizing them as beings with their own legitimate interests.

Don't plants, also, have interests and something like preferences? This problem might be handled by treating the preferences of *sentient* agents as special (that is what Korsgaard does). This move might be questioned, both in principle and in how it handles some cases, but let's accept it for now.

The way I want to motivate an end to factory farming is a little different from both of those more familiar paths (though those theories will return to the discussion). I'll do it with the idea of a *life worth living*—a life that's better than no life at all. Imagine that after you die, you can choose between coming back for another life as an animal—the particular kind of animal is not your choice, but is determined for you—or not coming back at all.

Suppose you would come back as a pig in a factory farm, or CAFO (the term "farm" really is a bit out of place in this setting). I sketched what that life would be like a page or two back. It's a life of about six months, removed early from your mother, with the amount of time spent in behavior that's typical and preferred by pigs in the outdoors being zero, not one day. All of the days are days of crowded confinement and some combination of stress, monotony, and pain.

The situation of cows raised for meat in intensive farming tends to be somewhat better. Dairy farming includes both better and worse options, where the worse ones, as for pigs, involve confinement for the animal's entire life and a round of forced pregnancies followed by immediate removal of your calves. Would you rather come back to a life like one of these after you die, or not come back at all?

This reincarnation test is obviously an imperfect thought experiment. Given that in some sense it has to be *you* returning, what sort of mental life do we assume? Your mind in a chicken's body, or a chicken's mind that somehow has hints of you? I suppose the second is the more realistic way to do it. There has to be enough continuity between you, in the present, and a hypothetical future mind for you to feel the choice as one where your own interests are at stake. An imperfect thought experiment, yes, but perhaps a useful one. In my own case, I find that *however* the details are filled out, I'd choose not to come back at all rather than to come back as a factory-farmed animal of those kinds. There is no way for me to get the other answer.

You might prefer another way of asking the question about whether the lives of factory-farmed animals are worth living. The reincarnation test has a good deal of potency for me, though. It is a way of making vivid the fact that some of the lives that we humans now initiate and control seem unbearable. And *this is where our human powers have brought us*, along the road described back in chapter 5, the road from life as just another medium-sized mammal to what we are now. Along the way, we have become able to create unbearable lives for other animals, and we do this to them in huge numbers.*

We can see how this happened, as our scope for control became greater, human populations increased, and agribusinesses shaved their costs and increased their scale. We can see how it happened, and we can stop and think: Should we continue to do this? Ending factory farming should be our highest priority in animal-human relations. This shift will have consequences for human diets. I don't think that people should be expected to abandon high-protein diets, so we do need to find better ways of enabling diets of this kind. I expect lab-grown meat to become a major component of food production, along with new plant-based options. In lab-grown, or "cultured," meat, a few cells from an animal are used to generate billions more, without any need for killing. Though these shifts cannot take place immediately, there can be immediate pressure to move away from the worst practices. Factory farming benefits from government subsidies—that is, from the money of taxpayers—in many countries. Ending these would reduce the price distortions that make modern farming hard to shift.

Suppose we agree on this. And imagine that we've reached

---

* Here is a passage from Michel Houellebecq's novel *Serotonin* (translated by Shaun Whiteside), about chickens in intensive farms: "the permanent look of panic that the chickens gave you, that look of panic and incomprehension; they didn't ask for pity, they wouldn't have been capable of it, but they didn't understand, they didn't understand the conditions in which they had been called upon to live."

a point where the worst excesses have gone or are receding. We then reach another set of questions about farming. Does this line of thought take us to a conclusion in which all farming of nonhuman animals, or perhaps all that involves killing, should end? Does humane farming make a difference or not?

In my discussion of factory farming I used the idea of a "life worth living." My opposition to those practices is not primarily based on the badness of killing; in modern farming, we control not just the animal's death but its entire life. The animal comes into existence, lives, and dies under our control. We are responsible for the whole life, and the whole life is what we should assess. This is part of the point of the reincarnation test; you are not coming back just to be killed, but to live an entire life. When asking ethical questions about farming, it is common to focus just on death. Death is big, but it's not the only thing.

In the humane farming of animals, many of the lives are worth living. Returning to the reincarnation test, I would feel fine about coming back as a cow on a humane farm. Certainly I'd prefer that, in the thought-experiment, to no reincarnation at all. Here I assume that life would be spent in the fields just about all the way through, with veterinary care, no threats, and a pretty quick death at the end. This is nothing like what we imagined earlier.

Given this, opposition to humane farming has to come from different reasons from those above. I think of our situation as one with two "rounds" of reflection or discussion. The first round, which is about factory farming, is comparatively easy. Once that stage is behind us—not that factory farming has ended, but once we agree it should end—we face a new round of questions. What kind of relationship do we want to have to the lives of nonhuman animals? Is a controlled, custodial relationship of the kind seen in humane farming acceptable, or should we just walk away?

In this second round, disagreement is probably inevitable, even when people are trying to be as reasonable as they can. Different moral theories, and different ways of thinking about the relationship between happiness and control, lead to different conclusions. A utilitarian perspective can approve of humane farming, even when it involves killing. Given that utilitarianism tries to consider *all* the effects of an action, this also depends on questions about environmental effects of farming, the economic side, and so on. But it is not hostile to humane farming itself. The other ethical theory I mentioned, the modernized Kantian approach, will probably never accept it. Humane farming, for a Kantian, still treats an animal "as a means," as something whose role is merely to serve our interests. This is most clear at the stage of killing, as animals usually have an interest in staying alive.

I didn't sign on to either of those views in that earlier discussion; instead, I used the idea of a "life worth living," as explored with the reincarnation test. I also insisted on thinking about the whole lives of animals, not just their deaths. The attitude embodied in that part of my discussion is a kind of "welfarism": we should ask about the overall welfare of the nonhumans, and humans, affected by farming, and try to avoid significant harms to their welfare. To say this is not to offer a general ethical theory—what do we do when welfares clash? Conflicts and trade-offs are at the heart of most problems in this area, and utilitarianism and the Kantian approach have a lot to say about them. For utilitarianism, you bring together all the good and bad consequences of an action, and consider the outcome as a whole. Kantianism looks for ways to enable everyone to pursue their goals without interfering with others doing the same thing. A general ethical theory has to grapple with questions like this. But although conflicts are very important, they're not always present. A welfarist can approve of humane farming when the animals involved have a good life.

In arguments against humane farming, people often make use of the idea of exploitation. This is related to the Kantian concept of "treating someone as a means," but people who object to farming because of exploitation can do so without working within a Kantian ethical theory. The argument can be more direct: we know exploitation is bad, and humane farming is a form of exploitation. So is keeping bees for honey, and other practices that don't seem to involve much suffering. People often say to me that all farming of animals is exploitation and is hence wrong—they view this as overriding other arguments.

I see why the idea of exploitation can motivate us to question a practice, but I don't think this argument is compelling. The idea of exploitation is one that we import from human social life, from our attempts to establish fair arrangements between people, especially in situations of unequal power. We can bring this concept over into the nonhuman domain, but it doesn't automatically have the same ethical significance when we do. (This is an example of the flexibility of parity judgments, which I discussed earlier.) Or, if we insist that exploitation must always be bad, then its presence might have to be detected differently. Humane farming can include mutual benefit, an exchange of protection for food. The fact that nonhuman animals are controlled in these arrangements, the fact that they are not equal partners in setting the arrangement up, can make things look like exploitation even when the animals have good lives. A welfarist might not mind about that.

A different concept that can be exported from human social relations has more impact on me. That is the concept of *betrayal*. Modern industrialized farming is a high-tech descendant of a relationship that humans formed with some other animals about 10,000 years ago. The relationship can have genuine reciprocity in it, when we give animals protection and a peaceful life. But modern factory-farmed animals are the victims of an immense betrayal of this relationship. I can see how this importation of a concept from human social relations might be questioned, but I don't want to be a part of this kind of betrayal.

A more revolutionary response to these problems is to take on an ideal of disengagement. We might decide to get as far out of the lives of nonhuman animals as we can. Quite a few philosophers find themselves in a place like this. The ideal might not be achievable, and perhaps we can't expect to even get close to it, but it still might be seen as our goal. We would abandon the farming of animals, also hunting and fishing, and probably even having companion animals—this last move takes the disengagement idea quite far from utilitarianism and the welfarist approach. We would allow wild nature to continue, and treat what happens there as not our business. Aside from abstract arguments about respecting animals' autonomy, this might be seen as a gigantic apology for the steadily escalating harms we have perpetrated, especially over the last few hundred years.

That is one choice we might make. An alternative ideal is to stay more engaged with nonhuman animals and continue farming, but do so in a better way. We do not step away from the control that we have, but we put that control to better use. The ideal would be a relationship that is mutualistic, one that benefits both sides. We ensure that all the animals under our control have lives that are clearly worth living. This might be seen as the restoration of an earlier relationship between humans and nonhumans, if we think that early animal husbandry and domestication were mutualistic. But even if the past was not like that, mutualism is still a goal that we can reasonably pursue.

This would be a future in which killing would remain part of what we do. For some people thinking about this topic, killing remains a unique harm, no matter what else is going on, and we should just turn away from it. I feel this pressure. But just about every response to the problem gets itself into an odd place somewhere. Animal advocates often contrast life on a modern farm or CAFO with a different life for animals, "the life they dream of," as one campaign had it, a carefree life in the fields. This is used in promotions to support veganism or something similar—a plant-based future. But if the future of human food is entirely plant-based, this won't give cows and chickens a new, carefree life, but something closer to no life at all. All of this does depend on decisions we might make about "rewilding," a topic I'll look at in the next chapter. We might encourage the descendants of some domesticated animals to head back into a life closer to that of their wild relatives. But at least for some domesticated species, if animals of their kind are are to continue on in any numbers, then some kind of farming will be in the picture. Perhaps all views in this second round of discussion end up encountering some perplexing or disturbing moments.

People sometimes reach a stage in the discussion like this and say, "Oh well, the issues are just not clear—we're back to square one. Maybe we should just continue with what we've been doing." But we're not back to square one at all; we're at a place that's quite far down the track. If we can apply in practice the conclusions reached in the first round of discussion, we'll have solved the most pressing problem in this area, the problem of the suffering caused by factory farming.

Questions about humane farming can sometimes come across as obsessing about a practice that can only end up as a middle-class indulgence, not something that's likely to feed large numbers of people. I am not sure if we know that to be true—that humane and regenerative farming practices can't scale up—but even if this is so, the question remains an important one. In developing countries, some traditional forms of farming are much more humane than factory farming. Should those traditional practices be continued? The middle class is also growing globally. Should humanely farmed meat be part of their lives or not?

My own view is that humane farming is okay. It can be justified by a whole-life argument and the possibility of genuine mutual benefit. My thinking in this area is also affected by my attitude toward death. Some people who write on these topics appear to have a horror of death itself that I do not share.

I like life very much, but I am comfortable with being a part of an omnivorous web, part of a cycle in which turnover and consumption are inherent to the system. Each of us, a pocket of bioenergetic order, passes into and out of being. Having an animal life means that one will die somehow.

This section of the book has looked at farming rather than hunting and fishing, and has concentrated on the farming of mammals and birds. In the case of hunting and fishing, the whole-life reasoning that I've been using does not apply, or not in the same way. In those cases, we are cutting short a life that was spent mostly out of our control. The ethical question is about our action at the final stage. Fish farming, which now accounts for about half of the fish we eat, has welfare problems in many cases, though it's probably not as bad as the worst farming of mammals and birds. The main thing for me in this area, the central priority, is to oppose the use of our powers to give rise to immense numbers of lives that are not worth living. The idea that an animal might die to feed me and other humans is not the big problem. Everyone dies. The idea that an animal should live in misery and stress for its entire life, because of our choices, is a completely different matter.

Animals in Experiments

The other problem this chapter will wrestle with is the use of nonhuman animals in experiments in biology and medicine. This problem is made especially acute by the fact that some of these experiments, over many years now, have been a means by which we have learned much of what we know about the minds of other animals. These findings have often shown that there's more going on in there than we might have expected. We have learned a lot from "noninvasive" work that does not involve surgeries, implants, and the like, but the invasive work has often been crucial. The experiments that I'll look at in this section include others, like drug testing, that don't have a role of this kind, but some of the work I'll question does include a continuation of research that got us to where we are now, with our richer understanding of animal minds.

In earlier chapters of this book (and my previous book, *Metazoa*), I have made use of work on "maps" discovered inside the brains of rats. The idea of inner maps had been conjectured in the 1940s by the psychologist Edward Tolman, who was looking just at the animals' behavior. A few decades later, the neuroscientists John O'Keefe and Lynn Nadel found that Tolman's inner maps were more physically real than might have been expected. As the rat moves through its environment, "place cells" that form a map-like structure light up. A continuation of this work found more surprises, including the dream-like—or not just dream-*like*—traversing of paths in sleep, the rehearsal and recollection of journeys, and mental exploration. This work has truly given us a look inside. But once this work went beyond Tolman's first steps, it involved tracking what individual neurons in the rats' brains are doing, with surgically implanted electrodes connected to wires leading out of their heads. I am not sure how bad this experience would be for the rats—perhaps much better now than it was in earlier decades. Animal neuroscience has also been full of "lesion" studies, however, where some part of the brain is destroyed to see what the animal can still do after it wakes up. I have frequently described "split-brain" research in these books. Human split-brain surgery was done for medical reasons, helping patients with severe epilepsy. But a lot of surgical experiments were done on animals as well, especially primates. These included tests of procedures, studies to see what happens if a split-brain cut is deeper than it would be in humans, and so on. Some of that work would, I assume, have informed the medically beneficial surgery done on people, but much of it appears to have been done more out of scientific curiosity.

Now that we know more about the animals, what sort of policies should we choose for the future? I do think change is needed. I won't go through horror stories here in this chapter's main text, but I will put some links in the endnotes, making sure they are fairly recent, for those who want to look closely. Dogs are still used in a lot of harmful testing, especially tests of the toxicity of chemicals. Most of these dogs are beagles; tens of thousands of beagles are used in research each year in the United States alone. Beagles are known for their amiable, trusting disposition, and that very fact has doomed them to awful experiments. As with factory farming, I see this practice as squarely, and almost unbearably, in the realm of human betrayal of animals who have made a life with us.

The vast majority of mammals used in testing are mice and rats, though, and within animals as a whole, a large number are fruit flies, small fish, nematode worms, and some others. Octopuses are used as research animals more than they were in the past. They now tend to get more protection than other invertebrates, but I hope octopuses never become "model organisms" in biology, as some people have suggested.

Let's focus on animals that are pretty clearly sentient. I take this to include many animals beside mammals, but mammals raise the most urgent questions. As in the discussion of farming, I want to focus not only on the experimental procedures the animals have to go through, but on their whole lives and likely experience. These lives include confinement and deprivation of opportunities for normal behaviors. They tend to also include a regular food supply, warmth, and so on, at least outside the tests. We need to think about the whole life.

A first response we might make, when troubled by the treatment of lab animals, is to insist on a stringent accounting of the benefits and harms associated with an experiment of a particular kind. Is the work likely to do more good than harm? This accounting would be done in a utilitarian way, counting total harms and benefits and allowing that harm to one can be offset by benefits to another. Such an accounting could not pretend to be exact, but it might give us guidance. Several philosophers have used the example of early-twentieth-century work on the role of insulin in diabetes. About thirty dogs were used in the experiments, and the benefits to humans were enormous. The diabetes case is extreme, and we're also not dealing with questions that can be answered by looking backward, knowing how the work turned out. Decisions have to be made ahead of time. But a case like that still might provide a model; perhaps sometimes we have good reason to think that things will turn out like this.

How would reasoning of this kind relate to "basic" research and work driven by curiosity, where animals are harmed but there is no clear path to a beneficial therapy? A simple response would be to say that the cost-benefit test is failed and the work should end. But once we start to press a little on the distinction between practically oriented and basic research, this whole approach becomes problematic. Scientific investigation is cumulative; a project that has good cost-benefit accounting now will have it in part because of earlier work, much of it probably "basic" or exploratory, that set up the background knowledge used in later rounds of research. The usual situation is one where different studies interlock; you learn a bit here and a bit there, and the pieces start to fit together in a way that allows you to do something useful. If we stop curiosity-driven work and only do work with clear practical benefits, we will lose out on the next round of knowledge about the basic workings of living systems, work that is likely to make all sorts of other future work beneficial.

For a person concerned about cruelty in experiments, this response can engender frustration. It is too open-ended; it will allow too much. In science, there's a strong tendency for work to breed more work of the same kind. Papers often conclude with "More research is needed," and funding agencies are approached in those terms. The result can be a lot of routine work that follows a path and adds small pieces with diminishing returns. In many parts of science, this is not a problem, as there's no reason not to keep probing away, following small leads. But in the sort of work we are talking about here, it does become a problem, because work of this kind can use a lot of animals.

Let's try a different tack. Does the discussion of farming in this chapter give us any guidance? Suppose we drop the distinction between "basic" science and research directed on specific harms and therapies, at least for a moment, and consider all the work together. In the case of farming, I insisted on using whole-life reasoning, not just looking at deaths, and said that humane farming of some kinds is acceptable. Can such a model be applied to the lab animal case? The proposal would be to make each animal's life a good one as a whole, a life clearly worth living. If this is acceptable in the farming case, it should be acceptable here, too.

In the case of some, perhaps many, laboratory animals, this may be impossible. The lives within humane farming envisaged earlier in this chapter were lives spent wandering around outdoors and experiencing little constraint most of the time (paddock fences, yes, but not cages and crates). Laboratory life, in contrast, generally involves confinement and the curtailing of normal behaviors, with no unconstrained wandering and no interaction in the sun. In the case of primates, cats, and dogs, I am doubtful that a life of the right kind could be achieved. Being well-fed, and well-numbed during the bad stuff, is nowhere near sufficient.

With mice and rats, things might be different. The philosopher Philip Kitcher wrote an article in which he suggests a regime of the right kind could be possible for those animals, given their normally short lives and the kind of environment that might be built for them. When there's a choice between making circumstances natural and just making them good for the animal, we might do the latter. We'd give them food and day-to-day security of a kind that most mice would envy, if they could. We could also try to ensure that typical behaviors can be expressed (if they don't harm other animals in that setting). Given the spatial scale at which these animals live, he thinks this might be feasible. Such an approach is much more difficult in the case of those beagles and primates.

Macaques, which are small monkeys, are still quite widely

used in research. Could they be given a life that would justify experimental work on them? In a case like this, it would require deciding that giving them a life that is *very* far from a normal, wild one is all right, if they end up in extremely benign, comfortable conditions for most of their time. We'd have to accept that it's okay for most of the ongoing projects that a normal macaque life involves to be lost. (This idea about the role of "projects" in wild animal life is one I'll come back to in the next chapter.) One of the heartbreaking things about animals is what they are able to adapt to. The fact that an animal can adapt does not make the thing they are adapting to defensible.

A few initiatives have built and supported retirement facilities for laboratory animals; we try to make it up to the animals afterward. This attempt at balancing is the converse of what is seen in humane farming, as the good part of life comes later. This will surely be better than nothing, but in a fair bit of animal research, the testing stage seems so bad (not just the procedures, but the confinement and deprivation) that I doubt that measures of this kind could be enough for a whole-life justification.

Whether this whole-life approach might allow ongoing use of animals in research is also affected by changes in technology. So far here, I've been assuming that confinement and constraint are part of the picture. In the future, perhaps it will be possible for brain recordings and the like to be done with tiny, harmless, self-contained implants that don't require wires connecting the animal to machines, and that allow the animal to live, freely moving, in a sanctuary rather than a lab. That would transform the problem.

Where does all this bring us in the meantime? It makes it reasonable to oppose a large amount of animal experimentation. At least until testing methods and the lives of the animals are greatly improved, a lot of work should stop. Again, I am focusing on mammals here, and am not sure at all about some of the invertebrates. But I would bring to an end just about all the harmful work on primates and dogs. What about work that has an unusually clear justification in utilitarian terms—research in which a small number of animals suffer harm to achieve great benefits to others? In any policy debate, there will be special cases and hard calls, but if work of that kind is to proceed, it should be done in a way that comes as close as possible to being justifiable in whole-life terms.

In both the farming case and the laboratory one, what I oppose most is humans setting things up, using our powers, to create ongoing misery, stress, and fear for other animals. We humans have emerged from the long history of animal evolution with unique capacities. How do we use them? Some uses of our powers are grotesque in the relationship they establish to the other animals who have come through this history with us, perhaps especially those who have lived among us. Factory farming of pigs and chickens, together with the worst practices used with cattle; the use of dogs, cats, and primates in harmful experiments—those are the most important cases.

If there is a scaling-back of the sort that I have in mind, scientific progress will be slower. We should accept this. Information will still come in, from work of many kinds that doesn't involve this kind of harm. The pace will be different. An objector might say, "Some people will be worse off because of the delay." Yes, but that argument has little force—things would go even faster if we used prisoners. We usually accept that the speed of progress is not the only thing to consider. Nearly everyone thinks that *some* degree of license for harmful scientific research would be too much to grant, and it's a question of the amount.

I advocate this package of views in the spirit of the discussion of ethical choice at the start of this chapter. In this area, there are some paths that are shortsighted, factually uninformed, inconsistent with other values and projects that the defenders would endorse, and so on. Arguments can be made where we show that someone has been making a mistake, or doing something that can't be defended. But as in the case of farming, a round of relatively clear improvement is followed by another round of decisions, and that later stage might offer several defensible paths. We should not let the existence of those harder questions prevent the earlier round of progress. Don't let the question "Is it okay to deliberately breed mutant flies?" deflect us from ending research that inflicts months of pain and stress on monkeys and beagles.

I can imagine a more permissive view for the future, one based on arguments about the overall benefits that come from more knowledge. If someone thinks we have evidence that harmful experiments of some kind that I'd put an end to will work out well, given how broadly the new knowledge could be applied, this, in some cases, could be a defensible position. I think these things are very hard to know, but uncertainty about outcomes is not the heart of the matter for me. I'd just not want to keep doing work of that kind—work that is clearly bad for the animals but *might* pay off in some important way. Scientific curiosity is insatiable, and we should not allow this curiosity to trump everything else. So I would end invasive and otherwise harmful experiments on mammals, certainly cats, dogs, and primates but also rabbits, rodents—and octopuses—unless a whole-life justification can be given. I accept that some of the work that I would stop might lead to important breakthroughs; I just don't want it to be done. I would like future generations to look back on our time and say: They decided to give up this kind of work, decided to let it rest. Those looking back would probably also say: This medical advance X (whatever it might be) came more slowly as a consequence of their decision. But, again, we could always go faster by being crueler. I suggest that we just put these practices behind us. Why don't we make this into one of the choices that these years in history are remembered for?

8

WILD NATURE

Jackson Pollock, on being asked whether he painted from nature: "I *am* nature."

LEE KRASNER: "When I brought Hofmann up to meet Pollock and see his work which was before we moved here, Hofmann's reaction was—one of the questions he asked Jackson was, do you work from nature? There were no still lifes around or models around and Jackson's answer was, 'I *am* nature.' And Hofmann's reply was, 'Ah, but if you work by heart, you will repeat yourself.' To which Jackson did not reply at all. Now then, this is what was happening to me: as I had worked so-called, from nature, that is, I am here and Nature is out there, whether it be in the form of a woman or an apple or anything else, the concept was broken and you faced a black canvas. Well, with the knowledge that I am nature and try to make something happen on that canvas, now this is the real transition that took place."

Nature and the Natural

The point made by Pollock and Krasner in the epigraph to this chapter is right. Human action should not be contrasted with "nature," should not be set against it. The evolution of human action is part of the evolution of the transformation of environments by living activity. This starts out as a near-inevitable consequence of life, takes new forms in animals, then reaches the extravagances made possible by human minds, societies, and cultures.

People sometimes suspect that a rethinking of "the natural" has immediate consequences for how we should behave. I don't think it tells us what to do, but it does make a difference. This chapter, like the last one, is about some problems we currently face, but the problems are on a different scale: climate, habitat protection, and the future of wild nature.

In many settings, we are used to the idea that the natural is good, or at least that to go against it might be bad. If we do think of ourselves and our decisions as fully part of nature, then that idea becomes empty. "Empty" is the right word, too. It's not that seeing human action as part of nature brings an excusing or approval. *Whatever* we might do is part of nature in this sense; this way of thinking can't distinguish one action from another.

Here is an example that goes back to chapter 2. That chapter looked at the burial of carbon and release into the atmosphere of the oxygen that animals need. Carbon atoms cycle through the Earth in several linked processes. In one of them, carbon is taken up into plant matter through photosynthesis, and is then either returned to the atmosphere as carbon dioxide or, in smaller amounts, buried in the Earth. At particular times, such as the Carboniferous, more carbon is buried and eventually forms deposits of coal and other fossil fuels.

The carbon sits down there while animals continue to

evolve, eventually developing complex societies and technology. Fossil fuels then become a useful source of energy. The oxygen and carbon, separated long ago, now reunite.

That story can make the whole sequence seem "natural," including our actions as the fuel users. The Earth has a stage when fuel will be stored, and a stage when it will be burned. A person might say: Yes, that's the natural sequence, and given its naturalness and our place in the process, we shouldn't be bothered by it.

This sequence of stages does make sense. But that doesn't mean that the fuel once stored will inevitably be burned, or that this is an especially natural (apt, good) way for things to go. Suppose we decide *not* to burn that coal and gas, as a result of reflection on the consequences of this action. If we decide to leave these fuels in the ground, that would be an expression of "nature," just as much as burning it would. This, too, would be a reflection of the history of animal action, leading to human foresight.

We are deciding what to do. Whatever we decide is an expression of nature in this broad sense, an empty sense as far as the decision-making process goes. The embedding of our thoughts and actions in nature does not bring a kind of absolution. We should just work out how we want things to go.

The idea of the natural as a guide becomes empty once we think on this scale, but I see what people are aiming for when they make this appeal, and some of the actions that are advocated on behalf of "nature" are good ones. I would like to preserve some of those choices within a different framework.

What people have in mind by "natural" is often the *non-human*, the part of nature that human technology and intelligence have not (or not much) reworked and transformed. We can choose to align ourselves, in part and in some settings, with the nonhuman side of things. We can decide to value it. This might be poorly expressed by saying we are protecting or supporting "nature," but that doesn't mean it makes no sense as a choice. It is valuing the older forms, life outside of the human technological realm.

Why might we make this distinction, setting ourselves apart in this way? Because we *are* different in what we do, because the effects of our actions are so unusual. I am going to use the term "wild nature" for the nonhuman side. It could equally be called nonhuman nature. Much of this chapter is about why we might choose to protect and support wild nature in this sense.

Even if this idea of wild nature is meaningful, we might wonder whether such a thing is still real. Martha Nussbaum has argued that wild nature no longer exists, because human control extends even over places we *call* wild: "All land in our world is thoroughly under human control." What we think of as wild lands are protected by governments, and dependent upon them.

Places like game parks and nature preserves are, as she says, set aside as deliberate acts, and in some senses we continue to control what happens there. But the Earth still contains wilder places than those, and even in reserves, our "control" tends to have a different role than usual. Much of the time, we act there to prevent other human actions, especially poaching and exploitation. That fact that we have to spend human effort to keep people from wrecking a place, to keep certain human activities *out*, doesn't mean that what is inside is thereby compromised as an instance of nonhuman, wild activity. Our aim can be, and often is, to keep most human influences at bay and to let things go on as they would have without us.

This is not true, or is less true, if you provision or provide other care to the animals in a reserve. Then we have human intervention in a stronger sense. The cheetahs in the Maasai Mara that I described at the end of chapter 6 have a conservancy program that is mainly aimed at preventing human interference but can occasionally involve some veterinary care, as cheetah numbers are so low that every loss is significant. That is taking a step in a different direction, toward the active management of nonhuman species. But many cases are not like that, and follow an ideal of little or no human impact, even if human effort is needed to keep that situation in place.

Habitat Protection and Climate Change

Our time is often now described as a new geological epoch, the "Anthropocene," a period in the history of the Earth distinguished by the impact of human activity. There are different ways of marking this epoch out, from the start of farming about 12,000 years ago to the first atomic bomb tests during World War II. I quite like James Lovelock's way of recognizing the border. He dates the Anthropocene from the first time a reasonably efficient coal-burning steam engine was used, around the dawn of the Industrial Revolution in 1712. Thomas Newcomen's coal-burning engine ran a pump. It pumped water out of a coal mine.

The human effects recognized in the idea of the Anthropocene are a continuation of a tradition of the transformation of environments by life. The effects that have prompted the introduction of this term, though, are largely *problems*, not just changes.

The most-discussed problem is climate change, an ongoing overall warming of Earth due, in part, to the trapping of heat by carbon dioxide released by the burning of fossil fuels, along with effects of human agriculture (which releases methane) and other factors.

Carbon dioxide makes up a very small part of the atmosphere, a fraction of 1 percent, but it has powerful effects on temperature. As its concentration rises, more of the sun's heat is retained by the Earth. Carbon dioxide levels rise and fall for various reasons independent of human action, and have done so for ages. Our activities are superimposed on those.

Once we have a dynamic picture of the Earth, why is climate change a problem? Temperatures have always fluctuated. The Cretaceous, the time of the formation of chapter 3's forests, was five to ten degrees Celsius warmer than the present; those forests extended above the Arctic Circle. The amount of warming projected as a result of what's happening now, even in more pessimistic projections, is not out of bounds if we go some distance back. The pessimistic scenarios have us fairly soon (within a century) reaching temperatures last seen about 15 million years ago, around the time when great apes began evolving from other primates.

The problem, in large part, is speed—that "fairly soon" in my previous sentence. The pace of change will probably create a great deal of disruption, both to humans, especially in developing countries that are already warm, and to other animals. This is not a situation where we are pouring a poison into the atmosphere; we are modulating, with our actions, some larger and ongoing processes of change. But the effects of our actions, especially in their speed, are a problem for us and many other species. Turning our eyes to the oceans, as carbon dioxide levels rise in the atmosphere, the sea absorbs additional carbon and becomes more acidic. This is a problem for many shell-building invertebrates.

The other planet-scale problem we face is the degradation of habitats and a great loss of numbers in many animal species. In the case of birds, a recent report covering the United States and Canada found an overall loss of about 29 percent (of birds, not of species) since 1970 levels. Over half of US bird species are in decline. In chapter 3, I looked at the steep decline in many groups of insects—butterfly numbers are down by about 50 percent in the United Kingdom since 1976, and so on. In the case of the cheetahs of chapter 6, only about 7,000 remain. Among the many species of birds drinking at the water hole described in chapter 3 were some Gouldian Finches. These are extraordinarily colorful birds, with purple or mauve chests, a sun-like yellow lower on their bellies, green wings, and face masks of several different designs (red, black, or yellow). Only about 2,500 are thought to remain in the wild. People sometimes disapprove of heightened concern for these charismatic species, but imagine how it will be if they are gone—gone as a result of our steady, complacent encroachment—or live on only in zoos and cages.

The present time is sometimes described as a "sixth mass extinction" and compared to events like the catastrophe at the close of the Cretaceous. That is an exaggeration; the mass extinctions of the past were on a different level, with over three-quarters of species lost. This might happen, but we are still a long way from it. There's a tendency to conceive of our time using labels pulled directly from history, when what's happening now is different. The Earth, surprisingly, is now a bit greener overall than it was in the recent past. This seems due mainly to land-use changes, and also, to some extent, to the increase in carbon dioxide itself. A "CO_2 fertilization effect" seems to have also had a role in softening recent climate change; this is another feedback loop in the system.

Our problem is not a general de-greening of the world, but a loss of forests in the tropics and a loss of other habitats such as wild grasslands—a loss of ecologies. This is bringing with it a massive loss in numbers within many wild species. A creep of greenness in developed countries sounds encouraging, but it doesn't help animals that need particular habitats that are being steadily cleared. Species have always been lost, but there was usually scope and space for renewal. What is happening now is different, with wild ecologies destroyed and the numbers of animals steeply declining. Under our watch, everything is just being squeezed.

These problems are so multifaceted and change so quickly that commenting on them in a useful way is difficult. But I will offer some ideas. Climate change dominates nearly all current discussion, and I want to make a case for elevating the priority of habitat protection, for a partial shift in emphasis in that di-rection. This is partly because of what I think we can reason-ably hope to do, and partly because of how I see the relations between the two problems.

A rapid global move away from carbon-based fossil fuels with present technology seems more difficult than it once did.

Developing countries want portable, convenient fuels that can be used in transport and industry, as the developed world has enjoyed for over 200 years. Who can insist that they not try to make their people's lives better sooner? Though the move away from fossil fuels may be slower than many people now hope, the move will come, probably with the aid of new technology. A technology that might truly enable a change of course may be a storage medium rather than a source of power—ideally, a synthetic fuel that is made using energy from solar and wind but that can be transported and stored at normal temperatures and pressures, like coal and diesel.

When it comes, a move away from fossil fuels will bring a host of benefits. Air pollution is discussed less now than it once was, perhaps because in developed countries it's not as visible as it used to be. But air pollution does great harm worldwide. The hidden health costs of diesel have become clearer in recent years. And in developing countries, the problem of air pollution is often still in front of one's eyes.

Now we reach a point that may be more contentious. The push for action on climate has dominated environmental discussion for years now. The issue has a massive presence in progressive politics. This is where nearly all the attention, the resources, and political capital are directed. Many courses of action in this area involve significant sacrifice that will be felt especially by lower-income people. The stock of goodwill is being drawn down very far. I wish that more of this effort and energy was going into habitat protection. When climate is seen as *the* issue, and dominates discussion, a lot of other harm can be done to the environment in the background.

While we can mitigate many effects of climate change if we

have the will to do so, especially by assisting developing countries, the effects of extinction and the breakdown of ecological
systems are of a different kind. Here, there is no technological
fix, and not much can be done after the fact. Once a species is
gone, it's gone. The fact that the Earth is getting greener is not
preventing population declines, and it doesn't prevent loss of the
habitats that wild species need. The aim should be to protect
ecosystems as wholes.

When a case is made for a renewed focus on this problem,
it is common to reply that climate change and habitat loss are
so closely linked that the issues can't be separated. This is used
as a reason to stay with the priorities in place now. I do not
think they are tied as tightly as people often say. Certainly they
are connected—deforestation releases carbon, and reforesta-
tion during the growing phase stores it. Climate change pushes
some species toward extinction by changing their conditions of
life in adverse ways. But there is more of a choice of priorities
here than people sometimes admit.

First, we could solve the problem of climate change but also
wreck habitats. We might achieve a breakthrough technology
and reduce emissions to near zero, while allowing land clearing, deforestation, overfishing, and the pollution of waterways.
Then we have a bad outcome for habitat, even as we do as well
as we possibly could on carbon and climate.

Alternatively, we could create a large network of reserves and
prevent their exploitation, while continuing to use fossil fuels
indefinitely. These choices are separate. In this case, a continuing warming could put more pressure on the "saved" habitats
and the species within them, and that is the scenario that leads
people to say that the climate problem is more fundamental

or the issues are not separable. But whether that is how things would go depends on the amount of land that might be set aside for wild nature. Animals and plants can adapt to climate change by migrating to an area that's cooler, wetter, or more suitable in some other way. Sometimes they will be unable to do this, and will go extinct, but if there is room to move, they often have a chance. This requires that there *is* room, and corridors linking different regions. Large populations are also more likely to make it through these crises than small ones.

On an Earth where species can freely move around, climate change will still be disruptive, especially when it's rapid. On an Earth where habitat destruction has made it impossible for animals to migrate and numbers are reduced, the disruption will be greater.

When I say "we could create a large network of reserves while continuing to use fossil fuels indefinitely," that is not what I think we *should* do. We should reduce our use of fossil fuels where we can; we should turn diesel, as soon as possible, into a rarity with a few niche uses, rather than the fuel in just about every truck. Rich countries should also be willing to give considerable aid to developing countries that have to deal with the consequences of climate change as it happens.

Temperate countries will probably have to accept a good deal of migration, too. Large-scale change is a normal feature of the Earth, but the changes we're looking at now are unusual in their speed. One of the main reasons this is problematic is the fact that humans, through the creation of national borders and also through sheer numbers, have made movement very hard for people looking to leave deteriorating environments. In general I am not an "open borders" person; I think that nation-states with borders have been valuable inventions. But one of the most salient injustices we confront in this area is that rich, temperate countries have been responsible for most of the increased carbon in the atmosphere, while less wealthy, warmer countries will experience most of the problems, and migration has been made increasingly hard.

I understand the alarm that many feel about climate change. We should do what we can, encouraging the development of new technologies and working for international agreement when it's feasible. But we should also press hard on habitat preservation, much harder than we have during the recent years of intense concern with climate. We should act to reverse those steady, increasingly precipitous losses in wild species.

The last point I want to make as part of this plea is a practical one. Local action is entirely meaningful in the case of habitat protection. A single country, a single state, or even a single local government can do things that are consequential. It can establish reserves and protect habitat within its bounds. This can be effective whether or not other states or other countries do anything similar. Each reserve is a genuine contribution that does not get washed out by others' failures. In the case of climate change, local action does not have this significance. If a single state or country makes significant moves in reducing carbon emissions, this has very little effect, unless we are talking about one of the countries responsible for massive emissions: China, the United States, India. When action by one party inspires or motivates action by others, that's admirable, and sometimes a small contribution might inspire larger ones. Every small local reduction in emissions does bring emissions a little below what they otherwise would have been, too. But in the case of habitat protection, the global problem is a collection of local ones, and that is not true of climate change.

Here is a reminder of how effective measures taken on a local scale can be. New York Harbor, and the Hudson River that runs into it, used to be as much a sewer and waste disposal pathway as anything else. Swimming there in the 1960s and 1970s was unthinkable. The Clean Water Act (as it is commonly known) became law in 1972. Fifty years later, the harbor is a completely different place. People do now swim in it, and in 2020 a humpback whale was seen cruising along the Hudson just off midtown Manhattan, a few blocks from where I used to live.

Choices

All through that previous section, I was supposing that the preservation of wild nature is a good thing. It is common to think so, but we should not take this for granted or see it as unassailable. Perhaps things only look that way through a foggy lens of romanticism. Concern about climate change is at least partly concern for the human community, and this does not raise special "Why care?" questions. Habitat protection is different.

Defending the value of wild nature is easier when we consider its *instrumental* value—its value for human projects. This is often the basis for good arguments, especially given the typical shortsightedness of the destruction of wild places for economic reasons. The Great Barrier Reef in Australia could easily have been completely wrecked as a result of the pro-development policies of the local state government in the late 1960s and early 1970s; much of it was slated for mining. The reef was saved by a small but energetic conservation movement. Aside from any value we might say that the reef has in itself, I doubt that anyone, soon after, thought that the reef might have been more valuable to humans if it was mined rather than protected. Here I have in mind both its economic value to the locals and its value to many more as a source of rapturous experiences—the two are linked, of course. When I first went to the reef in the 1980s, the near miss was palpable, and digging the place up seemed unthinkable.

Cases like that are powerful, but if all we recognize is the instrumental value of a wild place, then when the scales tip differently, we should act differently. The harder problem is whether there are reasons to protect wild nature that extend beyond this.

I'll approach this question by looking at a challenge that arises even before we ask about balancing values and forgoing human projects. Is wild nature worth concern and protection at all? Is it instead a place dominated by suffering and pain? Perhaps the cruel chaos of wild nature was needed, in evolution, to get us here as humans, but now that we *are* here, should we just take charge? Should we either actively transform what remains of wild nature into something more benign, or perhaps just permit its disappearance as human projects expand?

When the question of wild animal experience and suffering is put on the table, people tend to think immediately of mammals as predators and as prey. Philosophical discussions keep coming back to antelope and lions. Those need to be considered, but along with all the rest, invertebrates as well as vertebrates. We have evidence that a capacity to feel something like pain is far more widespread in animals than has often been supposed. It is probably present in fish and crustaceans. Insects also seem much more likely to have experiences of this kind than had been realized before.

Fixating on the negative side of experience is misleading, though. A lot of discussions tend to do this; they focus on pain and death, and don't give much consideration to good experiences in animals that might balance the bad. When I have discussed animal pain in public talks, someone often asks: What about the upside? Human life can contain plenty of pain, and in some cases, at least, that does not make it all worthless. I am always glad to be reminded of this, and of course the point is right. We need to think about the balance.

Might experience in some animals not have this other, positive side? Might life for some animals be either neutral or negative, at each moment, and that's it? Special cases are always possible, but this seems unlikely in general. Learning by reinforcement is very common in animals. Actions with beneficial consequences tend to be repeated, and those with adverse consequences are not. If we think that negative reinforcements are felt, why should the positive ones not be? More generally, it makes sense that experience is a matter of contrasts, between better and worse. That encourages us to recognize the apparent moments of peace and comfort in animal lives as genuine—as felt positively rather than neutral.

The next step seems to be to think about an overall accounting of the good and bad in wild animal lives. The utilitarian approach to this problem is to think about all the good and bad experiences that wild animals have as a kind of block or sum, with positive and negative contributions. We'd ask whether the totality of pleasure in wild nature outweighs the totality of suffering. In this scheme, situations where everyone does fairly well can be treated equivalently to situations where some suffer for the greater good of others. I mostly rejected that kind of accounting in the previous chapter, when we looked at farming. The approach I took then, one that might also be applied here, is to retain the idea of tallying good and bad experiences but do this in a way that focuses on how individual lives tend to go—what a typical path looks like. This would have to be done separately for each kind of animal. How do things tend to go for an elk, an albatross, an octopus? Do each of these lives tend to be worth living?

Initially, at least, it does seem to make sense to ask about summaries of this kind. I don't say that an exact accounting might be done in practice—tallying up the usual mix of good and bad octopus-hours or elk-hours—but we might be able to get a sense of the overall picture. We might be able to ask, for animals of some kind, whether negative experiences tend to dominate life or not. Then we might step back and see whether there's a general pattern visible in the whole. We'd ask whether wild nature tends to be a scene of suffering for most animals or not.

However this attempt to do an inventory of experience in wild animal lives might be conceived, it runs into a complication. I'll introduce it by thinking first about how all this looks in the case of an individual human, rather than a nonhuman, life. Here, we might initially imagine going through an accounting of a particular person's life, hour by hour, looking for good and bad events, and then realize that we shouldn't really think of it this way. Whether a human life is a good one depends on more than the balance between momentary experiences of different kinds. Particular events of great significance, even if they are brief, can cast what went before them into a new light. Eventual success can make early struggles meaningful, or turn suffering into a sacrifice that the person was glad to have made. Vindication might look short-lived in experience, compared to what has gone before, but if the person is asked whether the early stages were worth it, they might say, emphatically, *yes*. They would not change a thing.

We are encountering here a new intrusion of something that came up back in chapter 6, the role of narrative in human life and our sense of who we are. Whether the good outweighs the bad within a person's life will depend, often, on the way those events are framed by the person's sense of the meaning of those experiences—the meaning of the failures that led eventually to success, or the other way around. A person might also change their view of the meaning of events over time. When a person does a summing-up of this kind, sometimes they might seem to make a mistake—perhaps ignoring for no reason the good things that happened to them, letting positive events recede in a mist of depression. They might forget, and then re-member, important events. They may come to rethink the whole in the light of new factual information (as in the movie *It's a Wonderful Life*). But in many cases, there doesn't seem to be a lot of sense in the idea that a person might get their personal summary *wrong*. Experiences differ from one another not only in basic value and raw intensity but also in kind, and in felt significance. When a person looks over the whole, they have to give a weighting to vastly different episodes—frustrations, vindications, disappointments, sublime moments—in any attempt to say whether the whole was worthwhile. Their narrative-building self *imposes* this weighting, to a large degree, constructing it on the basis of their views at that moment. Sometimes the balance might be obvious from the outside, being dominated by the good side or the bad. It's when life has many complicated ups and downs that these questions of overall meaning become more indefinite, more narrative-dependent. And the survey that a person makes, looking over what has happened up to that stage, is itself another experienced episode in their life.

You might then say: This is a human peculiarity, something that only applies in our case. This dependence that the significance of one event has on other events is important for humans, but only for us. It applies in our case because of the complex projects we have, and because we have the ability to come up with narratives that thread things into a whole. Nonhuman projects are not as elaborate, and other animals can't come up with narratives that tie them together. Given this, it seems that the accounting should be easier in their case. All we need to ask is: How much pleasure was there, and for how long? How much suffering, for how long?

But I've come to think that this response would be a mistake, and many wild animal lives can be similar to ours in a crucial respect. I don't mean that they can come up with narratives that make sense of events in the way we do (though I will come back to this in a moment). I mean that in wild animal life, as with us, differences in the value of experiences are not just differences on a scale, a scale from good to bad. Some events, good or bad, can lend significance to others. Wild animal life has projects, frustrations, and culminations, not just momentary ups and downs. I don't mean this to apply to all animals, and it's probably best to start out thinking about mammals and birds, and consider extensions from there.

Back in earlier chapters of this book, I described the avian goings-on down behind our house, featuring several species of parrots and other birds. Two Rose-breasted Cockatoos raised a family of two chicks while I watched. They prepared a nest in a tree hollow, stripping bark around it and bringing in fresh green twigs with leaves. When the chicks emerged, both adults fed them from their mouths. I saw one of the chicks fly. The other was slower to leave. Once the first one flew, it seemed never to return—the first flight was the exit. After both chicks had gone, a week or so after I first saw them and several months since the nest was started, the adults departed, too. A month later, two Rose-breasted Cockatoos visited the empty nest briefly. I don't know if it was the same pair, but they certainly seemed at home. I wondered if the pair came back to revisit their success, and perhaps also to see if their nest might be usable again next season. That is a life of projects, of fulfillments and frustrations, of some events giving meaning to others.

A case like this is an extreme one, but it illustrates what I am talking about. A picture of life consisting only of ups and downs that might be counted and summed is inaccurate not just for humans but probably for many other animals as well. I don't say that all these animals can *plan*, that they can represent their projects as wholes, but I suggest that many events in their lives have their experienced significance tied together in a certain way. (I note, also, that a number of nonhuman animals have recently been shown to exhibit a kind of self-control, forgoing immediate rewards for later larger ones. This is the sort of thing that many philosophers used to say animals just can't do.) In cases like the birds, and many others, the way things went for an animal during its life might, in principle, be formed into a narrative and understood as a whole, even if the animal cannot construct the narrative. The animal just *lives* the events, in all their diversity.

The animal may well remember some or many of these events. "Episodic" memory, the memory of particular events and experiences, has also been controversial outside of humans, but experiments suggest it is probably present in some other animals. And whether or not particular events are remembered, an animal might emerge from the sum of events over its life with an overall orientation—bold or nervous, for example. Some non-human animals certainly appear to reach an overall gestalt—a kind of peace, or an unease—that reflects much of what has gone before. This might be seen as a first-person distillation of the complexity of their personal history. In a few cases—and this is now going quite a bit further—a nonhuman animal might have, in the absence of language, something like a considered sense of its life so far. In dolphins and chimps, we certainly might wonder about this. But my point is not that nonhuman animals can do the narrative sense-making that we can do when we reflect on the path of our life; my point is that the diversity in experience and links between events that prompt our own narrative sense-making is probably a part of their lives, too. And in a complicated life of this kind, one with frustrations and culminations, victories and disasters, the idea that an individual wild animal's life was "mostly good" or "mostly bad" is often a problematic one.

Where does this twist in the path take us? What happens to the attempt to work out whether lives within wild nature are generally worth living? The place we've gotten to is the idea that for some animals, an hour-by-hour accounting of ups and downs, even in principle, would not answer the question well. (For other animals, it might be fine.) We might then think: If these lives are not clearly *bad*, we should not be tempted to eliminate wild nature, and should protect it. That thought would probably be a mistake, though; we've not decided that the lives are *okay*, just that we often *can't say*. Why would that give us reason to protect them? Maybe it gives us reason not to actively wipe out wild nature for the animals' own good, but that's not the most relevant question. Protection is the more important issue.

Perhaps we need another idea on the table, the idea of the richness of a life as opposed to its balance of good and bad events. Richness, the pursuing of projects even if they fail, is itself something we might want to protect. We'd then have two different respects in which a life can be worth living, or two factors to weigh, one that involves positive experiences and another that involves the pursuit of projects. I arrived at this idea through difficulties in accounting the ups and downs of experience, but it can have its own importance—it does not depend on problems with the other approach. I suspect that animal life tends to have more positive experience than people sometimes suppose, but that is not the only thing worth considering. Perhaps many lives in wild nature are tough but rich, and we might choose—I would choose—to protect wild nature in part because of this richness. Thinking about the animals I've encountered, and putting myself in their shoes, I find that even when things don't go well, I'd rather be in the fight.

How do these ideas relate to the arguments of the previous chapter? Back then, I said that many lives within intensive factory farming are not worth living. Do the points made in this chapter about the difficulty of summarizing the overall goodness of a life undermine what I said in the earlier one? They don't, because the lives of animals within factory farming are so different. Especially in the cases I emphasized back then, pigs and chickens, those lives are just awful, comprising some combination of stress, monotony, and discomfort, along with episodes of acute pain. Reproduction is controlled, food is delivered, and no significant choices need to be made. The projects characteristic of wild life are absent. The question of whether some special positive experiences might outweigh difficult times, or at least balance them, does not arise, because there are no experiences of that kind.

The relationship between the ideas in this section and *humane* farming is more complicated. A life under close care and protection might lack complexity and projects of the kind seen in wild animal life. Then we'd have to ask how bad it is for an animal to lack a good deal of the richness I talked about a moment ago, and instead experience a "flattened" but benign life within farming. That's a harder question to answer. These ideas about ongoing projects within animal life provide a way to make sense of the persistent (for some people, for me) but always uncertain intuition that *dignity* is something we should have our eye on in this area—dignity and meaningfulness, even in nonhuman lives. I see this as a reasonable source of unease about humane farming.

I won't leave questions about suffering in wild nature behind yet. There's more to explore, including arguments given by other philosophers. For example, we might move away from thinking about suffering in general and look at more specific policies, ones that intervene in wild nature in a targeted way. The obvious case to think about is predation, especially where the prey is likely to be sentient.

The philosopher Jeff McMahan has argued that we should take seriously the possibility of interfering with predators that cause a lot of suffering. He thinks the reticence that people usually feel about such actions doesn't have much warrant. People say that interfering in nature is "playing God," but as McMahan says, no actual God is having his work interfered with. If *we* don't do something in a setting where we can see that some good might be done, no one else will. The spirit of McMahan's discussion, in this respect, is reminiscent of the Pollock and Krasner passages in the epigraph to this chapter: we are part of this system, and we have as much business to be acting on it as anyone else. The fact that we have greater capacities to affect what happens should make us wary of unintended consequences stemming from our ignorance—Lori Gruen has emphasized this problem, in response to McMahan. But overstepping is not the only thing we could get wrong; we might also worry about doing nothing when we could prevent real harm.

McMahan thinks that it may soon be feasible to actually do some of the things that have been speculated about. We might work out which predators in natural systems cause the most suffering and take them in the direction of becoming herbivores though genetic manipulation, or humanely sterilize them if we can't change them. Our intervention need not be a matter of shooting the lion to save the gazelle; we can instead push the lion's descendants toward a different lifestyle. If we choose it, then sometime in the future, "the wolf will dwell with the lamb," as the biblical Isaiah said. We wouldn't eradicate wildness, but would change this side of animal behavior.

McMahan advocates this, and Martha Nussbaum seriously considers it. Nussbaum's view of how animals should be treated is based on the importance of their "striving," and the injustice in thwarting this striving. Her view recognizes something similar to what I discussed as animal "projects," and for her, we should try to protect the striving of animals from harms due to *other animals*, not only from humans. The "predators" that McMahan and Nussbaum discuss tend to be the big-toothed African mammals. If we ask—What about sea eagles? Sharks? Octopuses?—the reply can be that we need not target all predation. Each case can be considered in turn.

Preventing an animal from dying in one way is exchanging that death for another. If we eliminate a form of predation that we think is cruel, the animals saved will still die in some way. McMahan acknowledges this; wild animal life contains death by "disease, parasites, malnutrition and starvation, dehydration, freezing." Whether the wolf dwells with the lamb or not, both will die somehow. McMahan's response is that we should try to prevent other forms of suffering as well. Reducing predation can cause prey populations to grow very large and face deaths from scarcity. As well as controlling carnivores, we could control fertility in herbivores.

The ideal need not be an impossible future in which no one dies at all. Instead, we might imagine lengthy herbivorous lives, without much population pressure. The fact that this is different from what life for animals of this kind used to be like does not matter. Authenticity is not the goal.

What *is* the goal? The outcome seems like an enormous zoo, a reminder of some of what used to exist in wild nature, now in a more benign version. For McMahan, the aim is to reduce suffering, and whenever we can do that without untoward side effects, it's sensible to try. But once we're following this logical path, what is the reason for keeping this quasi-wildness at all? Why not push toward a different world, one with a large human population, few nonhuman animals of any kind, and hence little animal suffering? This path would not require an aggressive eradication of wild animals. The process of human encroachment would simply be allowed to continue. Wild populations in many species would fade away over some number of generations. We would embrace our capacity for control and try to minimize suffering as the process moved along.

We might call this a "Huxleyan ecology," in reference to Aldous Huxley's novel *Brave New World*. The world of that novel is dystopian, but in a relatively gentle way. Huxley's world is one of drug-aided indoctrination and conformity within overtly pleasant human life. The scenario I am imagining here need not be so constrained for humans; they might still have plenty of free rein. Wild nature, though, has been nonviolently flattened out. The world (at least on land) is one of well-managed crops, forest plantations, lab-grown meat, and well-fed companion animals. This is not a cruel place, by most standards, but it's very tightly controlled, and little is left of the unruly, scrappy side of animal life. It's that combination of tight control and an absence of physical suffering that I think of as Huxleyan.

We can compare these two possible futures—McMahan's managed wilderness and the more radical Huxleyan ecology—to a third one. In this alternative, we actively protect wild nature on a large scale. We do not interfere with predation or the other harms that wild animals encounter. We not only protect the wilderness that remains but also encourage some other parts of the Earth to head back toward a wilder state; we engage in "rewilding" as well as protection.

If all you care about is reducing suffering, the Huxleyan ecology might be best. If one thinks that biological diversity itself is good, then McMahan's managed wilderness would be better than the Huxleyan ecology. So would the third option of preserving and fostering wild nature, including its darker side. The McMahan picture will look good for a person who cares a lot about both suffering and diversity. When I grappled with difficulties in assessing the goodness of a life earlier in this chapter, I recognized the richness of a life, and the pursuit of projects, as things worth valuing. In McMahan's scenario, many animal projects will still exist; the cockatoos I watched raising a family could continue (as long as they don't overdo it). But animal projects would in many cases be transformed; part of the point of McMahan's scenario is reduction in the suffering that results from failed projects. McMahan's future is a "flatter" one in this respect.

A future of protecting habitats and rewilding might be seen as the most authentic to Earth's history. Authenticity sounds good, but in some forms, at least, this appeal would fall afoul of ideas endorsed in the first section of this chapter. We should not mark our own actions off as separate from what is natural, or deny the dynamic nature of the Earth.

Authenticity is not the right concept, but something related, less easy to summarize, guides my attitude here. When we preserve a diverse wild nature, we preserve, as far as we can, a great creative engine. This engine gave rise to us, along with other forms of life. (When I think about the Huxleyan ecology, I find myself reflecting on how precious the last uncontrolled deep-sea ecosystems would be.) We humans are a recent stem on the tree of animal evolution, one that has acquired the ability to look over the whole. There's a kind of ingratitude in allowing the extinctions, the narrowing, the reduction of animal life. I am proposing that we take some responsibility for this creative engine, and value its continuation. This system includes a lot of suffering, along with positive experiences and fruitful lives. I would choose to preserve and strengthen it, where this includes all its contrasts. Whether we like it or not, we have ended up as custodians of this astounding system. We can choose to protect it, and that is the choice I advocate.

I'll finish this discussion of wild nature with a few other thoughts. First, how unqualified, or pure, is the defense of preservation of wild nature that I want to give? Is there some amount of wild-nature awfulness that would change my thinking? What if we found that the inner lives of wild animals were much worse than we had thought? What if we found another inhabited planet where the natural order of things looked very grim? Is there *something* we might learn, in this or some other case, that would push me into accepting a suppression of wild nature for welfare reasons? I find myself saying yes, but partly just because "*something* we might learn" is so broad.

Second, I supported "rewilding," not just preservation. We don't just stop the destruction of habitats, but encourage some parts of the Earth to return to a wild state. How do we handle feral animals and invasive species that have become established in a place? For example, wild horses now roam in some large Australian national parks. They are not native, and they do a lot of damage, especially around waterways. Should we see them as bona fide parts of nonhuman nature who have made their way in and now can stay, or as an intrusion due to human action, in which case we might move, sterilize, or kill them? This is a hard question, especially as there is a gray area between ordinary movement of animals and human-related invasions. Feral cats are a disaster in Australia and New Zealand; they need to be aggressively controlled, or the cost to the ecology is too vast. But species do come into new areas and successfully compete, and it's not always something to oppose. I see this as a case-by-case issue. In the case of the Australian national parks, I'd at least try to establish some horse-free and horse-proof areas.

Third, philosophers and others often address questions in this area using the idea of a *right*. They might say, "Wild animals have the right to be left on their own," or "We don't have the right to interfere." In response, I think that we might sensibly decide to establish rights of some kinds for nonhumans, but rights are not given out by nature itself. If an animal has the right not to be interfered with by us, does it also have the right not to be interfered with by predators? A person might say that wild nature as a whole has the right not to have us interfere with it, but if this is a natural right, why has nature put us on one side, as interferers, and the other animals on another?

More generally, people who discuss the topic of wild nature and how we should treat it are often looking for a principle that will just *resolve* the matter, something we have to respond to once we recognize it. McMahan draws on a view offered by the philosopher Thomas Nagel about the special significance of suffering. Nagel and McMahan think that when we see suffering, we see something that we know *should not exist*. The fact that suffering should not exist, its essential badness, is "part of reality." This is true, McMahan thinks, whether the suffering is found in human affairs or wild nature; we should prevent suffering whenever we can. On the other hand, Tom Regan, one of the most influential thinkers in environmental ethics, expressed just as much confidence about something very different. Though wild nature is full of suffering, "our ruling obligation with regard to wild animals is to *let them be*." Our obligation is not to reduce suffering; our obligation is not to interfere. In an earlier version of the same discussion, Regan said that this is because of our role, our proper place in the world; humans are "neither accountants nor managers of felicity in nature." McMahan himself quotes these passages from Regan and contrasts his own view based on the special importance of suffering.

I agree with McMahan that we can choose to focus on suffering without worrying about whether this is our job or not. We can choose to make suffering (or overall welfare) our priority. But we're not making a mistake about reality, failing to recognize a real feature of suffering (its *should-not-be-ness*), if we don't do this. We can choose the Regan role, the McMahan role, or some other. Regan and McMahan are both wrong that there's a moral feature in this situation that we *have* to recognize and respect (note again that they disagree entirely about what this is), but each describes an attitude we might reasonably choose to take. When we make our choices in this area, we should try to work out how these choices fit in with other things we believe, other things we value, and so on. But if we hold out for an objective imperative, something that instructs us to intervene or not to intervene, to look after animals or to let them go their own way, then we are holding out for something that will never come. We don't need such a thing anyway; we should just try to make our valuations as reasonable as possible, and decide what to do.

Instead of Us

As I was getting close to the end of writing this book, several people writing to me on other topics expressed, unprompted, an enthusiasm for the idea of human extinction—the end of humanity. In some ways they look forward to it.

The first two were not people I'd thought of as especially negative or misanthropic—although looking forward to human extinction must make you, technically, very much a misanthrope. The third person does have a darker outlook on the world. Three of them spontaneously saying this certainly started me thinking.

The third friend, when I followed up with him, offered a definite argument. Life for animals within factory farming is much worse than nearly any animal experience would be in our absence. Huge numbers of animals live under this regime, and we are unlikely to stop this kind of abuse in the next few hundred years, he thinks. Nature without us would certainly be "red in tooth and claw," but the rest of animal life would still be better off without humans in charge. And for my friend, the heights of human culture (whatever you take these to be) don't compensate for this cruel side of what we do.

The argument is reinforced when we think about numbers. In the previous chapter I looked at figures for the overall amount of biomass, or living matter, in various kinds of organisms. Most biomass today, about 80 percent, is in plants. Animals as a whole make up less than 1 percent, and most of animal life is in the form of arthropods (like insects) and fish. But when we get to mammals and birds, the skewing due to human action becomes apparent. Livestock, animals of the kinds that we confine and control, make up about ten times the biomass of wild mammals and birds.

The total number of poultry, pigs, and cattle alive on farms and in feeding operations across the world at any given time is around 30 billion. The total for farmed land animals is a couple of billion more. The majority of these animals probably live within some form of factory farming, broadly defined—one estimate is about 74 percent. That suggests that over 23 billion animals, at any time, are found within factory farms.

What proportion is this of the total number of mammals and birds on Earth? Here I'm asking about the number of individuals, not biomass. When thinking about human impact, it makes sense to ask about biomass. But when thinking about experience and suffering, it makes sense to switch to the number of individuals—one cow should not count the same as a large collection of smaller animals, just because of their sizes. Then we find a surprise. Especially in the case of mammals, although the biomass of farmed animals is much larger than that of wild animals, the relationship when we consider numbers is reversed. This is because the world still contains huge numbers of very small wild mammals, especially rodents and bats. More than half of all wild mammals are bats! That is an estimate, but a careful one. It leaves out, as non-wild, the species of mice and rats that tend to live in cities. Wild mammals, mostly very small, outnumber livestock by something like eighteen to one.

If we just think about mammals with bodies larger than one kilogram (a bit over two pounds), then the wild numbers and the livestock numbers might be pretty similar (4 to 5 billion).

The relationship between the numbers of small and larger wild mammals has probably not always been this skewed. We're seeing here another effect of human action. As humans spread across the globe, we wiped out a lot of larger wild animals, and have replaced them with livestock.

Farmed mammals include a fair number of sheep, goats, and others that have been able to stay outdoors and not too con-fined (though sheep are often subjected to other cruel practices, especially live export, crammed into sweltering ships). The lives of cattle are a mixture, as I said earlier, and the situation of pigs is the real disaster. The proportion of farmed mammals living within intensive factory farming is growing, but probably not yet a majority.

In the case of birds, farmed birds make up much more bio-mass than wild birds, but the numbers of individuals are again reversed, because there are, at least in estimates, so many small wild birds. If fish farms are counted as factory farming, then fish are the most numerous of all factory farmed animals, but still a small proportion of wild fish.

We're still a fair way from a situation where *most* verte-brate animals on Earth are stuck within factory farming. But the numbers themselves are huge—many billions—and grow-ing. (These wild-versus-farmed comparisons are affected also by the fact that animals in industrialized farming have such short lives; the population of chickens alive at any time is much smaller than the number killed each year.)

I found myself thinking that my main disagreement with

my pro-extinction friend was over the prospects for change. I expect us to be able to start doing better in this area within a few decades. If I thought we could not, especially if I thought things would keep getting worse, I might find myself saying similar things to him.

Another of the friends who commented on this topic, a biologist, thinks about the desirability of our extinction in conjunction with the fact that it is probably going to happen at some stage anyway. It's not that our extinction's being likely makes it good, but if we are going to leave the scene, there's a question about how much damage we do before we go. If biological diversity is shredded as a result of the actions we're taking now, then when we eventually depart, we will have already closed off the Earth's future to a significant extent. My friend wrote: "If we keep going on our current path, I picture our post-human world covered in a thin skin of archaea, nematodes, tardigrades, viruses, and some algae. But if we checked out now, before we've done too much damage, the Earth could go on without us and recover itself." Her picture of how the Earth might end up when we finally leave it is indeed troubling. Archaea are similar to bacteria. Tardigrades (microscopic "water bears") have both charm and tenacity, but they are a long way from the thrumming muscle of the cheetahs and the flower-like giraffes. It's hard to summon any enthusiasm at all for nematodes. "Life on Earth now is astonishingly beautiful and a bottomless well of surprises," my friend continued. "It feels morally inexcusable to wreck it when there are alternatives."

As with my other friend, part of my disagreement here concerns what we might expect in the near or medium-term future—in this case, whether human extinction is likely. *Even-*

tually it becomes likely, as the sun heads toward swallowing us and other large-scale changes take their toll. But humans are so adaptable that I don't think arguments from the general rates at which animal species tend to go extinct have much purchase on our case. We may live on for a long time. If I thought that we were likely to leave the scene fairly soon, after rapidly doing a lot more damage, then I might think more like she does. My friend's reasoning is certainly consonant with things I've said in this chapter about the tragedy inherent in the destruction of so much of the creative engine we find around us on Earth.

With these questions on the table, this is also the right point to think for a moment about the distant future. I said back in chapter 2 that life is a long-term tenant, not just in relation to the age of the Earth but also in relation to the age of the universe. More accurately, we've been long-term tenants so far. Matters will eventually look different.

As we peer forward from our current vantage point, on a 100-million-year timescale, we see some endings that are unavoidable, or at least very hard to avoid, and imposed by factors that we don't much control. Something like four of these might be looming. First, one of the carbon cycles that I've discussed several times in this book, the slow, or "geological," carbon cycle, is expected to eventually become unfriendly to life on Earth. This is the cycle in which rocks are weathered, carbon is laid down in sediments at the bottom of the sea, and volcanoes return that carbon to the atmosphere. Eventually, the carbon-returning part of the cycle will fail to keep up (for reasons involving the slowing of plate tectonics, as well as the warming sun), and carbon dioxide in the atmosphere will fade to levels unable to support photosynthesis and plant life. When plants go, animals should follow. This will include us, or any form of life like us, unless we can devise a new way of using the sun to build living material. All this is projected to happen half a billion to a billion years from now.

The next imposed ending is the loss of the oceans, through evaporation, followed by the engulfing of the Earth by an expanding sun. The loss of oceans is expected in about a billion years, the engulfing around 7 billion years on—though that engulfing is apparently a little uncertain, as the planet has some chance of drifting away first. To escape this further round of disasters, we'll need to travel to a new solar system. Finally, stars and planets themselves will probably be lost, as the universe expands into a gray entropic fuzz. There's probably no way of avoiding that one.

All this does bear on my friend's reasoning. Suppose humanity does wreck much of the Earth fairly soon, and also goes extinct. Then the amount of time the Earth would have to rebuild, before the demise of plants, would be roughly similar to the period from the origin of animals until now. We might think of this as enough time for one more run, one more long opera, though it would take place in increasingly challenging circumstances. This would be a bit like one of those global crashes-and-restarts that we encountered at the end of chapter 2, except that this time, it would be us, and the malign side of our place in the history of living action, that brought it about.

9

SEAMOUNT

Manta

Through empty blue water like space, you come down onto a dive site in the Raja Ampat archipelago. Below an expanse of open water, "Blue Magic" is a huge mound, flat like a mesa, rising from the seabed.

The top of the reef, oval-shaped and slightly hunched, looks about seventy yards long or so, with steep sides falling away. Approaching, you can see the jumbled living mesa, but not the terrain below and around it. It is a "seamount"—a reef that comes up from the ocean floor and sits there like a world.

A couple of years after that dive, I swam down onto another seamount, Roma, near the Indonesian island of Sulawesi. Roma has barrel sponges that look like the bases of ancient stone columns, with ornate, thickly grooved sides. On that dive, I remembered Blue Magic and had a sense, silently in my mind, of why these sites seem significant. It is that world-like character. You come in and the seamount seems to rise from nothing. But you know it is supported from below, and its life is sustained and suspended in energy flows.

The reef is a collection of countless animals, bodies building on bodies. A depression in a corner has an anemone with anemone fish. A little over from there is a cleaning station, where a nervous, dark-blue sickle-tailed fish is having its skin cleaned of unwanted life by a smaller fish while another large fish waits. Coral is stacked in plates and folds or grows in branches like a tree. The animals are barrels and filaments and stars, each pursuing its projects, also completely tangled and connected, each touching neighbors, who touch others.

These places summarize some features of the Earth as a system: the seamount is isolated spatially, but embedded in flows of many kinds—light, nutrients, oxygen. It is not a single organism, but is made largely out of interconnected life. Collaborations and conflicts are jumbled together, with organisms dependent on others they can't see, but link to in long chains and webs.

At Blue Magic, an oceanic manta came in. These rays can be thirty feet long. I don't know how big this one was—smaller, certainly, but still huge, and an impossibly graceful animal, a wing extended in the sea. Its movement was effortless, weightless, gliding in like an idea, a passing thought.

Though massive as an animal, the manta seemed to have been created from quickly made lines. Its body's markings were white on a near-black gray, with rough edges, very much as if the manta had been drawn with charcoal on coarse-grained paper. I am an atheist; I think that religion is a mistake. But if I wasn't, I'd think this was God sketching in charcoal.

Looking Back

Life, pockets of order and the control of energy, appeared early on Earth. Life exists within flows, in traffic, using resources and changing its environment. Life includes reproduction, along with the metabolic control of processes. With reproduction comes recurrence and multiplication: a few give rise to many. With multiplication, variation, and the inheritance of traits comes a Darwinian process of evolution by natural selection. This sets in place a process, the first of several, in which innovations can be retained, and spread, because of their beneficial effects.

Several paths lead out from there. Two paths, interlocking, mattered especially to this book. In one of them, some bacterial cells invent a form of photosynthesis that establishes a flow of oxygen gas into the atmosphere. These cells are taken up as symbionts in algae, and their descendants become part of the cells of land plants. Green plants spread and carpet the Earth with solar panels.

These organisms, by filling the atmosphere with oxygen, also make a different kind of life possible. That path starts with another group of single-celled creatures, who came to live in colonies, then in more integrated groups, becoming animals. A controllable internal skeleton, used in single-celled protists to change body shape and act, becomes the basis of muscle, and hence of action on a multicellular scale.

Initially, this part of the tree of life shows just glimmers of the active cohesion of animals; the path starts with frond-bearing creatures fixed to the seafloor, or creeping slowly along it, while film-bodied beings hover above. Then, with the aid of growing levels of oxygen, this cluster of evolutionary experiments runs rampant, giving rise to the rest of animal life, including its transformative power.

Animal action is controlled by nervous systems—not all animals have them, but the exceptions are very few. Nervous systems in some groups become elaborate, and the scope of action grows. As bodies, nervous systems, and senses become more sophisticated, actions become more targeted and have new kinds of effects. Learning enables past successes to shape future behavior. Useful habits can later be augmented, and partially replaced, by plans based on inner models. Animal culture arises, and takes on a special role in a small group of primates who make a home on African grasslands. They develop language and deliberation. Plans are directed on mere possibilities, represented and discussed. Their technologies change the reach of animal action.

All this is part of an account of the place of mind in the natural world. Minds are private, the home of perspectives and points of view, inner ramblings and quirks. But minds evolved in a common space, and they affect that common space, our common world. Our minds inhabit an ecology of action, a scene where actions arising from many different perspectives converge and play out.

How likely or unlikely was this to happen? I've covered a few questions of that kind explicitly, and other answers are suggested by things learned along the way. It is striking that life appeared quite early on Earth. This suggests that life might arise readily when conditions are right. While some form of life may not be too hard to get, finding a form of photosynthesis that fills the atmosphere with oxygen, or anything that could play a similar role, might be a much rarer step, one that life on other planets may not hit on. As things went, life on Earth changed just about everything, but some of the scientists whose work I used in chapter 2 might say that even after life was established, that cascade of further changes was far from inevitable. It needed something like our water-splitting, oxygen-releasing form of photosynthesis. This enabled the Earth to generate many *more* inhabitants, in more environments, and it made the animal way of living possible.

I discussed all this with the biologist Andrew Barron, after these ideas were in place in the book, and his reply was that I was being "oxygenist"—coining this term to refer to an unreasonable chauvinism. Who knows how things might go elsewhere, or might have gone here? Maybe there's another path by which life could become planet-changing, using different chemical pathways. Many of the other biologists whose work I've used here would probably plead guilty to oxygenism.

If the animal way of life can become established, with oxygen or without it, we might then expect it to explore all sorts of paths. Simple forms of culture, like simple forms of life, might be quite accessible. Although this is uncertain, there's a good chance that learning by tracking the good and bad consequences of one's actions evolved several times, independently, in different groups of animals. This is clearly true of learning by imitation, given that bees, as well as birds and mammals, can do it. Once nervous systems are in place, they can discover a range of ways for actions, and their beneficial consequences, to be retained and spread. It's harder to know whether a human-like path, with language, society, and technology, would be likely to arise if the experiment was run again, though I suspect that it would.

Likely or not, it happened with us. We have emerged from the thicket of animal evolution with unusual powers, with reflection, debate, and foresight, and also with unusual efficacy in our actions. We have these powers, and can explicitly ask: How should we use them?

The scope of human influence over other animals has gradually become enormous. The majority of mammal and bird life on Earth is either livestock we control, or *is* us—humans themselves make up a large fraction of vertebrate life on land. We have squeezed out much of wild nature. In the last part of this book I argued for habitat preservation, rewilding, an end to cruel factory farming, and a massive reduction in the use of animals in experiments.

Especially in the discussions of wild nature and why we might protect it, I found myself moving away from familiar and worked-out options in ethical theory. For example, the goal of prevention of suffering might encourage us *not* to protect wild nature. In many settings, reducing suffering is a good goal, but in this case it should be balanced against other goals. I criticized appeals to natural rights, such as a right to live free of interference. I tried instead to work out how we might act if we are guided by an appreciation for the vast creative engine that got us here. This includes not just other animals, the present outcomes of the many paths of animal evolution, but the whole ecologies in which life took and continues to take new forms.

The motivation I offer for protecting wild nature can look

a bit like an aesthetic matter, but it's not that we are standing back and noting some object's beauty or impressiveness, then deciding to protect it for that reason. It's not that we want to keep wild nature around just so that we can appreciate it. I am not sure what the best words are for what I have in mind, but gratitude and a sense of kinship have a role here, and these are quite different from an aesthetic interest. It's more a matter of *identifying* with a process than appreciating it as an onlooker. I don't deny the aesthetic side, and can imagine an alternative world in which we, reflecting together, look back on what we arose from and find it gross or horrible. That would raise new questions. We might then decide to cut ourselves loose, as much as we can. But our actual situation is not like that.

A picture of our place—in evolution, in the history of the Earth—does not tell us what to do. It can point to actions, to commitments we might make, but all of this is very much a choice. We can take on the project of protecting wild nature, but we could also head in a different direction, looking for a future Earth that might be more benign in some ways, but also impoverished. The future I worry most about is not so much one in which people actively try to "civilize" the Earth, but one in which we don't make much effort to protect natural eco-systems because we don't see much reason to look after what might be lost. We need positive reasons to resist those tenden-cies, to act against them. In this book I've tried to make the out-lines of these choices clearer, and tried to motivate, as a task we might embrace, the protection and restoration of wild nature.

Given all that's gone before, there's one more topic that it makes sense to look at. This is the span of our individual lives, in space and time.

Lives and Minds

Our human lives have a fair degree of definiteness to their boundaries. Where each of our bodies begins and ends in space is pretty clear (give or take the bacterial colonies inside our guts—those might be in some ways part of us and in other ways distinct). The same is true of our beginnings and endings in time. Each of us begins from a fertilized egg. The new individual grows up and develops, while keeping a fairly constant form, before growing older and dying.

Other organisms are less definite in their beginnings and ends. When a bacterial cell divides, is the result two daughters and the death of the parent, or does the parent live on in one of them? If so, which one? A tree might send out a root that initiates a new stem, and if the root breaks, the two trees are entirely separate. Is that something like a birth? And where are the spatial boundaries of "the" tree while the two stems are still attached?

For life to continue, there needs to be a way of preventing metabolic processes from diffusing away into the surrounding chaos. Compartments and borders of some kind are necessary. This is the role of cells. But when many cells are working together, there's no need for these larger units to be always neatly marked off from one another. In chapter 2, I talked about the "circus of forms" that evolution has produced at this multicellular level: clusters of coral polyps with algae inside them, colonies of cyanobacteria, symbiotic associations (ant and acacia) that can be loose or tight. Living things often have vague boundaries, and this is another reason why it's common to think about ecological systems using biomass rather than counts of individual organisms; in a lot of cases, it's not at all clear how the count of organisms would go. This applies to plants, corals, and many others.

Now let's turn to the mind. It seems, at least, that our minds also have pretty definite boundaries, tied to those of our bodies. If there is no afterlife, then when I die, that will be the end of my mind. Each of our minds is, it seems, "owned" by an individual person, and private to that person in many respects. This relationship might have some exceptions and qualifications. In chapter 6 we looked at the synchronization of brain activity across individuals. There I discussed some radical possibilities, including a literal merging of minds, but even those views would allow that one person's mind is mostly pretty distinct from another's. In rare and fascinating cases, physically conjoined twins seem to have a partial unity, or at least very unusual contact, across their two minds. "Split-brain" patients are another variant.

All these phenomena shake up our expectations in a useful way. And they lead to a question about how things might have been, or how they might be elsewhere. Could the mind, as a feature of life on Earth or another planet, have evolved in a massively spread-out and extended way, merging and blurring rather than being tightly associated with distinct individual bodies and forming individual selves? Is it an evolutionary accident that matters are the way they are here? I want to suggest that it's not much of an accident. The kind of individuality present in animal lives like ours has connections to the evolution of the mind, including felt experience, and the messages here relate to our boundaries in both space and time.

Here is a broad distinction between kinds of living things at the multicellular scale. I'll call it the distinction between *modular* and *unitary* kinds of life. These are standard terms in biology, though I am broadening them a little.

Modular organisms include oak trees, corals, fungi, and marine animals such as bryozoans that form colonies that look like moss or spaghetti. Unitary organisms include ourselves, ants, and octopuses. Colonies of bacteria, if we think of them as units, are also modular in the sense I have in mind. In all these modular cases, there's a collection of small repeated units that work together to some extent, and the details of how they are organized are flexible—it doesn't matter much whether an oak tree has ten branches or twenty, or how the spaghetti of a bryozoan colony is arranged. In a unitary organism, like us, the details matter more. People differ a lot, but they can't stay alive unless they have the same basic physical organization, with a heart connected to other organs in a certain way, and so on. As a unitary organism grows, its parts get bigger while keeping their general patterning. As a modular organism grows, it makes more copies of the small units ("modules") that comprise it.

It's the modular organisms that have vague boundaries, that merge into one another, that raise problems about whether we have one of them or many of them. Unitary organisms, like us, are usually easier to count.

These two kinds of life also behave differently. Modular animals can't move well, and there are no modular animals on land. A modular animal is a bit like a bee colony in which the bees are all stuck together, and each bee buds off new bees. It would be hard for such a being to fly, though perhaps it might walk. Unitary animals can act as wholes, if it makes sense to do so. They are more centralized in their organization, though with plenty of eccentricities and partial departures from this principle. (An octopus, again, is a unitary organism.)

Action is more elaborate in unitary organisms, and their bodies, as wholes, repeat over generations. When the form of an animal body is repeated in this way, it allows the steady evolution of behavior on that recurring platform. All this implies that complex behavior and nervous systems go with the unitary body organization. Given the link between those features and felt experience, it's no accident that felt experience is found in our kind of body. I don't mean just that *our* kind of felt experience goes with our kind of body, but that experience itself, given that minds are controllers of action, goes with our kind of body. Minds came to exist to enable action in animals with bodies of roughly our kind—unitary, well-bounded bodies.

That first set of ideas was about our shape and boundaries in space. There's also a link between this line of reasoning and how we are located in time. Some parts of what I'll say next have theoretical steps that can be questioned, but here is how the story could go.

A crucial fact about reproduction in animals like us is that we each emerge through a "bottleneck," a one-celled stage. Our bodies are rebuilt in each generation from scratch. This seems in some ways a waste. If you want to grow up and get big, why start out as small as you possibly could? But the one-celled stage has a lot of importance in individual development and in evolution. The rebuilding from scratch, the fresh start, enables a small mutation in the genes of one cell to ramify through all the cells as they divide to make the new organism. A small change can affect everything in the body.

In many animals, like corals, reproduction only occasionally goes through a bottleneck in this way; you can bud off copies of yourself for much of the time, and then occasionally take things back to one cell, often at a stage when sex enters the picture. When reproduction is sexual, the one-celled stage also has the role of uniting the genetic contributions of the two parents.

All this gives rise to something close to a discrete start to each life in animals like us. It also has consequences for aging and decline. For various reasons—competition, external risks and threats—it makes sense to grow up and become able to reproduce earlier rather than later, as long as you're able to do the job well. It's also worth taking on costs that come due later in life, in order to do well at earlier stages. For many animals, this means that a natural decline tends to happen after reproduction, on a rough but reliable schedule.

I don't want to oversimplify. The "immortal jellyfish," *Turritopsis*, reaches a particular stage in individual development and then turns around and runs backward toward a more juvenile state, and can turn around and run forward again. But there's a general pattern here: Animals who are capable of felt experience will be behaviorally complex and mobile, hence unitary in organization, reproducing through a one-celled bottleneck, and with a pretty definite beginning and end to life. It's no accident that felt experience is associated with our kind of body, and also with our kind of path from birth to death.

Might all this change in the future, with new technology? Even if the shape of our lives and deaths makes sense in this way, even if it's all biologically comprehensible, we can still step back and ask what we think of this arrangement. Should we just accept it? Or should we fight it, and try to take a different course?

Glass Tunnel to Open Air

Here are two philosophers on life and death. First, Derek Parfit, a classic eccentric academic figure, always in the same white shirts, making his way back and forth between universities in England and the United States, working on problems of the self, ethics, and identity. He died in 2017.

Parfit's interest in philosophy was prompted, he said, by "split-brain" cases of the kind discussed a few chapters ago. His 1984 book, *Reasons and Persons*, is a long exploration of how ethical questions and choices about action relate to what kind of beings we are, especially what kind of continuation we have over time. Suppose that an efficient future means of transportation is one where your body is annihilated on Earth and rebuilt, exactly and near-instantaneously, on Mars. But on one occasion, the machines do not work right and your original body is not destroyed, so you wake up in both places. I said "you" wake up, but how can it be *you* who does this, if two of you wake? Science fiction writers have explored these cases. Parfit worked through the philosophical side, especially questions about the self, very carefully. He seemed to have endless patience as a philosopher, forever revisiting the same questions and never tiring of them.

He ended up arguing for a kind of deflation, a destabilizing revision, of selfhood and identity. Some questions of the form "Who in this scenario is *me*?" do not have real answers. At each time, you have beliefs, memories, wishes, and projects. You pursue the projects that seem good ones at the time. Across different times, there can be links—continuities and connections—between the mind you have now and what happens in the "same" mind later on. Your physical body also normally continues, but Parfit thought that this fact is not very important compared to the psychological side, and whether we are looking at physical bodies or felt experiences, there is no deep fact of your *you*-ness, a you-ness that stretches through time as a permanent identity. There are just various psychological links, which your brain is responsible for, between experiences now and experiences later on. He also thought that the links of experience and memory that connect us at different times are all that we should care about when we reflect and make decisions; you shouldn't worry about how the decisions you make now will affect some definite future *you*. In unusual cases, like the teletransportation case I mentioned above, a single mind that exists now might have strong mental continuities to more than one mind in the future. Fine. Don't worry about which one is really you. It doesn't matter.

Thinking all this through, Parfit came to see survival and death differently. He encountered a kind of freeing, or opening up, and found himself seeing death as less bad:

> When I believed that my existence was such a further fact, I seemed imprisoned in myself. My life seemed like a glass tunnel, through which I was moving faster every year, and at the end of which there was darkness. When I changed my view, the walls of my glass tunnel disappeared. I now live in the open air. There is still a difference between my life and the lives of other people, but the difference is less. Other people are closer. I am less concerned

about the rest of my own life, and more concerned about the lives of others.

The "further fact" he refers to at the start of the passage is the idea that there is a definite identity, a fundamental Parfitness, underlying all the mental changes that might take place. Giving up a belief of this kind, which Parfit did because of arguments, not because of how he wanted to feel, led to a kind of peace.

Thomas Nagel is another philosopher who has written about death, immortality, and what it is to have, or be, a self. Nagel has also been willing to go against trends in philosophy that have taken many of us down hardheaded, reductionist roads; he has long been suspicious of all that.

Nagel opposes Parfit's view of survival and death entirely. He rejects Parfit's view of what the facts are in this area, insisting that there *does* have to be a deeper fact about the continuing identity that each of us has over time. And he writes that if he did agree with Parfit's view of what a person is, rather than finding Parfit's sense of freedom, he'd probably find it depressing:

> [Death] is a great curse, and if we truly face it nothing can make it palatable except the knowledge that by dying we can prevent a greater evil. Otherwise, given the simple choice between living for another week and dying in five minutes I would always choose to live for another week; and by a version of mathematical induction I would be glad to live forever.

Mathematical induction works like this: If you have a series of things that have an order to them (first, second, third . . .), then even if the series is infinite, you can sometimes prove that all of them have some notable feature. You do it by showing that the first one in the series has the feature, and then showing that if any one in the series has it, then the next one does, too. That is enough to show that they all do, even if their number is infinite. This is an "induction" in a sense, but not in the sense where inductions are always uncertain and provisional. Here Nagel imagines being asked, over and over again, whether he wants to go on. He does want to now, and he thinks that at every later stage, he'd always choose to go on for a bit longer (unless going on was awful in some particular way). Because he wants to go on now, and thinks he will always want to go on each time the choice arises, he must want to live forever.

One reply to this argument applies an idea from another philosopher, Bernard Williams. If you are looking at choices way off in the distant future, even if you are sure that in some sense it's still *you* making this choice, that person will probably be very psychologically different from you now. Just about any amount of change could happen along the way. This observation might be seen as questioning the step where Nagel says he knows that at each stage he will choose to go on: Who knows what he'll choose? Or, and this is closer to what Williams had in mind: Why does it seem relevant to Nagel now that this future person, with a very different mind, would make a particular choice? After a long time and lots of psychological change, what is the practical difference between the chooser being Nagel and being someone else, who might make their own choice whether to continue on?

Like Parfit, I doubt that the kind of deeper sameness of a person over time that Nagel believes in is real, and I agree that this recognition can change our view of survival and mortality. Something akin or allied to Parfit's attitude might also be reached by zooming out and thinking about the biological side of things, especially the way organisms and their minds come and go on Earth. In a way, the message here is different; Parfit's change of perspective came through a loosening of ties between the stages making up a single "self." The message I've been trying to get across is not one that proceeds first by fragmenting us, but one that points directly at connection—at our material continuity and kinship with the rest of life on Earth, and the significance of turnover, the coming and going of individuals.

How do these reflections relate to the possibility of an endless continuation of one's mental life and experiences enabled through technology? We should set aside the idea of literally "endless" continuation, as events at the scale of the universe as a whole might not allow that. But we can certainly think about lives that run for several millions of years without running into issues of that kind. Then there are a number of scenarios to consider, including some in which a person takes up scarce resources each time they go on for another century, and some where they do not.

Suppose first that whenever you choose to go on, Nagel-style, you are choosing to take up a "slot" rather than make space for a new arrival. Do you always want to go on? I don't. What if there was no exclusion of others by your own continuation? Your mind is uploaded as software, and the computing that keeps you going is cheap, using a huge solar array. A great many of us can be up there in the machines at once, and you are not squeezing anyone out.

First, I do not think of this as an easy supposition, a nearby possibility, in the way that many people do. I don't think our minds could be transformed into bits of software that could be run on a suitable machine indefinitely. In order for your, or anyone else's, mind to continue on, the right biology has to be in place. The view of consciousness sketched in chapter 6 has this consequence.

Even if something like this continuation scenario is possible, some versions of it seem rather empty to me. If I lack a body materially involved in the affairs of the world, a great deal would be missing. On the other hand, social engagement might continue, at least in some manner. You could be with your partner forever, if they'll have you.

At several points in the discussion so far, I have imagined that one person's endless continuation would squeeze out the possibility of other lives. But the human population may peak and decline before long, due to the "demographic transition" taking place in more and more countries of the world (a drop in birth rates due to economic development and a freeing of women from traditional roles). Perhaps a materially based immortality would have none of those imagined costs to others, after all?

If human numbers dropped enough, my view of immortality (or a dramatically extended life) might indeed shift. I might start to worry about losing the human project and see a need to stretch each life out as far as possible. When I say this, I assume in this scenario that we have started to do better with our care of the Earth, in ways discussed at the end of the previous chapter. But whether we imagine a future with a great many humans or fewer of them, I would rather retain a world with turnover, with new lives, not one where the same individuals go on and on and on. In nearly all cases, I would want to give up my place, hand on the baton, myself.

I understand the point of thinking through the more far-fetched scenarios—the endless, disembodied, cost-free mental continuations. I can vaguely imagine a completely different physical basis for my existence, and then I might see the idea of turnover and endings differently. I might then want something more like what Nagel wants. But we can also think about our situation in a more realistic way, with our physical nature on board. Here we treat our minds not as barely housed, floating, ghost-like beings, but as parts of the material world as a whole, embedded in evolution and the Earth's development. When we see our nature in this way, you *might* still take on an attitude of total resistance to mortality, but you might instead find yourself at home in this coming and going, this coming onto the scene and departing from it. It's not just that thinking through the biological side of our existence shows that it would have been hard to have things any other way, and this might make acceptance of our lot easier. That's not what I have in mind. Rather, this coming and going is part of the Earth's history, with all its creative character. I identify with that process, including the turnover and renewal, the flow of new arrivals who then depart and leave room for more.

At the very start of this book is an epigraph from a poem by Walt Whitman. The poem is a reflection on death and renewal, written during the US Civil War. Whitman worked, on the Union side, as a volunteer nurse. His collection of poems about the war, *Drum-Taps*, was published in 1865, just after the conflict ended. The Whitman epigraph is an encapsulation of some central themes of this book: turnover, continuity, atoms reused, making their way round a cycle and into new life.

Some parts of the poem were left out of my epigraph. (The full text is in an endnote.) The poem's aesthetic includes an affection, on the part of the "Mother of All," for death—"O my dead, an aroma sweet!" This is not just an affection for the dead men, something that is also part of the poem—"my young men's beautiful bodies." Beyond this, he writes of "sweet death" itself. I didn't want that idea in the epigraph. One can have awe at the renewal that Whitman describes without this sensual attraction to death.

Whitman also tried to have some things both ways; he seems to have had a hankering for personal, spiritual immortality despite his appreciation for turnover and renewal: "without immortality all would be sham and sport of the most tragic nature." He said that not in a poem, but in conversation with his biographer Horace Traubel. Regardless of what Whitman himself thought (and one recalls his famous comment about containing multitudes), there's no need to try to have this both ways. Why must mortality and renewal, the ongoing creation of new individuals with their new beauty, involve a sham? As Whitman expressed in the poem, one can appreciate and celebrate these transformations—"let not an atom be lost!" One can feel an identification with the processes characteristic of our enlivened Earth. Those processes include, for beings like us, lives that take the form of a journey, being brought into existence by nature's energies and then dissolving back into them, as others have before.

End and Beginning

Most of 2022 was a hopeless time for scuba diving all over my usual sites on the east coast of Australia. It was a year of torrential rain, floods, and more. One day I went down to Cabbage Tree Bay, just north of Sydney, not to dive but to see some friends. This bay was the site of many of the meetings with animals, especially octopuses and cuttlefish, that led to the writing of the trio of books of which this is the third. This is where I began to think about the lives and minds of animals far from us in their evolutionary path.

I walked down the hill. To my surprise, the water, having recently been dull green, was sparkling, clear, and calm. Faint ripples at the surface seemed to hide a world of life below. A cormorant, an air/sea traveler, was sunning on the rocks between fishing expeditions. I had no scuba gear with me, but in the late afternoon I was able to get hold of my wife's snorkeling mask, a too-small wetsuit vest, and an old camera setup I'd used years ago when working on the book *Other Minds*.

I swam out, and encountered giant cuttlefish right away. No matter how often I have seen then, I am always amazed by these eight-armed, color-changing, spaceship-like creatures. Big males were touring and displaying. I followed them up and down the shore, watching the long, whole-body stretches and the colors, all the shifting reds and oranges. It was a Sunday, and the water was full of people. I was delighted that even with all the geared-up free-divers, wary tourists, young kids, and startled passing swimmers, not one person bothered the cuttlefish. A bemused-looking but untroubled animal was being visited for a while, at a good distance, by five or six different snorkelers. The animals were treated with complete respect by everyone I saw, and I think with a good deal of awe, too.

There we were, living on Earth, all ages from tanned old locals to young children first encountering the sea. The sanctuary, Cabbage Tree Bay, had been established about twenty years earlier, a small reserve that has been almost miraculously successful in bringing sea life back and providing animals a home.

I followed a few of the cuttlefish back and forth along the rocks, watching them change their colors for a bit over an hour, until I was freezing in the too-small vest. I then stayed with one as he tucked in his arms and swam away from the crowded area near the seawater pool, out through the reef, jetting backward like a relaxed and eccentric missile. With no one but me following, he headed out to sea.

The sand soon dropped away. I could see a few scattered rocks below. The cuttlefish was in the middle of the water column, still swimming backward.

After a while, I put my head up to look around in the gentle slosh of waves. We were farther out than I had thought. We were where the Pacific began, with the whale sharks and mantas, all the beasts below. I waved goodbye to the disappearing cuttlefish, turned, and swam in.

NOTES

This book has two sets of endnotes. The notes below contain basic references to some of the scientific and philosophical work that informed this book, along with comments and reflections. The other set of notes is online, here: https://petergodfreysmith.com/living-on-earth-online-notes. Those notes have additional references and go further on some philosophical and scientific paths. The online notes include all the material in the briefer notes and give full citation information for journal articles and books, including internet links. Below, journal articles are referenced with just the journal and the year.

1. SHARK BAY

3 *Sometime around 3 billion years ago*: My early chapters have been informed often by Tim Lenton and Andrew Watson's book *Revolutions That Made the Earth* (2011). For cyanobacteria, see Patricia Sánchez-Baracaldo and Tanai Cardona, "On the Origin of Oxygenic Photosynthesis and Cyanobacteria," *New Phytologist*, 2020.

7 *Below that level, you will be poisoned by oxygen itself*: As you descend, the oxygen is not chemically concentrated, but each breath taken at depth brings in more of everything, including more oxygen, cramming it into your body. Some of what comes in under pressure in this way does not do too much in larger doses, but oxygen does, because of those "oxygen radicals."

2. EARTH ENLIVENED

17 *The age of the universe*: Unsurprisingly, there's some controversy. NASA's number is about 13.8 billion. https://lambda.gsfc.nasa.gov/education/graphic_history/age.html.

18 *Animals might be 650 million years old or so*: Here, as in other cases discussed in this book, there's a gap between estimates based on fossils and those based on

molecular genetic data. In the case of animals, the first fossils are around 575 million years old, while estimates of their origin based on molecular genetics stretch back to 800 million years ago, or older. Some of my correspondents are becoming more skeptical about molecular genetic estimates. The dates I use in this book tend to be compromises. For the animal case, see Ross Anderson et al., "Fossilisation Processes and Our Reading of Animal Antiquity," *Trends in Ecology and Evolution*, 2023.

19 *One setting in which this might get started*: See Eugene Koonin and William Martin, "On the Origin of Genomes and Cells Within Inorganic Compartments," *Trends in Genetics*, 2005.

19 *Darwin imagined a warm pond as the site*: See Cairns-Smith, *Seven Clues to the Origin of Life: A Scientific Detective Story* (1985). The Darwin speculation is in a letter to Joseph Hooker, 1871.

20 *The choice between the origin stories I compared just now*: For a discussion of "metabolism first" and "replicator first" scenarios, see Freeman Dyson, *Origins of Life* (2nd ed., 2010).

20 *the "century of the gene," as the historian of science Evelyn Fox Keller*: See her book *The Century of the Gene* (2002).

22 *One place to see this is a coral reef*: Here I draw on J. Scott Turner's book *The Extended Organism* (2000).

22 *For Bohr, complementary properties of an object*: See, for example, his "Natural Philosophy and Human Cultures," *Nature*, 1939, which is discussed in Henry Folse's "Niels Bohr, Complementarity, and Realism," *PSA: Proceedings of the Biennial Meeting of the Philosophy of Science Association*, 1986.

23 *I am sitting out in the garden*: This is another area where I was helped by Lenton and Watson's *Revolutions* book, and by discussion with Jochen Brocks.

24 *Andrew Knoll, a Harvard biologist*: See Knoll's "The Geological Consequences of Evolution," *Geobiology*, 2003.

24 *James Barber, who admittedly worked for much*: See Barber, "A Mechanism for Water Splitting and Oxygen Production in Photosynthesis," *Nature Plants*, 2017.

25 *The light-harvesting molecules in bacteria and plants*: See Minik Rosen et al., "The Rise of Continents—An Essay on the Geologic Consequences of Photosynthesis," *Palaeogeography, Palaeoclimatology, Palaeoecology*, 2006.

26 *this change was still important enough to be called "The Great Oxygenation"*: See Lenton and Watson, *Revolutions* (though they call it, as some do, the Great Oxidation). The early stages may have seen an "oxygen overshoot" that briefly took the level much higher. This is still controversial. Here, and in other places in this chapter, I have been helped by Andrew Knoll and Jochen Brocks.

26 *New kinds of minerals*: See Robert Hazen et al., "Mineral Evolution," *American Mineralogist*, 2008.

27 *The rainforests are the lungs of the Earth*: For clarification of all this, see Scott Denning, "Amazon Fires Are Destructive, but They Aren't Depleting Earth's Oxygen Supply," *The Conversation*, August 26, 2019. Another article along similar lines is Jean-Pierre Gattuso et al., "Humans Will Always Have Oxygen to Breathe, but We Can't Say the Same for Ocean Life," *The Conversation*, August 12, 2021. They give different numbers for thought experiments where photo-

synthesis instantly ends and we have to keep breathing. The Gattuso article says we'd be okay for millennia, the Denning article for millions of years. They have different scenarios in mind. I continue along this path in the online notes.

28 *This slower "inorganic" carbon cycle*: See James Kasting, "The Goldilocks Planet? How Silicate Weathering Maintains Earth 'Just Right,'" *Elements*, 2019.

30 *Some corals have also been found with cyanobacteria*: See Michael Lesser et al., "Discovery of Nitrogen-Fixing Cyanobacteria in Corals," *Science*, 2004.

31 *As oxygen levels increased*: See Douglas Fox, "What Sparked the Cambrian Explosion?," *Nature*, 2016.

32 *We are also a* material continuation: In philosophy, Jim Griesemer is the person responsible for pressing the importance of this point. See especially his "The Informational Gene and the Substantial Body: On the Generalization of Evolutionary Theory by Abstraction," *Poznan Studies in the Philosophy of the Sciences and the Humanities*, 2005.

32 *Back in the 1970s, James Lovelock and Lynn Margulis*: See Lovelock and Margulis, "Atmospheric Homeostasis by and for the Biosphere: The Gaia Hypothesis," *Tellus*, 1974, and Lovelock's *Gaia: A New Look at Life on Earth* (1979).

33 *it was Margulis who rescued this idea*: Her original paper, published under the name Lynn Sagan, is "On the Origin of Mitosing Cells," *Journal of Theoretical Biology*, 1967.

34 *Ford Doolittle, one of the early critics of Gaia*: See Doolittle's "Is Nature Really Motherly?," *The CoEvolution Quarterly*, 1981.

34 *Although salt water is in many ways friendly*: For the saltiness of Martian water, see Nicholas Tosca et al., "Water Activity and the Challenge for Life on Early Mars," *Science*, 2008.

35 *Lovelock wondered whether the Great Barrier Reef*: See *Gaia*, chapter 6. Lovelock said in this book that 6 percent is an upper limit for almost all organisms, but this was perhaps an exaggeration. The water around the stromatolites at Shark Bay is apparently around 6 percent salinity, and there's quite a lot of life there (including the fish I watched). Ordinary seawater is around 3.5 percent. See the online notes for more detail.

35 *The biologists David Queller and Joan Strassmann*: Queller and Strassmann, "Beyond Society: The Evolution of Organismality," *Philosophical Transactions of the Royal Society B*, 2009.

36 *These acacias build living quarters*: I discuss these cases in "Agents and Acacias: Replies to Dennett, Sterelny, and Queller," *Biology and Philosophy*, 2011.

37 *That led to objections from evolutionary biologists*: See Doolittle's "Is Nature Really Motherly?" and Richard Dawkins, *The Extended Phenotype* (1982).

39 *Talk of Gaia invites us to think the Earth will* take care of itself: Here's another point along the same lines. The Earth does seem to have a good amount of life-friendly feedback in its processes. If the Earth is not like an organism, then the existence of one feedback process of this kind gives us no reason to expect another. There's no reason why there should be a general pattern. If the Earth is organism-like, then it has been shaped to have a general capacity for self-maintenance, to some extent. Then we *should* expect a pattern—not an exceptionless one, probably one with many gaps, but this is the sort of thing we'd expect to see.

39 *Sometimes people just want to use talk of Gaia*: For a simple discussion of "weak" versus "strong," see Ian Enting's "Gaia Theory: Is It Science Yet?," *The Conversation*, February 12, 2012. For versions of Gaia, see also Tim Lenton and David Wilkinson, "Developing the Gaia Theory: A Response to the Criticisms of Kirchner and Volk," *Climatic Change*, 2003. I mentioned Ford Doolittle earlier, as a Gaia critic. Doolittle has been rethinking the question and defends the possibility of Darwinizing Gaia, partly through selection processes based on survival or persistence. Doolittle has a somewhat organism-like way of thinking about Gaia. See his "Making Evolutionary Sense of Gaia," *Trends in Ecology and Evolution*, 2019.

On the other side, I've seen scientists keep the "Gaia" term around as a nod to Lovelock and the broadening of perspective that he introduced, even if they reject anything like an Earth-as-organism view.

40 *In this case, when conditions are warmer*: For these feedback processes, see Lenton's book *Earth System Science: A Very Short Introduction* (2016). For the effects of life on weathering, see David Schwartzman and Tyler Volk, "Biotic Enhancement of Weathering and the Habitability of Earth," *Nature*, 1989.

41 *How about the salt in the oceans?*: Here I draw on Eelco Rohling, *The Oceans: A Deep History* (2017). On the question of whether feedback is present, and the uncertainties, this passage is notable, from Stephanie Olson et al., "The Effect of Ocean Salinity on Climate and Its Implications for Earth's Habitability," *Geophysical Research Letters*, 2022: "The salinity evolution of Earth's ocean is not yet well constrained, but constant salinity through time would be a notable coincidence or imply some currently unknown feedback." I don't think people believe salinity was constant, but it might have been kept in a fairly narrow range.

42 *Much of it was probably brought in on asteroids*: See Lenton and Watson, *Revolutions*. Rohling, in *The Oceans*, views this as less clear, as a fair bit of water might have been in place when the planet formed.

44 *an event like a flow of adrenaline has a purpose*: This example is used often by Ruth Millikan, in her classic book *Language, Thought, and Other Biological Categories* (1984).

45 *the American philosopher Larry Wright*: See his *Teleological Explanations* (1976). Wright is the main source for me here; Millikan's *Language, Thought, and Other Biological Categories* is also important. The broad way I am applying these concepts is reminiscent of Daniel Dennett's concept of a "design stance," but I see his treatment of these ideas as more instrumentalist. For Dennett, the language of goals and functions provides an interpretive stance, a way of seeing complex phenomena that is justified if it helps us discern patterns. The framework doesn't have to be understood in terms of a definite set of mechanisms. See his *Darwin's Dangerous Idea* (1995).

47 *This rehabilitation does not carry over*: In a traditional way of using teleological concepts, the function of something is what it is *supposed* to do, and if it does not have that effect, something has gone *wrong*. This link might be seen as a bridge to a moral theory. I am not endorsing inferences of that kind at all.

48 *we can find borderline cases*: Some of these borderline cases were discussed as problems for Wright's analysis of biological functions—see Chris Boorse,

"Wright on Functions," *Philosophical Review*, 1976. They were seen as problems because Wright seemed to be committed to saying that biological functions were present in cases where they appear to be absent. I discussed this as a problem in one of my first papers, "A Modern History Theory of Functions," *Noûs*, 1994. I wish I'd not approached these interesting cases in this way. It was an opportunity to explore the borderline and marginal cases in themselves, rather than worrying about how they are categorized.

49   *conversations with the evolutionary theorist William Hamilton*: See Lenton et al., "Selection for Gaia Across Multiple Scales," *Trends in Ecology and Evolution*, 2018.

50   *The possible snowball Earth events were rare*: In the more powerful kinds of learning by trial and error, a learner adds improvements in stages while keeping the good elements of what they had. The snowball Earth events seem more like a crash plus a new roll of the dice—not with respect to features that make for individual advantage, but those that are helpful to life as a whole. I explore this further in the online notes.

3. THE FOREST

51   *The young Charles Darwin*: The account is in his *Journal of Researches*, known also as *The Voyage of the Beagle*. This wording is from the 1845 second edition. The 1839 first edition (*Journal and Remarks*) is very similar in the quoted "bold sea-coast" passage, but does not have the geological speculations.

52   *central to the work of Charles Lyell*: The crucial work was his *Principles of Geology: Being an Attempt to Explain the Former Changes of the Earth's Surface, by Reference to Causes Now in Operation*, 3 volumes (1830–33). Darwin dedicated the second edition of his *Beagle* book to Lyell.

52   *the geologist Charles Wilkinson hypothesized*: See J. L. Pickett and J. D. Alder, *Layers of Time: The Blue Mountains and Their Geology* (1997), and J. Milne Curran, *The Geology of Sydney and the Blue Mountains: A Popular Introduction to the Study of Geology* (1899). Darwin: "To attribute these hollows to the present alluvial action would be preposterous," *Voyage of the Beagle*, second edition, chapter 19.

53   *Ted Hughes, in his poem "Sugar Loaf"*: Published as "Sugar-loaf" in *The Atlantic*, 1962, and as "Sugar Loaf" in *Wodwo*, 1967.

53   *The Bark-Palaces We Call Plants*: "Mayer of Bonn, basing his theory upon molecular motions, considers the smallest granules of the cell-contents as individuals possessing animal life (biospheres) which build up plants for their dwellings. 'Like hamadryads these sensitive monads inhabit the secret halls of the bark-palaces we call plants, and here silently hold their dances and celebrate their orgies.'" Alexander Braun, *The Vegetable Individual, in Its Relation to Species* (translated by C. F. Stone, 1855).

53   *A forest of this kind*: See Graeme Lloyd et al., "Dinosaurs and the Cretaceous Terrestrial Revolution," *Proceedings of the Royal Society B*, 2008; Jose Barba-Montoya et al., "Constraining Uncertainty in the Timescale of Angiosperm Evolution and the Veracity of a Cretaceous Terrestrial Revolution," *New Phytologist*, 2018.

54   *Land plants arose from colonies*: See Karl Niklas, *The Evolutionary Biology of Plants* (1997), and Tais Dahl and Susanne Arens, "The Impacts of Land Plant

Evolution on Earth's Climate and Oxygenation State—An Interdisciplinary Review," *Chemical Geology*, 2020.

54 *A new group, flowering plants*: The evolutionary line that led to flowering plants probably branched off from others well before this, though the date is controversial. For one discussion, see Daniele Silvestro et al., "Fossil Data Support a Pre-Cretaceous Origin of Flowering Plants," *Nature Ecology and Evolution*, 2021.

55 *Insects are sprinkled through the fossil record*: Dates using molecular genetics push the origin of insects back to around 479 million years ago, but the fossil record starts much later. See Bernhard Misof et al., "Phylogenomics Resolves the Timing and Pattern of Insect Evolution," *Science*, 2014.

55 *something like 85 percent of species*: See Geerat Vermeij and Richard Grosberg, "The Great Divergence: When Did Diversity on Land Exceed That in the Sea?," *Integrative and Comparative Biology*, 2010. Eighty-five percent is their lower estimate; it could be as high as 95 percent. This number does not include microbes.

56 *Rivers, however, are not just inevitable consequences*: Apparently the fossil record shows quite a dramatic effect on river shape of the evolution of plants— see Neil Davies and Martin Gibling, "Paleozoic Vegetation and the Siluro-Devonian Rise of Fluvial Lateral Accretion Sets," *Geology*, 2010, and the more recent Alessandro Ielpi et al., "The Impact of Vegetation on Meandering Rivers," *Nature Reviews Earth and Environment*, 2022. Thanks to Mark Westoby for comments on this. Soil, too, was largely a product of plants themselves, along with fungi.

57 *This list is not supposed to cover everything*: What about drinking at a water hole? I include that as feeding. I leave out "elimination" behaviors, such as defecation, and also some self-directed behaviors such as grooming and cleaning oneself. Wound tending is important in other contexts; it is evidence for felt pain. I am trying to keep the list as simple as I can, in order to focus on some categories that matter most to the themes of this book. As will be evident, I don't think "four Fs" summaries suffice.

59 *All of these forms of action are probably very old*: For building by unicellular organisms, see Mike Hansell's *Built by Animals* (2009) on *Difflugia coronata*. The case I am not sure about, in unicellular organisms, is action with the goal of information gathering. There are cases where protists hunt in a way that is informationally efficient, sampling the environment (see Scott Coyle et al., "Coupled Active Systems Encode an Emergent Hunting Behavior in the Unicellular Predator *Lacrymaria olor*," *Current Biology*, 2019). This is not the same as acting with the sole or main purpose of information gathering. But perhaps there is a case of this kind.

59 *Now a cell can crawl, swim quickly*: Although a cytoskeleton with this sort of power is usually seen as a eukaryotic innovation, it, too, has precursors. The Archaea are a bacteria-like group of organisms, and a rare variety called the Asgard archaea have an internal skeleton that is similar to the ones within cells like ours. These archaea are seen with long, tentacle-like projections coming out from their bodies. See Thiago Rodrigues-Oliveira et al., "Actin Cytoskeleton and Complex Cell Architecture in an Asgard Archaeon," *Nature*, 2023.

Bacteria do have a form of cytoskeleton. In addition, engulfing is not wholly absent in bacteria: see Takashi Shiratori et al., "Phagocytosis-Like Cell Engulfment by a Planctomycete Bacterium," *Nature Communications*, 2019.

59 *The term "niche construction"*: See John Odling-Smee, Kevin Lala, and Marcus Feldman, *Niche Construction: The Neglected Process in Evolution* (2003).

60 *A few small worms may have hunted*: I discuss this in more detail in *Metazoa*, chapter 3. See James Gehling and Mary Droser, "Ediacaran Scavenging as a Prelude to Predation," *Emerging Topics in Life Sciences*, 2018.

60 *the British biologist Nicholas Butterfield*: See his "Animals and the Invention of the Phanerozoic Earth System," *Trends in Ecology and Evolution*, 2011.

61 *The phrase "ecosystem engineer"*: See Clive Jones, John Lawton, and Moshe Shachak, "Organisms as Ecosystem Engineers," *Oikos*, 1994.

61 *Earthworms, present-day descendants*: See Renée-Claire Le Bayon et al., "Earthworms as Ecosystem Engineers: A Review," in *Earthworms: Types, Roles and Research* (edited by Clayton Horton, 2017).

63 *Action is different on land and in the sea*: See Geerat Vermeij, "How the Land Became the Locus of Major Evolutionary Innovations," *Current Biology*, 2017. I discussed these ideas in *Metazoa*, chapter 9.

63 *The novelist Arthur C. Clarke, of* 2001: A Space Odyssey, *said this*: This is in his 1956 book *The Coast of Coral* and various biographies (e.g., https://www.imdb .com/). The screenplay of *2001: A Space Odyssey* was written by director Stanley Kubrick and Clarke, based on some Clarke stories, especially "The Sentinel" (1951).

64 *Early animals in the sea, and their*: There's more on this in *Metazoa*, chapter 3. When I say there are no radially symmetrical animals on land, I exclude anemones who live in the intertidal zone.

64 *Termites don't usually live inside the towers*: See Turner's *The Extended Organism* and Lisa Margonelli's *Underbug: An Obsessive Tale of Termites and Technology* (2018).

64 *There are tube-building worms, and shrimp-like animals*: For the amphipods, see Nikolai Neretin, Anna Zhadan, and Alexander Tzetlin, "Aspects of Mast Building and the Fine Structure of 'Amphipod Silk' Glands in *Dyopedos bispinis* (Amphipoda, Dulichiidae)," *Contributions to Zoology*, 2017. For the pistol shrimp, see Hansell's *Built by Animals* and references he gives (also my online notes). The pufferfish are the white-spotted pufferfish (*Torquigener albomaculosus*); see Hisoshi Kawase et al., "Spawning Behavior and Paternal Egg Care in a Circular Structure Constructed by Pufferfish, *Torquigener albomaculosus* (Pisces: Tetraodontidae)," *Bulletin of Marine Science*, 2015.

65 *At "Octopolis" and "Octlantis"*: These sites are described in detail in my books *Other Minds* and *Metazoa*. Storms and floods have affected the bay where the sites are located in recent years. When I last visited Octopolis, in early 2023, it was very quiet, with only a couple of octopuses present. Octlantis was livelier on that trip, with five octopuses, though well below the maximum we've seen there, which is around fifteen.

66 *A tunicate or sea squirt called* Oikopleura: See Hansell, *Built by Animals*.

68 *Why do I think there were tunnels?*: See Takeshi Takegaki and Akinobu Nakazono, "The Role of Mounds in Promoting Water-Exchange in the Egg-

Tending Burrows of Monogamous Goby, *Valenciennea longipinnis* (Lay et Bennett)," *Journal of Experimental Marine Biology and Ecology*, 2000.

69 *The feature that is basic to tool use*: In my earlier discussion of categories of action, I said that often the goals of an action form chains—you might move in order to interact with another person, and might do all that in order to make some change to the environment, and so on. I said that my categorization looks to the first goal, when there are chains like this. Why isn't the first goal, in some cases, the use of a tool? Then tool use could become a sixth element added to the earlier list. You might set things up like this, but I think the other way is also okay. I am treating tool use as how you might pursue another goal, rather than ever being a goal of its own.

70 *I learned of a wonderful case from David Scheel*: He sent this in an email.

70 *Chimps, bonobos, and crows are the most adept*: For the compound tool and "metatool" use of New Caledonian Crows, see Auguste von Bayern et al., "Compound Tool Construction by New Caledonian Crows," *Scientific Reports*, 2018, and Alex Taylor et al., "Spontaneous Metatool Use by New Caledonian Crows," *Current Biology*, 2007.

70 *The list of seagoing tool users is short*: For a review, see Janet Mann and Eric Patterson, "Tool Use by Aquatic Animals," *Philosophical Transactions of the Royal Society B*, 2013.
    Octopuses are on the list. Our study of projectile use by octopuses, first mentioned in *Other Minds*, is now published: Godfrey-Smith et al., "In the Line of Fire: Debris Throwing by Wild Octopuses," *PLOS ONE*, 2022. Another notable case is their carrying and assembling of half coconut shells for protection: see Julian Finn, Tom Tregenza, and Mark Norman, "Defensive Tool Use in a Coconut-Carrying Octopus," *Current Biology*, 2009.

72 *the neuroscientist and engineer Malcolm MacIver*: See Malcolm MacIver and Barbara Finlay, "The Neuroecology of the Water-to-Land Transition and the Evolution of the Vertebrate Brain," *Philosophical Transactions of the Royal Society B*, 2022, and other papers.

73 *Still, I think MacIver might be onto something*: With respect to differences between land-based and seagoing brains, another factor to consider is warm-bloodedness. Warm-bloodedness, which is seen in all the plan-using animals that MacIver discusses, makes for a higher-powered brain. You might say that animals have more need for a higher-powered brain on land, and this may well be true, but warm-bloodedness is also easier to achieve on land than it is in the sea. I looked at this in *Metazoa*, chapter 9.

77 *This picture has impressed a number of thinkers*: The framework was influenced by cybernetics, the mid-twentieth-century theory of control systems and feedback that fed into computer science and robotics. The theory was developed by William Powers. For a recent exposition and defense, see Timothy Carey, "Consciousness as Control and Controlled Perception—A Perspective," *Annals of Behavioral Science*, 2018.

78 *the "predictive processing" framework*: See Karl Friston, "The Free-Energy Principle: A Unified Brain Theory?," *Nature Reviews Neuroscience*, 2010; Andy Clark, *Surfing Uncertainty* (2015); and Anil Seth, *Being You* (2021).

78 *The main problem has been expressed*: This is discussed in lots of places; see Andy Clark's *Surfing Uncertainty*.

80 *Uexküll was a German-Estonian biologist*: A new book looks more closely at his political side: Gottfried Schnödl and Florian Sprenger, *Uexküll's Surroundings: Umwelt Theory and Right-Wing Thought* (translated by Michael Taylor and Wayne Yung, 2021).

82 *His work had a wide influence*: Heidegger praises him in *The Fundamental Concepts of Metaphysics: World, Finitude, Solitude* (lectures from 1929–30). There's also a mention of the *Umwelt* in *Being and Time*. He is discussed in Merleau-Ponty's second lecture course on nature at the Collège de France.

86 *The insect situation is sometimes referred to as the "insect apocalypse"*: For butterflies, see Martin Warren et al., "The Decline of Butterflies in Europe: Problems, Significance, and Possible Solutions," *PNAS*, 2021; for the windshield effect, see Anders Møller, "Parallel Declines in Abundance of Insects and Insectivorous Birds in Denmark Over 22 Years," *Ecology and Evolution*, 2019, and Damian Carrington, "Car 'Splatometer' Tests Reveal Huge Decline in Number of Insects," *The Guardian*, February 12, 2020. For the forests, see https://ourworldindata.org/deforestation.

4. ORPHEUS

89 *From the Rose-breasted Cockatoos (or Galahs)*: Ornithology seems to have a special tendency toward controversy (perhaps following the lead of the birds of the chapter opening), and this extends to naming and capitalization. Some say that because birds, unlike other animals, have official common names, it's apt to capitalize the first letters (https://ornithology.com/upper-case-bird-names/). Others reject this. I am following my publisher's preference.

90 *Their evolution began in the Jurassic*: Through here, I use Stephen Brusatte, Jingmai O'Connor, and Erich Jarvis, "The Origin and Diversification of Birds," *Current Biology*, 2015.

92 *Communication has borders*: A lot of this is discussed in Ronald Planer and Peter Godfrey-Smith, "Communication and Representation Understood as Sender–Receiver Coordination," *Mind and Language*, 2020. It gives citations to a large recent literature, which stems in part from Brian Skyrms's revival of David Lewis's model of conventional signaling (see Skyrms's *Signals*, 2010), and also from Ruth Millikan's *Language, Thought, and Other Biological Categories* (1984).

93 *Vervet monkeys, for example, give alarm calls to one another*: Robert Seyfarth, Dorothy Cheney, and Peter Marler, "Monkey Responses to Three Different Alarm Calls: Evidence of Predator Classification and Semantic Communication," *Science*, 1980.

94 *The idea that nearly anything could be used*: The classic discussion of arbitrariness is Ferdinand de Saussure's *Course in General Linguistics* (1916).

95 *bacteria use chemical communication*: See Steven Rutherford and Bonnie Bassler, "Bacterial Quorum Sensing: Its Role in Virulence and Possibilities for Its Control," *Cold Spring Harbor Perspectives in Medicine*, 2012. There are many papers on this topic.

95 *In the unusual circumstances of Octopolis and Octlantis*: See David Scheel, Peter Godfrey-Smith, and Matthew Lawrence, "Signal Use by Octopuses in Agonistic Interactions," *Current Biology*, 2021. This paper discusses the Nosferatu behavior, though not under that name.

98 *The earliest two operas that have survived*: These are *Euridice* by Jacopo Peri and Ottavio Rinuccini (1600), and *Orfeo* by Claudio Monteverdi and Alessandro Striggio (1607). Peri's 1597 *Dafne*, which is mostly lost, is sometimes regarded as the very first opera.

98 *The ornithologist Richard Prum uses the phrase*: I draw especially on his paper "Coevolutionary Aesthetics in Human and Biotic Artworlds," *Biology and Philosophy*, 2013, as well as his book *The Evolution of Beauty* (2017).

101 *Once we put insects, and their all-important relation*: Insect consciousness is no longer a fringe idea. See Andrew Barron and Colin Klein, "What Insects Can Tell Us About the Origins of Consciousness," *PNAS*, 2016, and Matilda Gibbons et al., "Motivational Trade-Offs and Modulation of Nociception in Bumblebees," *PNAS*, 2022.

101 *But now it is thought likely that the initial role of feathers*: This is in Brusatte, O'Connor, and Jarvis, "The Origin and Diversification of Birds," and many other papers.

102 *The colors in a coral reef*: See Jörg Wiedenmann and Cecilia D'Angelo, "Revealed: Why Some Corals Are More Colourful Than Others," *The Conversation*, January 30, 2015, and (a more technical version of the same work), John Gittins et al., "Fluorescent Protein-Mediated Colour Polymorphism in Reef Corals: Multicopy Genes Extend the Adaptation/Acclimatization Potential to Variable Light Environments," *Molecular Ecology*, 2015. Also Alya Salih et al., "Fluorescent Pigments in Corals Are Photoprotective," *Nature*, 2000.

Thanks to Meryl Larkin for help here. This site has more information: https://www.gbrbiology.com/knowledge-and-news/how-corals-get-their-colour/. It raises the possibility that some coral colors may be matched to fish vision, and that would qualify the claim that coral colors are not produced to be seen. See also Mikhail Matz, Justin Marshall, and Misha Vorobyev, "Are Corals Colorful?," *Photochemistry and Photobiology*, 2006.

103 *They form long-lasting bonds*: See Amanda Vincent and Laila Sadler, "Faithful Pair Bonds in Wild Seahorses, *Hippocampus whitei*," *Animal Behaviour*, 1995.

105 *the whole enormous branch of passerines*: This section draws often on Tim Low's excellent book *Where Song Began* (2014).

105 *One study found that even other* birds *can't always tell lyrebird counterfeits*: Anastasia Dalziell and Robert Magrath, "Fooling the Experts: Accurate Vocal Mimicry in the Song of the Superb Lyrebird, *Menura novaehollandiae*," *Animal Behaviour*, 2012. Females also call, and mimic; the function of their calls is less clear, but they may play a role in nest defense and competition between females for breeding territories. See Anastasia Dalziell and Justin Welbergen, "Elaborate Mimetic Vocal Displays by Female Superb Lyrebirds," *Frontiers in Ecology and Evolution*, 2016. The females I've heard also seem to sing more softly than males.

109 *The smaller cluster includes another group of birds*: This cluster also includes the treecreepers (not included in my tree diagram). These early branchings seem

to attract some controversy. I use Carl Oliveros et al., "Earth History and the Passerine Superradiation," *PNAS*, 2019.

109 *Male bowerbirds build a nest-like structure*: In this section I draw on some books by Clifford Frith and Dawn Frith: *Bowerbirds: Nature, Art and History* (2008) and (more academic) *The Bowerbirds* (2004).

Charles Darwin, during the visit to the Blue Mountains I described in chapter 3, observed Satin Bowerbirds, and they informed his realization of the importance of female choice in his theory of sexual selection.

111 *In the case of preferences for blue*: See Gerald Borgia, Ingrid Kaatz, and Richard Condit, "Flower Choice and Bower Decoration in the Satin Bowerbird *Ptilonorhynchus violaceus*: A Test of Hypotheses for the Evolution of Male Display," *Animal Behaviour*, 1987. Prum does not endorse this view.

I emailed some experts to ask about all this, and they were cautious—no clear pattern has emerged. Thanks to Gerald Borgia for the "far from civilization" comment about blue objects; I have only seen these bowers closer in. The Great Bowerbird I saw had some dark green ornaments.

111 *Jared Diamond, in the course of some intrepid work*: See his "Animal Art: Variation in Bower Decorating Style Among Male Bowerbirds *Amblyornis inornatus*," *PNAS*, 1986. See also Joah Madden, "Do Bowerbirds Exhibit Cultures?," *Animal Cognition*, 2008.

112 *Their courting behaviors seem to employ*: As birds can see into the ultraviolet part of the spectrum, and different parts of the male's body reflect differently, what looks to us like a pretty uniformly blue-black bird dancing in unusual ways might look more psychedelic to a female.

113 *Gerald Borgia, after studying the birds extensively*: "Why Do Bowerbirds Build Bowers?," *American Scientist*, 1995.

113 *Biology has seen a long-running and sometimes tense*: This debate is central to Prum's *The Evolution of Beauty*.

116 *In 1964, the lyrebirds down there*: See F. Norman Robinson and Sydney Curtis, "The Vocal Displays of the Lyrebirds (Menuridae)," *Emu—Austral Ornithology*, 1996. While on the topic of whipbirds: their whiplike sound has a standard reply call from a partner, a bit like a cheery wave. Sometimes a lyrebird will include the reply as well.

5. HUMAN BEING

120 *The group we visited on this first encounter*: These gorillas are in Volcanoes National Park, Rwanda. The online notes contain links to resources about the park, the Kwitonda and Igisha groups, and other material. These are the gorillas studied by Dian Fossey, as described in her *Gorillas in the Mist* (1983) and the movie of that name. The tour operation is impressive. Each gorilla group can be visited by one small human group once a day for one hour, maximum.

120 *Mammals arose back in dinosaur-dominated times*: See Steve Brusatte, *The Rise and Reign of the Mammals* (2023).

121 *One branch within primates is the great apes, or hominids*: See Sergio Almécija et al., "Fossil Apes and Human Evolution," *Science*, 2021.

122 *But sometime over 5 million years ago, a primate line made its way*: From here I start to make use of Joseph Henrich's book, *The Secret of Our Success* (2015).

122 *The primatologist Sarah Hrdy offers*: See her *Mothers and Others* (2009).
123 *Culture in this sense refers to the establishment and development*: As well as Henrich's book, see Robert Boyd and Peter Richerson's pioneering *Culture and the Evolutionary Process* (1985).
124 *For Sterelny, human societies continually rebuild*: As well as *The Evolved Apprentice* (2012), see Sterelny's *The Pleistocene Social Contract* (2021), which bears on later topics in this chapter.
125 *Until recently, researchers tended to think*: See Andrew Whiten, "Blind Alleys and Fruitful Pathways in the Comparative Study of Cultural Cognition," and the accompanying commentaries, *Physics of Life Reviews*, 2022. The Whiten paper is rather combative in tone, but the whole collection is valuable. For the bees, see especially Sylvain Alem et al., "Associative Mechanisms Allow for Social Learning and Cultural Transmission of String Pulling in an Insect," *PLOS Biology*, 2016.
125 *Is it due to brainpower, or perhaps a more cooperative*: The suggestion about cooperation is made by Sterelny in his commentary on the Whiten paper just above.
126 *Children often seem to have an eye out for transgressions*: For one of the original studies, see Marco Schmidt et al., "Eighteen-Month-Old Infants Correct Non-Conforming Actions by Others," *Infancy*, 2019. More research is described in the online notes. Cecilia Heyes is a critic of some of this work; see her "Rethinking Norm Psychology," *Perspectives on Psychological Science*, 2023.
129 *practices involving the detection and punishment of sorcery*: See Ron Planer and Kim Sterelny, "The Challenge of Sorcery," forthcoming.
130 *This view was championed by the American linguist Noam Chomsky*: See, for example, his *Rules and Representations* (1980).
130 *This has come to seem unlikely*: See especially Michael Tomasello, *Origins of Human Communication* (2008). See also Ron Planer and Kim Sterelny, *From Signal to Symbol* (2021).
132 *John Locke, in the late 1600s, saw language*: See Locke's *Essay Concerning Human Understanding* (1689).
133 *a phrase from the philosopher Josh Armstrong*: See his "Communication Before Communicative Intentions," *Noûs*, 2021.
133 *The first evidence of stone tools dates*: Through here I follow Henrich's *The Secret of Our Success*.
135 *The scale of Göbekli Tepe is substantial*: David Graeber and David Wengrow's fascinating book *The Dawn of Everything* (2021) has much to say about many of the topics of this chapter from this point onward.
136 *Discussion in Australia, where stereotypes*: Bruce Pascoe's *Dark Emu* (2014) has been an influential contribution to this discussion. Pascoe argues that some Aboriginal Australian groups farmed and lived in settled societies. In *Farmers or Hunter-Gatherers? The Dark Emu Debate* (2021), Peter Sutton and Keryn Walshe criticize the book, not to reassert an old view of Aboriginal Australian life as simple and "primitive," but to argue that "the old people" of Australia were mostly complex hunter-gatherers ("hunter-gatherers-plus").
136 *The political scientist James Scott's book*: This is his *Against the Grain: A Deep History of the Earliest States* (2017). Graeber and Wengrow's *The Dawn of*

Everything is an absorbing counterpoint to Scott's book, and Graeber and Wengrow discuss Scott near the end. They are skeptical about the causal story and the account of typical transitions that Scott offers, arguing, for example, that many early states were not notable for a rise in inequality. See the online notes for more detail. The view I outline here is somewhat Scott-ish, informed also by correspondence.

136 *when I first learned that, in old hunter-gatherer skeletons*: This was in Jared Diamond, *The Third Chimpanzee* (1991): "Corn, first domesticated in Central America thousands of years ago, became the basis of intensive farming in those valleys around AD 1000. Until then, Indian hunter-gatherers had skeletons 'so healthy it is somewhat discouraging to work with them,' as one paleopathologist complained. With the arrival of corn . . . [t]he number of cavities in an average adult's mouth jumped from fewer than one to nearly seven, and tooth loss and abscesses became rampant."

139 *Play that involves explicit pretense*: See Alison Gopnik, "What Good Comes from Pretending?," *The Wall Street Journal*, January 19, 2023. For primates, see Juan-Carlos Gómez, "The Evolution of Pretence: From Intentional Availability to Intentional Non-Existence," *Mind and Language*, 2008, and Tetsuro Matsuzawa, "Pretense in Chimpanzees," *Primates*, 2020.

141 *The outlines of Lévi-Strauss's sketch*: Here I draw on Olivier Morin's work, especially "The Piecemeal Evolution of Writing," *Lingue e Linguaggio*, 2022, and Olivier Morin, Piers Kelly, and James Winters, "Writing, Graphic Codes, and Asynchronous Communication," *Topics in Cognitive Science*, 2020. The suggestion about proper names and sound-based codes is from Morin.

142 *The "memory palace" or "method of loci"*: See Frances Yates, *The Art of Memory* (1966).

143 *An older tradition of memorization*: See David Reser et al., "Australian Aboriginal Techniques for Memorization: Translation into a Medical and Allied Health Education Setting," *PLOS ONE*, 2021. For memory skills in Aboriginal Australian societies and others, see Lynn Kelly, *Knowledge and Power in Prehistoric Societies* (2015). The message-stick technology is discussed in Piers Kelly, "Australian Message Sticks: Old Questions, New Directions," *Journal of Material Culture*, 2020.

145 *Written language is not just a combination of sender-receiver interaction and engineering*: This passage is from "Writing, Graphic Codes, and Asynchronous Communication," by Olivier Morin, Piers Kelly, and James Winters (*Topics in Cognitive Science*, 2020): "Writing systems are the only graphic codes that can rival the richness and versatility of spoken languages, while remaining sufficiently productive [that is, organized with smaller elements that can be recombined in many ways] to be learnable. The only way that writing achieves this is by encoding a natural language, working as a meta-code (so to speak)."

145 *The twentieth-century biologist Richard Lewontin*: The essay can be found in Richard Levins and Richard Lewontin, *The Dialectical Biologist* (1985). While on the topic of loops, Fred Keijzer, Gáspár Jékely, and I wrote about how general the phenomenon might be in "Reafference and the Origin of the Self in Early Nervous System Evolution," *Philosophical Transactions of the Royal Society B*, 2021. Another person who has written richly about them is the computer

scientist Douglas Hofstadter. A "strange loop," for Hofstadter, is one in which the viewer views themself, or a sentence is about itself, or there is some other self-directedness that has this mind-bending, head-over-heels character. (Hofstadter says that when he was young, he went to a store selling the first video cameras that sent an image to a screen in real time and was going to aim the camera at the screen itself, and was told: "No!" See his *I Am a Strange Loop* [2007].)

146 *The Greek philosopher Socrates*: Socrates's comments about writing appear in Plato's *Phaedrus*. Socrates and his ideas were also described in writing by the historian Xenophon and the playwright Aristophanes.

147 *Literacy, in particular, has significant effects*: See Stanislas Dehaene et al., "Illiterate to Literate: Behavioural and Cerebral Changes Induced by Reading Acquisition," *Nature Reviews Neuroscience*, 2015. See also Cecilia Heyes's book *Cognitive Gadgets* (2018), which emphasizes the many effects of culture on our brains.

148 *The French composer Olivier Messiaen wrote "Quartet for the End of Time"*: This was the first of Messiaen's works to engage with birdsong. Aspects of his dramatic recollection of the first performance in the prison camp have been questioned by others who were there (in relation to the condition of the instruments and size of the audience, for example). See Rebecca Rischin, *For the End of Time: The Story of the Messiaen Quartet* (2003).

148 *I'm reminded of a quote from an interview*: This is from Malcolm Knox, "After the Booker: Why Richard Flanagan Isn't Playing Safe," *Sydney Morning Herald*, September 22, 2017.

149 *Stephen Jay Gould imagined a "replaying of the tape"*: This is in Gould's *Wonderful Life* (1989). See also Simon Conway Morris, *The Crucible of Creation* (1998).

150 *In a variant of this story, Sterelny sees the formation*: See his *The Evolved Apprentice*.

151 *Another biologist, Antone Martinho-Truswell*: In his book, *The Parrot in the Mirror* (2022).

152 *Dolphins are large-brained animals*: See Ann Weaver and Stan Kuczaj, "Neither Toy nor Tool: Grass-Wearing Behavior Among Free-Ranging Bottlenose Dolphins in Western Florida," *International Journal of Comparative Psychology*, 2016.

155 *Octopuses have trouble with these sorts of things*: For an imaginative exploration of a change in course, see Ray Naylor's *The Mountain in the Sea* (2022).

155 *In his book* Built by Animals, *which was helpful to me*: This is in his first chapter.

156 *Contrast all this with our primate-style life*: Here I echo and modify a phrase from the philosopher Donald Williams, in "The Argument for Realism," *The Monist*, 1934, within a passage that was somewhat celebrated when I was a student. "Philosophy is not 'higher' and suprascientific. It is the lowest and grubbiest inquiry round the roots of things, and when it answers real questions about the world, it is and can only be an inductive science."

156 *In Greek myths and later reflection on them, especially in writers like Nietzsche*: See his *The Birth of Tragedy* (1872).

6. CONSCIOUSNESS

157 *There's something it feels like to be us*: This well-known formulation of the problem comes from Thomas Nagel, "What Is It Like to Be a Bat?," *Philosophical Review*, 1974.

158 *I won't give arguments*: For more detailed discussions, and some defenses, see *Metazoa*; "Gradualism and the Evolution of Experience," *Philosophical Topics*, 2020; and "Evolving Across the Explanatory Gap," *Philosophy, Theory, and Practice in Biology*, 2019.

158 *Nervous systems may have first arisen*: Fred Keijzer's work has influenced me here, and Fred Keijzer, Marc van Duijn, and Pamela Lyon, "What Nervous Systems Do: Early Evolution, Input–Output, and the Skin Brain Thesis," *Adaptive Behavior*, 2013. See also Gáspár Jékely, Fred Keijzer, and Peter Godfrey-Smith, "An Option Space for Early Neural Evolution," *Philosophical Transactions of the Royal Society B*, 2015.

159 *More of what goes on in our brains matters than that, most likely*: Here I have been influenced by Rosa Cao. See her "Multiple Realizability and the Spirit of Functionalism," *Synthese*, 2022. The views of Anil Seth and Ned Block are also related; see Seth's *Being You* (2021), and Block, "Comparing the Major Theories of Consciousness," in Michael Gazzaniga (ed.), *The Cognitive Neurosciences* (2009).

160 *An example is the oscillation in electrical activity*: There's more about this in *Metazoa*. Also see Wolf Singer, "Neuronal Oscillations: Unavoidable and Useful?," *European Journal of Neuroscience*, 2018.

160 *Some decades ago, Francis Crick (of DNA fame), Christof Koch, and others*: See Francis Crick and Christof Koch, "Towards a Neurobiological Theory of Consciousness," *Seminars in the Neurosciences*, 1990; and Lucia Melloni et al., "Synchronization of Neural Activity across Cortical Areas Correlates with Conscious Perception," *The Journal of Neuroscience*, 2007.

160 *The large-scale rhythmic patterns that Crick and Koch wrote about*: See, for example, Bruno van Swinderen, "The Remote Roots of Consciousness in Fruit-Fly Selective Attention?," *BioEssays*, 2005.

160 *Back in the 1960s, the neurobiologist L. M. "Mac" Passano*: See his "Primitive Nervous Systems," *PNAS*, 1963.

162 *This oscillatory activity in the brain*: See Singer's "Neuronal Oscillations: Unavoidable and Useful?"

164 *The situation is different with another technology that is developing very quickly*: One example of this work: Ranmal Samarasinghe et al., "Identification of Neural Oscillations and Epileptiform Changes in Human Brain Organoids," *Nature Neuroscience*, 2021.

165 *Rats make use of map-like representations*: See John O'Keefe and Lynn Nadel, *The Hippocampus as a Cognitive Map* (1978), and (among much recent work) H. Freyja Ólafsdóttir et al., "Hippocampal Place Cells Construct Reward Related Sequences Through Unexplored Space," *eLife*, 2015. For a philosophical discussion, see Nicholas Shea, *Representation in Cognitive Science* (2018).

166 *A 2022 paper found that crows could learn to generate "recursive" patterns*: See Diana Liao et al., "Recursive Sequence Generation in Crows," *Science Advances*, 2022.

166   *Stanislas Dehaene, a French neuroscientist*: The paper is Dehaene et al., "Symbols and Mental Programs: A Hypothesis About Human Singularity," *Trends in Cognitive Sciences*, 2022. The paper is about "human singularity"—"We suggest that humans owe their singularity to [internal] symbols." The crow paper in the note above may push back a little on this.

166   *Language, especially speech, is lateralized in our brains*: Through here I make use of work by Michael Gazzaniga, Lesley Rogers, and Giorgio Vallortigara. Here are a couple of papers (the online notes have more): Michael Gazzaniga, "Shifting Gears: Seeking New Approaches for Mind/Brain Mechanisms," *Annual Review of Psychology*, 2013; Lesley Rogers, "A Matter of Degree: Strength of Brain Asymmetry and Behaviour," *Symmetry*, 2017; Giorgio Vallortigara, Lesley Rogers, and Angelo Bisazza, "Possible Evolutionary Origins of Cognitive Brain Lateralization," *Brain Research Reviews*, 1999.

166   *I have used these remarkable cases to work through some puzzles*: In both *Other Minds*, chapter 5, and *Metazoa*, chapter 6.

167   *Some simple but striking work has been done*: See Victoria Bourne, "How Are Emotions Lateralised in the Brain? Contrasting Existing Hypotheses Using the Chimeric Faces Test," *Cognition and Emotion*, 2010. This paper has a good series of photos showing the effect, as well as a review of hypotheses.

169   *The presence of this highway seems to allow specialization*: See Michael Gazzaniga, "Cerebral Specialization and Interhemispheric Communication: Does the Corpus Callosum Enable the Human Condition?," *Brain*, 2000.

169   *In one experiment, a patient had the word "bell" shown*: This case is in Gazzaniga's "Cerebral Specialization and Interhemispheric Communication."

169   *In some further experiments, split-brain patients were shown*: See Elizabeth Phelps and Michael Gazzaniga, "Hemispheric Differences in Mnemonic Processing: The Effects of Left Hemisphere Interpretation," *Neuropsychologia*, 1992.

170   *People have come up with a number of evolutionary sequences*: As well as the Gazzaniga, Rogers, and Vallortigara work, see Iain McGilchrist, *The Master and His Emissary* (2009).

171   *An intriguing difference that bears on conscious experience*: See Rogers, "A Matter of Degree: Strength of Brain Asymmetry and Behaviour," *Symmetry*, 2017.

171   *In the memory experiments I mentioned a moment ago*: See Michael Miller and Michael Gazzaniga, "Creating False Memories for Visual Scenes," *Neuropsychologia*, 1998.

172   *What I have in mind is conscious thought*: Here we reach the territory of "dual system" views of cognition. See Daniel Kahneman, *Thinking, Fast and Slow* (2011).

173   *the French cognitive scientists Hugo Mercier and Dan Sperber*: See Mercier and Sperber, *The Enigma of Reason* (2017). I commented on an earlier version of their view in a note with Kritika Yegnashankaran. See our "Reasoning as Deliberative in Function but Dialogic in Structure and Origin," *Behavioral and Brain Sciences*, 2011.

173   *An example of an error we all tend to make is confirmation bias*: Mercier and Sperber argue that the phenomenon is a bit misdescribed with this term—it would be better called "myside bias" ("myside" as in *my side*).

174 *A related way in which language and culture*: See Daniel Dennett, "The Self as a Center of Narrative Gravity," in *Self and Consciousness* (edited by Frank Kessel et al., 1992), and Anil Seth, *Being You* (2021).

175 *Over thirty years ago, Jyotsna Vaid and Maharaj Singh wondered*: See their "Asymmetries in the Perception of Facial Affect: Is There an Influence of Reading Habits?," *Neuropsychologia*, 1989.

176 *On the other hand, a leftward bias in looking at faces*: See Kun Guo et al., "Left Gaze Bias in Humans, Rhesus Monkeys and Domestic Dogs," *Animal Cognition*, 2009. See also Lesley Rogers, Giorgio Vallortigara, and Richard Andrew, *Divided Brains: The Biology and Behaviour of Brain Asymmetries* (2012).

176 *Giorgio Vallortigara, writing about animals*: "Comparative Neuropsychology of the Dual Brain."

177 *This has gone from being semi-implicit lore*: See Matthew Egizii et al., "Which Way Did He Go? Film Lateral Movement and Spectator Interpretation," *Visual Communication*, 2018; Roger Ebert, "How to Read a Movie," RogerEbert.com, 2008.

178 *In a study of how soccer goals were interpreted*: See Anne Maass, Damiano Pagani, and Emanuela Berta, "How Beautiful Is the Goal and How Violent Is the Fistfight? Spatial Bias in the Interpretation of Human Behavior," *Social Cognition*, 2007. As the authors say, this tells against the idea that a general, species-wide hemisphere asymmetry is behind the left/right distinctions people make in the interpretation of action. But, they add, it does not mean that there can't be a role for a different style of processing across the two hemispheres. Perhaps the way our brain hemispheres develop during socialization is affected by the way language is handled in one's culture? Other left-right differences, affecting how we perceive things other than language, might stem from that.

   Here is another study that complicates things: Anne Maass, Caterina Suitner, and Faris Nadhmi, "What Drives the Spatial Agency Bias? An Italian–Malagasy–Arabic Comparison Study," *Journal of Experimental Psychology: General*, 2014: "A comparison of 3 language communities (Italian, Malagasy, Arabic) differing in script direction (left–right for Italian and Malagasy and right–left for Arabic) and in subject–object order (subject–verb–object in Italian and Arabic and verb–object–subject in Malagasy) provides evidence for the assumption that both mechanisms contribute" to differences in how actions are perceived.

179 *You can, as the philosopher John Dewey said a century ago*: This is in his *Experience and Nature* (1925).

180 *A 2002 paper set a lot of work in motion*: P. Read Montague et al., "Hyperscanning: Simultaneous fMRI During Linked Social Interactions," *NeuroImage*, 2002.

180 *In fact, there was an earlier experiment, published in 1965*: T. D. Duane and Thomas Behrendt, "Extrasensory Electroencephalographic Induction Between Identical Twins," *Science*, 1965.

181 *The EEG method itself was introduced*: I discuss this episode in *Metazoa*, chapter 7.

181 *This study was done very informally, with no statistics*: Duane and Behrendt looked at fifteen pairs of twins. In the test, one twin would close their eyes in a lit room. Closing the eyes tends to initiate alpha rhythms in the brain. Would the other twin, in a separate room, enter the same brain wave pattern also? The other twin was about six meters away. The researchers said that two pairs of twins out of their fifteen could do it, and the others could not. One brain would start alpha rhythms, and the other would also. The pairs who could do this did so repeatedly. Unrelated pairs of individuals never did. The paper has no statistics or even detailed numbers. The authors just looked at the readouts to see if alpha patterns were visible and when they started. This experiment would have to be done carefully. The fact that most pairs of twins do not show the effect does not kill the result; if a few special pairs could do it over and over, that would be a big deal. In a response to critics, the authors gave a bit more detail: the channel between twins worked in both directions, and "in the successful twins transmission seemed to occur always." See Charles Tart, George Robertson, Thomas Duane, and Thomas Behrendt, "More on Extrasensory Induction of Brain Waves," *Science*, 1966.

181 *This 1992 experiment, using EEG scans*: See Jacobo Grinberg-Zylberbaum et al., "Human Communication and the Electrophysiological Activity of the Brain," *Subtle Energies and Energy Medicine*, 1992. The most detailed account of Grinberg-Zylberbaum's work and his disappearance I have found is a recent one: Ilan Stavans, "The Grinberg Affair: One of Mexico's Most Curious Missing-Persons Cases Involves a Scientist Who Dabbled in the Mystical Arts," *The American Scholar*, 2023.

182 *Several different kinds of scanning are used*: As well as EEG and fMRI, which are described in the text, there is MEG (magnetoencephalography) and fNIRS (functional near-infrared spectroscopy). MEG, like EEG, picks up electrical patterns but does so using magnetic influences. fNIRS, like fMRI, looks at changes in oxygen use, but does so with light. Though the original "hyperscan" experiment used fMRI, this method can't pick up fine-grained synchronization in temporal patterns.

182 *The picture emerging is a surprising one*: The online notes will have a lot of references; here are a few. Yan Mu, Cindy Cerritos, and Fatima Khan, "Neural Mechanisms Underlying Interpersonal Coordination: A Review of Hyperscanning Research," *Social and Personal Psychology Compass*, 2018; Edda Bilek et al., "Information Flow Between Interacting Human Brains: Identification, Validation, and Relationship to Social Expertise," *PNAS*, 2015; Adrian Burgess, "On the Interpretation of Synchronization in EEG Hyperscanning Studies: A Cautionary Note," *Frontiers in Human Neuroscience*, 2013.

182 *Two people playing a guitar duet do synchronize*: For teamwork, see Caroline Szymanski et al., "Teams on the Same Wavelength Perform Better: Inter-Brain Phase Synchronization Constitutes a Neural Substrate for Social Facilitation," *NeuroImage*, 2017. For the cocktail party effect, see Bohan Dai et al., "Neural Mechanisms for Selectively Tuning In to the Target Speaker in a Naturalistic Noisy Situation," *Nature Communications*, 2018.

184 *The most radical option*: See Ana Lucía Valencia and Tom Froese, "What Binds

Us? Inter-Brain Neural Synchronization and Its Implications for Theories of Human Consciousness," *Neuroscience of Consciousness*, 2020.

185 *Valencia and Froese also discuss an argument that was given*: See Andy Clark, "Spreading the Joy? Why the Machinery of Consciousness Is (Probably) Still in the Head," *Mind*, 2009.

186 *In an old experiment done first by chance in the seventeenth century*: See Burgess, "On the Interpretation of Synchronization in EEG Hyperscanning Studies."

187 *All this is very much on the edge*: See Antonia Hamilton, "Hyperscanning: Beyond the Hype," *Neuron*, 2021, and Clay Holroyd, "Interbrain Synchrony: On Wavy Ground," *Trends in Neurosciences*, 2022.

188 *a distinctive part of human life is the formation of shared intentions*: See Michael Tomasello, *Becoming Human* (2021).

189 *That evolutionary thicket has proved hard to fully resolve*: See James Tarver et al., "The Interrelationships of Placental Mammals and the Limits of Phylogenetic Inference," *Genome Biology and Evolution*, 2016.

190 *we see giraffes walking, as Karen Blixen said*: This is in her *Out of Africa* (1937). She wrote this book as "Isak Dinesen."

7. OTHER LIVES

194 *I'm going to begin by thinking about this in terms of the* biomass: Here, and often below, I use this fascinating paper: Yinon Bar-On, Rob Phillips, and Ron Milo, "The Biomass Distribution on Earth," *PNAS*, 2018.

195 *I am going to use "ethical" and "moral" nearly interchangeably*: Some people use "ethical" about issues that involve harm to others, equality, and so on, and "moral" for more personal questions (sexual morality). But I've seen people distinguish them with those two meanings switched. The terminology is all over the place.

195 *Behind many of these debates lies a deeper division*: In this area I have been influenced by Simon Blackburn's *Ruling Passions* (1998), though Blackburn's view is closer to traditional "expressivism" than mine. That is the view that ethical claims express an emotional response, or something like a preference, in the speaker, rather than making a claim that might be true or false. Christine Korsgaard's work has also influenced me, though more as a foil, as here the disagreements are larger. See her *The Sources of Normativity* (1996) and *Fellow Creatures* (2018). The literature here is enormous.

196 *A picture like this is seen in historical sketches*: See Philip Kitcher's *The Ethical Project* (2011); Kim Sterelny and Ben Fraser, "Evolution and Moral Realism," *British Journal for the Philosophy of Science*, 2017; Kyle Stanford, "The Difference Between Ice Cream and Nazis: Moral Externalization and the Evolution of Human Cooperation," *Behavioral and Brain Sciences*, 2018.

196 *The social psychologist Jonathan Haidt*: See Jonathan Haidt and Jesse Graham, "When Morality Opposes Justice: Conservatives Have Moral Intuitions That Liberals May Not Recognize," *Social Justice Research*, 2007. This is one of many discussions of these ideas, recommended by Haidt as an accessible introduction. Here they use these five categories: harm/care, fairness/reciprocity, ingroup/loyalty, authority/respect, purity/sanctity. In recent work Haidt and his

colleagues have sometimes recognized six "moral foundations": care, equality, proportionality, loyalty, authority, and purity. (See https://moralfoundations .org.)

198 *Ethical claims are a kind of valuation*: Back in chapter 4, I talked about "evaluation" when we looked at communication and sender-receiver systems. Evaluation there was a category of behavior seen in receivers of signals and displays. Here we're looking not at communication, but at a more general phenomenon.

199 *This view is closer to the made side*: I say a little more about this view in "Philosophers and Other Animals," *Aeon*, 2021. It's around here that I depart from Blackburn, whom I acknowledged above, as I see his view as too close to "expressivism" or "sentimentalism." My unpublished Whitehead Lectures (Harvard, 2022, available on my website) also discuss the topic.

201 *About 73 million pigs are alive at any time in the United States alone*: The numbers are always changing, and some are contested. The USDA's figure for 2022 was 73 million pigs. I make use of reports from the Humane Society, available here: https://www.humanesociety.org/resources/pigs and https://www.humanesociety .org/resources/poultry/, along with some others: https://sentientmedia.org/u-s -farmed-animals-live-on-factory-farms/.

202 *On questions about intensive farming of these*: A classic defense of utilitarianism is John Stuart Mill's *Utilitarianism* (1861). Peter Singer's *Animal Liberation* (1975; recently updated as *Animal Liberation Now*, 2023) is written from a utilitarian perspective. For the updated Kantian view, see Christine Korsgaard's *Fellow Creatures* (2018). For an introduction to all these issues, see Lori Gruen, *Ethics and Animals* (2011).

203 *Imagine that after you die*: This reincarnation test is also discussed in my article "If Not Vegan, Then What?," *Aeon*, 2023.

208 *A welfarist can approve of humane farming*: Welfarism, in this sense, has features in common with both utilitarianism and Kantianism, but it departs from both. Welfarism is akin to utilitarianism in its focus on experienced well-being, but it does not follow utilitarianism in its willingness to justify harm to one through benefits to another. In its focus on the individual rather than the total sum of an action's effects, welfarism sounds a bit like the Kantian view. But the Kantian and the welfarist may diverge about humane farming. Welfarism allows a kind of paternalism toward animals: controlling them can be acceptable when their lives are peaceful and good. That kind of paternalism is at odds with the Kantian respect for autonomy. As emphasized in the main text, welfarism in this sense is not an ethical theory that stands alongside utilitarianism and Kantianism, as it does not (yet) have anything to say about clashes of welfare, and trade-offs.

209 *That is the concept of betrayal*: On this topic, see Steve Cooke, "Betraying Animals," *The Journal of Ethics*, 2019.

209 *Quite a few philosophers find themselves*: For a discussion of abolitionist and various welfarist views, see Gruen, *Ethics and Animals*. Gary Francione is a prominent abolitionist. See, for example, "Are You a Vegan or Are You an Extremist?," *Think*, 2023.

210 *Animal advocates often contrast life*: I discuss an example in "If Not Vegan, Then What?"

213 *The idea of inner maps had been conjectured in the 1940s*: The early work was by E. C. Tolman, "Cognitive Maps in Rats and Men," *Psychological Review*, 1948. Central to the next round was John O'Keefe and Lynn Nadel, *The Hippocampus as a Cognitive Map* (1978). Recent work includes H. Freyja Ólafsdóttir et al., "Hippocampal Place Cells Construct Reward Related Sequences Through Unexplored Space," *eLife*, 2015.

213 *how bad this experience would be for the rats*: At a recent conference in New York City (ASSC 2023), May-Britt Moser, who won a Nobel Prize for her contribution to the "inner map" work, gave a talk in which, at several stages, she emphasized her lab's concern with their animals' welfare, and suggested, from their behavior in videos, that they were not in a traumatic situation.

214 *I won't go through horror stories here in this chapter's main text*: Here are a few examples. Tens of thousands of dogs are used in the United States each year in the testing of potentially harmful substances such as industrial chemicals, which they are forced to ingest in various ways, and also in the investigation of diseases, which are induced. In 2019, the USDA's number was about 58,000 dogs, most of which are beagles. Some of these studies involve many months of daily forced administration of harmful substances. The dogs are kept in small cages. A dog thirty inches long, for example, can be legally kept in a cage whose floor space is three feet by three feet. If the cage is a bit larger (4.25' × 4.25', doubling the floor area), the dog need never be let out of the cage for exercise.

For more detail, see Glenn Greenwald and Leighton Woodhouse, "Bred to Suffer: Inside the Barbaric U.S. Industry of Dog Experimentation," *The Intercept*, May 17, 2018. Regarding the theme of betrayal, see the *Intercept* article and also this news story: Maya Trabulsi, "Used, Reused or Euthanized: A Dog's Life in Animal Research," *KPBS*, August 12, 2022. "'The docile nature of beagles is what makes them the victim here,' said Kathleen Conlee, a former animal researcher."

In mice and rats, the "forced swim" is widely used to test antidepressants. The animal is put into a water-filled cylinder with no escape and watched as it tries to keep itself afloat and able to breathe. Eventually, it reaches what is sometimes called "behavioral despair" and gives up. Antidepressants tend to make the animal swim for longer.

A pair of studies looked at the creation of "nightmares" in rats, caused by either experiencing an electric shock to the feet or perceiving other rats experience the shock (a shock strong enough to make the rats scream). Well after this experience, rats froze when they were returned to the site of the trauma, and some exhibited sleep patterns suggesting nightmares. See Bin Yu et al., "Different Neural Circuitry Is Involved in Physiological and Psychological Stress-Induced PTSD-Like 'Nightmares' in Rats," *Scientific Reports*, 2015; and see David Peña-Guzmán, *When Animals Dream* (2022), for more detail on this work.

Margaret Livingstone's laboratory at Harvard studied the development of visual parts of the brain by suturing shut the eyelids of two baby macaques for their first year, and raising four more apart from their mothers in a way that gave them almost no experience of faces—their human keepers all wore welding masks. See Michael Arcaro et al., "Anatomical Correlates of Face Patches in Macaque Inferotemporal Cortex," *PNAS*, 2020. Controversy arose around this project in 2022, when Livingstone published some observations on maternal bonding, also in *PNAS*, and several hundred scientists called for the work to end; see David Grimm "Harvard Studies on Infant Monkeys Draw Fire," *Science*, October 2022.

214 *Let's focus on animals that are pretty clearly sentient*: Which animals can feel pain and can suffer? These are distinct—stress is suffering that need not involve physical pain, and, more tendentiously, some physical pain might not be minded much. In the food discussion in this chapter, all the animals discussed probably feel physical pain (and at least in many cases, other forms of suffering). There we were looking at mammals, a few birds, and fish. A longer discussion would include crustaceans. In the case of experiments, a lot of work takes place in the uncertain area populated by flies, worms, and others. People tend to look for a cutoff, a border. Who is sentient and who is not? Which side of the line are flies on? That question is understandable as a first move, but the more likely situation is one with no sharp border. The presence of sentience will be not a simple yes-or-no matter, but one with graded and indefinite cases. Papers about animal pain often use fairly similar charts and tables with lists of features that are taken to be relevant to the question—not decisive, but relevant. A list from Lynne Sneddon ("Comparative Physiology of Nociception and Pain," *Physiology*, 2017) includes features like avoidance learning, making trade-offs between different kinds of benefits and harms, wound tending, responsiveness to analgesic chemicals, and some others. In many cases, though, these capacities are found both in clear forms and also in borderline, just-barely-visible, or semi-visible versions. The traits involving learning are very much like this. Flatworms, with small and simple nervous systems, can show "conditioned place preference," avoiding locations where they've encountered adverse conditions, and so on. I doubt that a sharp line between *yes* and *no* cases will appear as we learn more.

215 *early-twentieth-century work on the role of insulin in diabetes*: Examples include Philip Kitcher, "Experimental Animals," *Philosophy and Public Affairs*, 2015, and Korsgaard in *Fellow Creatures*.

217 *The philosopher Philip Kitcher wrote an article*: This is also in his "Experimental Animals."

217 *Macaques, which are small monkeys*: In 2018, more than 70,000 nonhuman primates were used in research in the United States, according to the USDA. Most of these would be macaques.

218 *A few initiatives have built and supported retirement facilities*: In the United States, these include Chimp Haven, Chimpanzee Sanctuary Northwest, and Primates Incorporated.

8. WILD NATURE

222 *The point made by Pollock and Krasner*: This is from the transcript of "Oral History Interview with Lee Krasner, 1964 Nov. 2–1968 Apr. 11," at the Archives of American Art, Smithsonian Institution. The italics on *"am"* do not appear in the transcript, but the emphasis is clear if you listen to the recording.

224 *That story can make the whole sequence seem "natural"*: James Lovelock, in *A*

Rough Ride to the Future (2014), sometimes seems to be heading toward saying something like this, but I don't think he does.

225   *Martha Nussbaum has argued that wild nature no longer exists*: See her *Justice for Animals: Our Collective Responsibility* (2023), and especially "A Peopled Wilderness," *The New York Review of Books*, December 8, 2022.

226   *a new geological epoch, the "Anthropocene"*: The term's introduction is usually credited to Paul Crutzen and Eugene Stoermer, "The 'Anthropocene,'" *Global Change Newsletter*, 2000, though there were some earlier uses, often with slightly different meanings.

226   *I quite like James Lovelock's way*: This is also in *A Rough Ride to the Future*.

227   *The Cretaceous, the time of the formation of chapter 3's forests*: See Jessica Tierney et al., "Past Climates Inform Our Future," *Science*, 2020.

228   *This is a problem for many shell-building invertebrates*: I said earlier that the slow, "geological" carbon cycle works in part through sea creatures locking carbon away in their shells, which eventually become limestone. If the ocean becomes so acidic that many of these organisms can't function, then the laying down of carbon in limestone may slow. It won't stop, apparently; see James Kasting, "The Goldilocks Planet? How Silicate Weathering Maintains Earth 'Just Right,'" *Elements*, 2019.

228   *In the case of birds, a recent report*: See Kenneth Rosenberg et al., "Decline of the North American Avifauna," *Science*, 2019.

228   *In the case of the cheetahs of chapter 6, only about 7,000 remain*: The cheetah number is from the IUCN Red List of Threatened Species, 2021. The Gouldian Finch number is from the World Wildlife Fund. Also according to the World Wildlife Fund, a little over 1,000 mountain gorillas survive. See the online notes for more detail.

228   *That is an exaggeration; the mass extinctions of the past*: Peter Brannen, "Earth Is Not in the Midst of a Sixth Mass Extinction," *The Atlantic*, June 13, 2017.

228   *The Earth, surprisingly, is a now a bit greener*: See Abby Tabor, "Human Activity in China and India Dominates the Greening of Earth, NASA Study Shows," *NASA*, Feb 11, 2019.

229   *A "CO_2 fertilization effect"*: See Zaichun Zhu et al., "Greening of the Earth and Its Drivers," *Nature Climate Change*, 2016.

233   *I understand the alarm that many feel about climate change*: When I talk about mobility as part of a solution, I do not intend to minimize the stresses and costs of moving. A sense of place, of home, is a central source of purpose and well-being in the lives of many people. Losses of community patterns, of ways of living in a physical environment, are real and significant.

234   *The Clean Water Act (as it is commonly known) became law in 1972*: John Waldman, "Once an Open Sewer, New York Harbor Now Teems with Life. Thank the Clean Water Act," *The New York Times*, December 30, 2022.

234   *The reef was saved by a small but energetic conservation movement*: See Ann Jones and Gregg Borschmann, "Harold Holt, the Poet and 'the Bastard from Bingil Bay': How Reef Conservation Began," *ABC Science*, August 11, 2018.

235   *Insects also seem much more likely to have experiences of this kind*: If a form of subjective experience exists in some kind of animal, it should generally have

some *point*. It should be part of what helps those animals steer their way through the world. If there was a species in which pain had no useful role at all—if it could never guide an animal toward something better for it—then we might expect this kind of experience to fade as evolution went on. That fact probably does constrain the extent of negative experience in the natural world. But not much; even if pain does have to be selective in order to be useful, it could be extremely common in animal life.

236 *Might experience in some animals not have this other, positive side?*: Heather Browning and Walter Veit have written several articles on this topic; see especially "Positive Wild Animal Welfare," *Biology and Philosophy*, 2023.

236 *The next step seems to be to think about an overall accounting*: On this topic, see the Browning and Veit article cited in the preceding note.

237 *Whether a human life is a good one depends on more*: On this topic, see also J. David Velleman, "Well-Being and Time," *Pacific Philosophical Quarterly*, 1991.

240 *They prepared a nest in a tree hollow*: These two (probably—the identification is not certain) also engaged in physical battles with other birds while establishing the nest. I described these episodes on my *MetaZoan* blog (metazoan.net).

240 *a number of nonhuman animals have recently been shown*: See Alex Schnell et al., "Cuttlefish Exert Self-Control in a Delay of Gratification Task," *Proceedings of the Royal Society B*, 2021, both for a very interesting case and for a quick survey of what has been shown in this area.

244 *The philosopher Jeff McMahan has argued*: See "The Moral Problem of Predation," in *Philosophy Comes to Dinner* (edited by Andrew Chignell et al., 2015).

244 *Lori Gruen has emphasized this problem, in response*: This is in her *Ethics and Animals*, and McMahan responds in the paper cited in the preceding note.

244 *Nussbaum's view of how animals should be treated*: See her *Justice for Animals*. Here is a point of agreement with Nussbaum. In these recent writings, she is very critical of "safari" tourist experiences that feature the observation of animals being killed by predators. She finds this indicative of something wrong in many human attitudes to wild nature. I think that if one encounters a situation of this kind in an eco-tourism context, it is good to look away.

249 *McMahan draws on a view offered by the philosopher Thomas Nagel*: McMahan quotes these passages from Nagel and Regan. See Thomas Nagel, *The View from Nowhere* (1986), and Tom Regan, *The Case for Animal Rights* (1983, updated edition 2004). McMahan compares the two editions of Regan.

252 *The total number of poultry, pigs, and cattle*: Here I draw on the dissertation work of Rachael Banks ("Experimental and Theoretical Studies of Non-Equilibrium Systems: Motor-Microtubule Assemblies and the Human-Earth System," Caltech, 2023) and other sources (including https://ourworldindata.org).

252 *The majority of these animals probably live within*: The 74 percent figure is from the Sentience Institute, https://www.sentienceinstitute.org/global-animal-farming -estimates. Their estimate is based in part on the numbers of animals within farming operations of various sizes. As they note, animals can be confined in cruel ways within facilities that do not meet a "CAFO" criterion. In the main text, I emphasize modern chicken and pig farming as the paradigm cases of "factory farming." See the online notes for more detail.

I don't discuss fish farming and other forms of aquaculture much here. For some figures and arguments (the numbers are huge), see Becca Franks, Christopher Ewell, and Jennifer Jacquet, "Animal Welfare Risks of Global Aquaculture," *Science Advances*, 2021. From 2018: "The farmed aquatic animal tonnage represents 250 to 408 billion individuals, of which 59 to 129 billion are vertebrates (e.g., carps, salmonids)."

252 *Wild mammals, mostly very small, outnumber livestock by something like eighteen to one*: See Lior Greenspoon et al., "The Global Biomass of Wild Mammals," *PNAS*, 2023. The situation with birds is similar, but not quite as extreme in how the relationships change. Most wild birds are smaller than farmed birds, but the difference is not as big as with mammals. Two recent estimates of the wild bird population are 50 billion (Corey Callaghan, Shinichi Nakagawa, and William Cornwell, "Global Abundance Estimates for 9,700 Bird Species," *PNAS*, 2021) and 100 billion (the 2018 biomass distribution paper). Farmed birds are 25 billion or so. I don't discuss marine mammals here, but their biomass is large. See "The Global Biomass of Wild Mammals."

253 *If we just think about mammals with bodies larger than one kilogram*: See "The Global Biomass of Wild Mammals."

255 *With these questions on the table, this is also the right point*: My third friend was fairly close to the second, but also said that humans have had a natural span that is coming to an end, a fact that is reflected in our present destructiveness.

255 *As we peer forward from our current vantage point*: I'll put more in the online notes. See Jack O'Malley-James et al., "Swansong Biospheres: Refuges for Life and Novel Microbial Biospheres on Terrestrial Planets Near the End of Their Habitable Lifetimes," *International Journal of Astrobiology*, 2013. To add insult to injury, we'll apparently lose our oxygen as well. See Kazumi Ozaki and Christopher Reinhard, "The Future Lifespan of Earth's Oxygenated Atmosphere," *Nature Geoscience*, 2021.

9. SEAMOUNT

265 *In rare and fascinating cases, physically conjoined twins*: I have in mind especially Tatiana and Krista Hogan. They are described in Tom Cochrane, "A Case of Shared Consciousness," *Synthese*, 2020.

265 *Could the mind, as a feature of life on Earth*: Stanislaw Lem's *Solaris* (1961) explores this theme.

265 *Here is a broad distinction between kinds of living things*: I discuss this distinction in my *Darwinian Populations and Natural Selection* (2009), and apply it to the evolution of the mind in "Individuality, Subjectivity, and Minimal Cognition," *Biology and Philosophy*, 2016. For discussion of the spatial and temporal dimensions of this topic, I am indebted to Rebecca Mann and her forthcoming PhD dissertation, "Complex Individuality: The Spatial, Temporal, and Agential Dimensions of the Problem of Biological Individuality."

268 *The "immortal jellyfish," Turritopsis*: See Stefano Piraino et al., "Reversing the Life Cycle: Medusae Transforming into Polyps and Cell Transdifferentiation in *Turritopsis nutricula* (Cnidaria, Hydrozoa)," *Biological Bulletin*, 1996.

270 *Thinking all this through, Parfit came to see*: See his *Reasons and Persons* (1984). The glass tunnel passage is from chapter 13.

271 *Nagel opposes Parfit's view of survival and death*: This material is from his book *The View from Nowhere* (1986).

272 *One reply to this argument applies an idea from another philosopher, Bernard Williams*: "The Makropulos Case: Reflections on the Tedium of Immortality," in his *Problems of the Self* (1973). Thanks to Christine Korsgaard for alerting me to this discussion.

276 *Some parts of the poem*: This is the original 1865 version. Later versions have small changes, including deleting the word "beautiful" in the line that begins "My dead absorb."

> PENSIVE, on her dead gazing, I heard the Mother of All,
> Desperate, on the torn bodies, on the forms covering the battle-
>   fields gazing;
> As she call'd to her earth with mournful voice while she stalk'd:
> Absorb them well, O my earth, she cried—I charge you, lose not
>   my sons! lose not an atom;
> And you streams, absorb them well, taking their dear blood;
> And you local spots, and you airs that swim above lightly,
> And all you essences of soil and growth—and you, O my rivers'
>   depths;
> And you mountain sides—and the woods where my dear
>   children's blood, trickling, redden'd;
> And you trees, down in your roots, to bequeath to all future trees,
> My dead absorb—my young men's beautiful bodies absorb—and
>   their precious, precious, precious blood;
> Which holding in trust for me, faithfully back again give me,
>   many a year hence,
> In unseen essence and odor of surface and grass, centuries hence;
> In blowing airs from the fields, back again give me my darlings—
>   give my immortal heroes;
> Exhale me them centuries hence—breathe me their breath—let
>   not an atom be lost;
> O years and graves! O air and soil! O my dead, an aroma sweet!
> Exhale them perennial, sweet death, years, centuries hence.

276 *Whitman also tried to have some things both ways*: This discussion of Whitman's attitudes to death draws on David Reynolds, "Fine Specimens," *The New York Review of Books*, March 11, 2018.

ACKNOWLEDGMENTS

A book about octopuses led to a book about nearly everything. As a result, I needed a lot of help with this one and have many people to thank. High on the list must be Tim Lenton, who, undeterred by my skepticism about Gaia, helped extensively and generously as I slowly made my way into Earth science. In the same area, I am grateful to Jochen Brocks, Andrew Knoll, Minik Rosing, and Ford Doolittle.

Katherine Preston helped with forests and Kim Sterelny with humans. For contributions to the text and ideas I am also grateful to Andy Barron, Rob Bezimienny, Laurent Bopp, Gerald Borgia, Nicholas Butterfield, Tim Carey, Mark Collard, Scott Denning, Ute Eickelkamp, Mark Fisher, Cliff Frith, Tom Froese, Michael Gazzaniga, Steven Gross, Lori Gruen, Robert Hazen, Celia Heyes, Peter Hiscock, Catherine Hobaiter, Sarah Holland-Batt, Gaspar Jekely, Fred Keijzer, Matt Lawrence, Ron Milo, Jadran Mimeca, Olivier Morin, Rob Phillips, Lesley Rogers, David Scheel, Jeff Sebo, Nick Shea, Ana Lucía Valencia, Giorgio Vallortigara, Roman Werpachowski, Caroline West, and Mark Westoby. Dan Dennett died, after a stupendous career, while this book was in press. His thinking influenced all the books in this series, especially *Metazoa*.

Ena Alvarado did a fact-check of several chapters and, in addition to catching errors, made a number of other deft suggestions. Especially as I did not follow Ena's advice in every case, any remaining factual problems should not be associated with her work. I am grateful to Myles Archibald at William Collins both for his continual support and for significant improvements to the text.

The book has been enriched by the illustrative prowess of Rebecca Gelernter (the drawings on pages 36, 68, 96, and 112), Kylie Brown (tree diagrams on pages 92, 106, 121, and 189), and Linda Lunnon (chimeric faces on page 168). I thank Annie Gottlieb, once again, for much more than a copyedit.

My Africa trip was done with Ged and Teresa Caddick's Terra Incognita Ecotours, and the Sulawesi and Solomon Islands trips with Dive Center Manly. Thanks to everyone at Little Governors' Camp (Kenya), Sabyinyo Lodge (Rwanda), and the Nelson Bay dive shops Let's Go Adventures and Feet First Dive.

I would like to acknowledge the traditional custodians of places in Australia that figure in the book: the Gandangara people of the Blue Mountains; the Worimi people of the Port Stephens area; the Gumbaynggirr people of the Dorrigo area; and the Malgana, Nhanda, and Yinggarda people of Shark Bay. I acknowledge and thank the Wreck Bay Aboriginal Community for their continuing care of Booderee National Park.

My wife, Jane, was very much present in the earlier books in the series but her role is more visible in this one, and she contributed many crucial images and insights. These include the Pollock quote in chapter 8 and chapter 7's reflection on nonhuman animals' capacities to adjust to too much. ("Hang on, those are the two best bits of the book." Perhaps they are.)

Sarah Chalfant and her colleagues at the Wylie Agency were superlative once again. I am reminded often of Rebecca Nagel's crucial comment about the organization of the book's themes. Alex Star, my editor at Farrar, Straus and Giroux, was deeply involved in the development of some central ideas of *Living on Earth* as well as its edits, and Ian Van Wye has skillfully steered the book's production. All through this project I have continually felt the presence of a wonderful team of collaborators alongside me.

INDEX

Page numbers in *italics* refer to illustrations.

A NOTE ABOUT THE AUTHOR

Peter Godfrey-Smith is a professor in the School of History and Philosophy of Science at the University of Sydney. He is the author of *Other Minds: The Octopus and the Evolution of Intelligent Life*, which has been translated into more than twenty languages and won the 2019 Patrick Suppes Prize; *Metazoa: Animal Minds and the Birth of Consciousness*; and four other books, including *Theory and Reality: An Introduction to the Philosophy of Science* and *Darwinian Populations and Natural Selection*, which won the 2010 Lakatos Award.